C000254519

TO DARRYL

WEMBLEY WINS
WEMBLEY WOES

autobiography by

Jim McCalliog

Best wishes

Jim McCalliog

Langside Publishing

First published in Great Britain in August, 2021
by Langside Publishing, Langside B & B,
off Bowling Green Road, Main Road,
Fenwick, Ayrshire, KA3 6AL

ISBN 978-1-3999-0144-4

Langside Publishing

Printed and bound by CPI Group (UK) Ltd,
Croydon CR0 4YY

CONTENTS

ACKNOWLEDGEMENTS

I would like to thank the following people with all the help they have given me to make the writing of this book possible:

Denis Law for his readiness to write the foreword to my book. I am thrilled and honoured.

Alex and Gerda Gordon for their endless time & effort in putting the book together. I will be forever grateful.

David and Liz Instone for all their hard work against the clock. Their professionalism shone through.

Andy Howarth of CPI Printers. Great company.

Grant Jamieson from Creatur Ayr.

Suse McCallum for time spent with my wife Debbie.

Thanks to all the former players who gave up their time to write testimonials for the book.

My book is dedicated to:

My Mum and Dad, who encouraged and supported myself and all my siblings throughout our lives.

My children Mark, Nicola, Joely and Leah.
I am so proud of you all.

My grandchildren Finn, Myles and Caiden.

To my wife Debbie, Love of my life.
An amazing woman, wife, mother and daughter.

To Debbie's children Mark, Grant, Stewart and Rachel.
Growing up into wonderful human beings.

FOREWORD BY DENIS LAW

I KNEW Jim McCalliog would make it big in football following his very first kick on his Scotland international debut - he passed the ball to me.

The boy could do no wrong after that, as far as I was concerned!

Jim took the kick-off at precisely 3pm against England at Wembley that unforgettable Saturday afternoon of April 15 1967. What an occasion for the lad to make his first appearance for his nation at the age of twenty. I was playing for Scotland for the thirty-seventh time. He was the new kid on the block and I was the veteran - at the age of twenty-seven.

Following an hour-and-a-half of action and a fifteen-minute half-time interval, we were both cavorting around the pitch in absolute delight, the Scotland support was in a frenzy of joy, Lion Rampants and tartan flags and scarves fluttered everywhere you looked, fans danced on the field, hugging anyone fortunate enough to be wearing the dark blue shirt. The euphoria of the immediate aftermatch was simply one of overwhelming happiness.

I scored the first goal against the great Gordon Banks, Celtic's Bobby Lennox netted the second and Jim claimed the winner. It ended 3-2 for Scotland and, boy, did that triumph feel good. Over half-a-century later, I can't prevent a large grin from dominating my features when I recall that event. Did I remember to tell you England, with my Manchester United team-mates Nobby Stiles and Bobby Charlton in the side, were world champions at the time?

I was not one bit surprised at Jim's performance that day. I had known about his ability long before we teamed up at Wembley. I was aware of a young boy by the name of Jim McCalliog who had been at Chelsea. Maybe he didn't get as many first-team outings as he might have liked at Stamford Bridge, but his name was getting around in football circles.

In fact, back at the start of 1967 - even before Wembley - I was asked by a newspaper reporter to name the young player to look out for that year. I am quoted as saying: 'I would have rated Jim as an exciting arrival but for one thing. He really stepped into the big-time a year ago. At twenty, he is clearly going to be a power in the game for many seasons to come. He has one quality I prize above all others. He can always be relied upon to play the big game on the big day.'

Well, I got that spot on! Back then, you didn't get anything like the TV coverage of football we can enjoy today. There would be players you knew very little about until they were in opposition on match day. But Jim McCalliog, in his own quiet way, was making progress in the English top flight and the popular opinion was that he was a young lad with a fair bit of talent.

My United pal Pat Crerand told me Jim must be a good player because he came from the same part of Glasgow as himself, an area known as the Gorbals which, as an Aberdonian, I had only heard about. It was well known as being a tough, hard district of the city and Pat continually told the joke that rottweilers used to go around in pairs to feel safe. It certainly proved to be a breeding ground where budding sportsmen, blessed with a competitive edge at an early age, could emerge with that in-built determination to succeed. That sort of relentless spirit to overcome odds cannot be bought.

Benny Lynch, the world flyweight boxing champion in the late thirties, was born in the Gorbals and he was just one of the products of this part of the globe that emphasised Glasgow grit allied with Scottish steel could conquer most obstacles. It's not a bad combination, my friends. Jim McCalliog possessed those attributes.

I first met Jim during the week before the Wembley extravaganza when United were due to play Sheffield Wednesday, the team he joined after his two years at Chelsea. Immediately, I liked the look of the kid - especially when he told me I was his hero. I realised there and then that Jim knew his football.

The media, of course, saw the opportunity for a photograph of the two Scots who would be teaming up against England the following Saturday and the image of the two of us grinning away just before kick-off was seen in a few national newspapers. It was a polite handshake, but three days later there would be other pictures of us looking slightly more animated.

In the countdown to the big game, I spent a bit more time with Jim and he came across as a genuinely nice guy. He was polite and even a little bit reserved which I quite liked. I've never been a fan of blowhards.

Naturally, we had no inkling of what lay in store at Wembley, but I will say we were confident of achieving something. Trust me, we had no intention of going onto that field to be bit-part players. As Scots living in England, Jim and I had the fact England had won the World Cup in July 1966 rammed down our throats just about every day. They were unbeaten going into the match against Scotland, who were being managed by Bobby Brown for the first time.

The odds were heavily against Scotland, so we really had to respond. I never required any extra motivation when I played for my country. It didn't matter who or where we were playing, I wanted to be involved.

It's in the history books now what unfolded that glorious afternoon in London. Jim could hardly have dreamed of a more spectacular start to his Scotland career than a winning goal against the world champions on their own midden, as I liked to call it.

Unfortunately, we were destined to team up on only two more occasions for Scotland. That was a pity. I really would have enjoyed a few more games playing alongside Jim.

And I also missed the opportunity of lining up with the lad when he joined Manchester United in March 1974 after I had left the previous summer to cross from Old Trafford to Maine Road for my second stint at City.

So, the fates decreed that the first of a trio of appearances together should have been that memorable day at Wembley. I really do wish there had been a few more occasions, maybe a season or two playing alongside each other and getting a proper chance to get to know our individual preferences that can only come during a run of games.

Who knows what we could have achieved? First up, I thought Jim was a terrific player, gifted with a range of skills, He was a totally unselfish team player and that'll do for me. He could strike a good pass, had excellent vision, could be relied upon to give one hundred per cent in every single game. He had a first-rate career with a few clubs and the fact so many managers were persuaded to buy him is testimony to his qualities.

And Jim had an eye for goal, as he proved in a wee kickabout against the Auld Enemy on an April afternoon in 1967 in front of exactly 99,063 spectators, a sporting occasion that will be forever cherished by those who played in it and those who witnessed the spectacle that is now embedded in Scottish football folklore.

I am aware Jim says some very kind things about yours truly in the following pages of his marvellous life story.

Let me make this clear, please. I am proud to have called Jim McCalliog a team-mate. And prouder, still, to call him a friend.

Denis Law, July 2021

PROLOGUE

IT was a typical Sunday morning in the Sheffield Wednesday club house. The accommodation, a three-bedroomed semi-detached property which would have been worth around £15,000 - a lot of money in 1967 - was home to the team's twenty-year-old centre-forward and the McCalliog clan.

Mum Mary was busy, as usual, in the kitchen making tea and toast for my dad Jimmy and the family. I was milling around and my brothers Freddie, Danny and Eddie and sister Anne were somewhere in the vicinity. I had already scoffed my routine full breakfast. Some of that day's newspapers were scattered on the table amid the cups and plates and cutlery. A large cereal packet would normally have pride of place in the centre. There was the usual chatter as we talked about this, that and the next thing. A perfectly normal day on the Sabbath for the McCalliogs.

There was a telephone extension in the kitchen. Suddenly, it shrilled to life. I looked at the clock on the wall: 9.16am. I wondered who would be calling at that time on a Sunday morning, the one day a week a footballer could normally depend upon for some rest following the rigours of a game the previous afternoon. Quizzically, I picked up the receiver.

It was a phone call that changed my life.

'Jim, it's Tommy Docherty,' came the voice on the other end. I recognised the unmistakable rasping tones.

'Hello, boss,' I returned. I always referred to him in such a term, although, of course, I had left Chelsea, where he had been my manager, eighteen months previously to join Sheffield Wednesday.

'Just ringing to congratulate you - '

I didn't get the opportunity to ask for an explanation.

' - you've been picked for Scotland. You'll be playing against England at Wembley on Saturday. It'll be in the papers tomorrow.'

I stood with the phone in my hand. I was aware the kitchen had gone silent.

'Good luck,' was The Doc's parting shot. The line went dead.

I told my family what I had just been told. 'Is this a joke?' asked my mum. Like me, she was aware my old Chelsea gaffer had a misplaced sense of humour; not malicious just slightly mischievous. Immediately, there was a seed of doubt in my mind.

'Surely, Tommy wouldn't do something like that, would he?' queried my dad. My mum and I answered in unison, 'Oh, yes, he would.'

So, there I am, standing in the kitchen with my mum and dad, and I don't know if my dream of playing for my country is about to come true. Okay, I am aware it is a cliche. But anyone who knows me would tell you I had always wanted to play for Scotland. It had been my ambition since I had been a kid. Yes, I was aiming high, but why not? And you can be sure a certain Tommy Docherty, someone who had originally tried to get me to Chelsea when I was fifteen years old, was fully aware of my hopes and aspirations. God knows I had talked it over with him more than just a few times. So, was my old boss at it? You could never tell with The Doc.

To set the record straight, I had been mentioned with the Scotland international squad for a few months. Bobby Brown had come in as the first full-time manager of the nation and he had been quoted as saying it was a new ball game and everyone would get a chance to impress him. The jungle drums were beating and my name was mentioned. So, too, were about one hundred other hopefuls. I was aware the Scottish Football Association had representatives watching potential candidates in England most weeks. Back in the sixties, television coverage was not the saturation coverage it is today. Sometimes your team might be allocated all of two minutes on the BBC's Match of the Day or ITV's On The Ball. And that was if you were lucky. There were occasions when your game did not figure at all; no highlights, nothing.

So, a lot of it was word of mouth and you had to be hopeful - if there was a selector in the stand - you would perform well and get a mention in someone's report back to the SFA. I was aware a chap by the name of Andrew Hepburn, who had connections to Stirling Albion, had taken in a few Sheffield Wednesday games and you didn't have to be a genius to work out he was looking at me; I was the only Scot in the team. The previous season, Wednesday had played Everton in the English FA Cup Final and our line-up consisted of ten Englishmen - and me. Andrew Hepburn was not the only selector who had been watching me.

Coincidentally, the day before the phone call, I had a brief chat with The Doc. Wednesday had played Chelsea in the quarter-final of the FA Cup at Stamford Bridge and we had lost 1-0 when Tony Hateley rose to head down a ball in front of Tommy Baldwin and he lashed it into the net. The goal came in injury time and we thought we had done enough to earn a replay. Of course, it had been a disappointment and The Doc said all the right things afterwards when he spoke to me very briefly. Listen, I liked my ex-boss. That may be hard to believe when I tell you I had three head-to-head confrontations with him when I told him I wasn't satisfied about lack of first-team appearances following my debut on my eighteenth birthday in a 3-0 win over Birmingham City. One year later, I had added a mere six outings to that match. I knew he rated me, but he just didn't play me enough. Mind you, there were a lot of good young players at The Bridge back then with Peter Osgood, John Hollins and John Boyle among them, but that didn't ease the frustration. Eventually, he relented and I joined Wednesday. However, we had remained on fairly amicable terms.

And now, early on a Sunday morning, he had phoned to congratulate me on being called up for Scotland. Or was he pulling my leg? Honestly, I could not be sure. It was not outwith the bounds of possibility that Bobby Brown had mentioned a few names to sports scribes in Scotland and some news had filtered through to The Doc. As I said, he had at least a couple of Pressmen in the know who could make the right calls. Otherwise, I may have joined Celtic instead of Chelsea back in 1964, but that's a story for another chapter.

So, what was I supposed to do? Who could I phone? I hadn't seen this one coming, that's for sure. Up until that moment, it had been a typical weekend. A game on a Saturday and, on this occasion, a train journey home from Euston Station in London. I would spend some time with my Wednesday mates Peter Eustace and Wilf Smith and I always had friends outside football.

Now, though, I was in a bit of a quandary. Rather astonishingly, the Scotland game against the world champions was due in six days' time. That was the way it worked back then. One Saturday I'm playing in London against Chelsea in the FA Cup and the next I am back in the same city making my debut for Scotland against England in the Home Internationals. It was all a bit whistle-stop. On the Sunday, I decided to try to push it to the back of my mind. I didn't receive any calls from anyone else and I couldn't help but wonder if The Doc had been up to his old tricks.

On the Monday, I reported to training at Hillsborough, as usual. I was in with the lads and getting changed to go training when someone popped his head around the dressing room door and said: 'Jim, the boss wants to see you'. And that was all. 'Oh, what have you been up to, then?' came the response from my team-mates. To be honest, I didn't make the connection with Scotland, but I had a fair idea moments after entering the office of manager Allan Brown. He was sitting behind his desk and he looked up and smiled. 'I've got some good news for you, lad,' he said.

I didn't have a chance to say anything when he added without preamble: 'You've been picked to play for Scotland against England at Wembley on Saturday.' He stood up from his chair, stretched across his desk. put out his hand and shook mine and said: 'Let me be the first to congratulate you.'

Actually, Tommy Docherty had beaten him by about twenty-five hours to put in the phone call that made certain my life would never be the same again.

Tommy Docherty would possibly have had a phone call from the SFA telling him Eddie McCreadie was in the team. Tommy would have asked who else is in the team. This probably how he knew I was included.

This made me think back to when I was fifteen. One evening in the Boys' Club I overheard someone saying that he didn't fancy my chances of being picked for Scotland Schoolboys because I was from the Gorbals. This made me more determined. I wanted to be the first boy from the Gorbals to play for Scotland schoolboys.

Chapter One

FOOTBALLING CHILDHOOD IN GLASGOW

I WAS born in the Gorbals district of Glasgow on September 23 1946, the eldest of five children. My parents, Jimmy and Mary, had come to Scotland from Ireland and their lives revolved around my siblings and I as they tried to make the best of what could be a harsh life in the post-war urban sprawl of one of the most deprived areas in Western Europe.

We kids, of course, knew little about the poverty, inadequate housing and social injustices that blighted so many lives. This was the life we knew and I look back on my early years with huge affection, thanks largely to the love, support and encouragement of my parents. My father hailed from Donegal and my mother was born in County Fermanagh in the North. They had both moved separately across the Irish Sea to Scotland when they were young and met and married in Glasgow.

My surname is a rather unusual one. I haven't met too many other McCalliogs on my travels and, in fact, is a variation of McCallion, which in turn is derived from the Irish spelling of O'Cathgalain. My father's brother actually called himself McCallion, but my dad insisted on McCalliog. For my part, despite the fact I could have played for Eire as the country was known during my playing days, I have always considered myself Scottish, something that that was one of the major factors in my drive and ambition as a young boy to succeed as a professional footballer. I wanted nothing more than to play for the country of my birth. Scotland.

My dad worked as a motor mechanic and his wages allowed us the occasional treat such as a chip shop tea every Friday in an age when fish suppers were viewed as a treat. My mum and dad knew next to nothing about football, indeed my dad was a boxing fan, but they always encouraged me and were always eager to hear about my progress. We lived in a typical Glasgow tenement in 42

Caledonia Road, well perhaps it wasn't so typical, as unlike many tenements of the time, it actually had an indoor toilet. Luxury!

But the flat did have the bed that folded up into the wall in one of the three bedrooms that I shared with my three younger brothers. My sister had her own room as did my mum and dad, but my mum also took in lodgers now and again, so the house could get pretty cramped, but I loved it. I was able to play football outside and my mother always knew I was there. Playing outside the flat on the street had pros and cons. The street was bumpy and therefore ideal for perfecting balls skills, however it was usually covered in glass, dangerous to a person if you fell, and lethal for the ball you were kicking. Growing up, I always wanted a proper leather ball and I remember when I was about twelve and finally got one. I managed to burst it on the rails of a bordering fence, and despite the best efforts of my dad, it proved irreparable. The pitches we played on, even in organised football proved no less lethal to skin and bone, as most of them were black shale. Holyrood Senior Secondary school had red shale. Even the so-called grass pitches contained precious little of the green stuff and were usually rutted and full of holes.

As a young boy and living quite close to Shawfield Stadium, I was a Clyde fan and my early hero was their Scotland left-back Harry Haddock who captained the 'Bully Wee' to two Scottish Cup Final victories in 1955 and 1958, unthinkable nowadays.

Like so many boys of my age and background, I ate, drank and slept football and played as much as possible, whether it was on the street with my pals, avoiding the (very) occasional car, for the school, or in kickabouts with the older kids. I also practised on my own for hours, honing my skills with the ball. If I didn't have a ball, I would kick cans or stones, or make a ball out of the wrapper from a loaf. I loved my Primary school, St Francis, I couldn't wait to get there in the morning and although football was a big factor in this, I enjoyed lessons as well. In fact, school probably cemented my love of football once and for all one Friday afternoon when, as a ten year old, I was made captain of my Primary school team and, as was the custom at the time as captain I was allowed to take the match ball home with me. My duties as captain entailed looking after the ball and bringing it with me the next day for the match.

However, bursting with excitement on the way home with my pals, we couldn't help but give in to temptation and soon the shiny new ball was being used for an impromptu kickabout on a patch of waste ground with pillars acting as goals, as I kept a wary eye in case anyone caught us kicking the school ball around the streets, otherwise my captaincy could have been the shortest in history! When I arrived home, my mum remarked on how dirty the ball wa, obviously wise to to what just had transpired. Even then, however, my mother was careful to keep my feet on the ground. She was obviously delighted for me, telling me that it was a good start, but warned against getting too carried away. As well as the ball, I had been given my football kit for the next day, and as cliched as it sounds, that night I slept in the maroon and white jersey, giving my mum an extra ironing job in the morning.

I suppose I was quite the young budding footballer as at aged eleven I was playing for St Francis Boys Guild Under-16s, and it was with them that I collected my first winner's medal in 1958 when we won the Boys Guild Cup Final. I was injured during this match and had to go off, but with no substitutes in those days I came back on again and scored one of our goals. As a result of this, I received my first piece of publicity when the St Francis newsletter ran a story on the precocious eleven year old playing with and against much older boys.

On passing my eleven plus exams, I moved to Holyrood Secondary school, where I was to meet a teacher who would have a great influence on my career, but first of all I was in for a shock on my first day at Holyrood when a message came over the tannoy instructing James McCalliog to report to Mr Murphy, the head gym teacher. This, I duly did and I was astonished to be informed by Mr Murphy that he knew all about me and my football background, and that Celtic Football Club also knew all about me and were keeping tabs on my development. To say I was in a state of shock as I returned to class is a huge understatement and, of course, my classmates were all keen to know all about my meeting with Mr Murphy. I wasn't about to tell them, they probably wouldn't have believed me anyway. Instead, I waited until I got home and discussed it with my parents.

It was decided that at that stage of my life, school was more important than football and Celtic could wait for the time being. However, football remained a huge part of my life and I was soon made captain of the school under-13 side by the science teacher who ran the side, Dennis Cuddihy. Mr Cuddihy was young, confident and bubbly, and loved football, and as I mentioned above, became a huge influence on my career. He took us twice a week for training and stayed with us for four years, during which time I was selected for Glasgow Schoolboys under-13s, 14s and 15s sides. I was also training and playing with St Luke's Boy Club, ran by two dedicated men, Billy Wallace and Tam Daley, who, along with a host of volunteers, provided a marvellous outlet for kids, offering snooker, boxing and table tennis at the club, in addition to football. Tam and Billy's dedication to the cause was so deep seated that they even managed to set up makeshift floodlights for the dark nights when we trained in the Gorbals' gloom.

I have often looked back on my life and career and thought about the debt of gratitude I owe people like Tam Daley, Billy Wallace and others like Eddie Flannagan who put so much of their time and effort into organisations like St Francis Boys Guild and St Lukes. They helped so many boys off the street and gave so many opportunities to kids brought up in a tough environment, many of whom could have taken the wrong turning in life. Many of the kids I grew up with weren't really trouble makers, but found themselves caught up in the gang culture of the time. It was never an issue with me. If I misbehaved or spoke out of turn, a look from my dad was enough to stop any thoughts of straying from the straight and narrow. There is temptation in every era, but for me the over-riding principle was you don't shame your name or your house.

So I was steeped in football from a young age. It wasn't uncommon for me to play for Holyrood School on the Saturday morning, St Lukes on the Saturday afternoon and then again on a Sunday morning and quite often I would fit in a game on the Sunday afternoon as well. In the early days I played in whichever position I could get a game, but I was usually to be found in midfield as a wing-half at Primary School and inside-left (although I was predominantly right-footed) with Holyrood. Aged fourteen, I received another newspaper write-up when I was pictured with Celtic's Pat Crerand after he had presented me with the ten medals I had won with St Lukes in a single season. If I wasn't playing football, I was watching it.

Four famous stadiums, Shawfield, Hampden Park, Celtic Park and Ibrox, were all within a short walk or bus ride from my home and I would go to as many matches as possible. I have fond memories of being 'lifted' over the turnstiles, as was the tradition of the time and gaining free access to some of the greatest Scottish footballers of the era. My favourite players were guys like Harry Haddock, Archie Robertson and Tommy Ring, of Clyde, Paddy Crerand, Willie Fernie, of Celtic, and Ian McMillan, of Rangers. Often, after school, I would tear up to Hampden when there was an international being played there, and I vividly recall watching my great hero Denis Law from behind the goal, with his vivid blond hair, scoring twice for Scotland in a World Cup qualifier in 1961. I was fourteen at the time. How could I have possibly known that just six years later I would line up alongside Denis Law for Scotland? Many of these matches were watched by huge crowds, it was a fantastic experience.

The only match I wasn't allowed to attend by my parents was the Old Firm match. When you consider the many wonderful achievements by Scottish people in sport, science, industry etc, I don't believe that Celtic and Rangers represent us as a nation. Of course, bigotry and sectarianism have always blighted our society, and although I was fully aware of these two evils growing up, I have to say I was never hugely affected by them. My hairiest experiences in this regard was probably at Primary School, where I quickly discovered that although the quickest way to get to St Francis from home was along the Caley Road, it was actually smarter to take a detour so I didn't have to pass the protestant school. It took longer, but removed the possibility of any confrontations.

I was only interested in playing football, and my pals were just my pals regardless of which school they attended. I also didn't experience too much of the infamous Gorbals' violence, apart from one night when I was thirteen or fourteen. I had a job in the cloakroom of the Boys Guild, and was walking home along Cumberland Street, when suddenly loads of people tumbled out of a close wielding chains and axes, and generally knocking seven bells out of one another. I just pressed myself against the wall until it subsided and I was able to get away safely. The Gorbals was a tough, deprived area, no mistake., but I believe that it doesn't matter where you come from if you have ambition and get a couple of breaks. And by the time I reached my teens my ambition was to become a professional footballer. I didn't have to look too far for inspiration, with Tommy Docherty, Pat Crerand and Frank McLintock just some of the famous names who had been brought up in the Gorbals, and moved onto great things in the game.

As I grew older, in the time honoured fashion, scouts were knocking on my door, and my mother and father began taking note of their names and teams that they represented. Due to their lack of knowledge of football, mum and dad just felt it was the only way to keep track of the interest in me, and by the time I was fifteen, the total of scouts enquiring about me had reached 22. One of the scouts, Mr Barr, was from Leeds United, then a mediocre club in England's second division. But Don Revie had just taken over as manager and was in the process of putting into place his wonderful nationwide scouting network, and Mr Barr would soon bring outstanding young talents such as Eddie Gray, Peter Lorimer and Jimmy Lumsden to the club. Aged fourteen, I was invited to spend a week at the club along with my brother Freddie, a talented footballer himself, and totally undaunted by the prospect, we accepted the offer. We made our own way down to Yorkshire, and were very much left to our devices, but we were Gorbals streetwise, so it didn't faze us in the slightest. I didn't see too much of Don Revie on this occasion, but had quite a lot of dealings with Les Cocker, his trainer and coach.

I certainly caught a few breaks along the way, one of which was being nominated by Mr Jamieson the Glasgow Schools manager for the Scotland schoolboy trials. I had been playing regularly for the Glasgow boys under 13s, 14s and 15s sides, and felt my game was really coming along and Mr Jamieson obviously agreed. I then made a bit of history in 1962 by becoming the first Gorbals' boy to play for Scotland Schoolboys when I was selected for the under 16 side against Northern Ireland at Windsor Park. We won 5-1 and I scored the first goal and there was a great surprise and thrill for me after the match when I discovered that unknown to me, my dad had flown from Glasgow to the match and was waiting outside to see me. To this day, I have no idea how he managed to raise the money to come and see me, and I never did ask him. I can only surmise that my parents somehow found the money by making some other financial sacrifice or perhaps by doing some extra work. But it was a huge emotional experience for me to discover that he had travelled all that way to support me.

Mr Cuddihy was delighted for me when I told him that I would be going to Leeds in the summer, and gave me a nice going away present by suggesting me for the Holyrood under 18 side for a forthcoming cup final. One of the usual team was cup-tied and he wanted me as a replacement. I wasn't too sure as I hadn't played in any of the other ties at that age group and felt that perhaps one of the reserves deserved a chance, but Mr Cuddihy prevailed and I played in the match at Hampden Park which we won 5-1. On returning home I was greeted by a Manchester United scout. I had to tell him that I was heading for Leeds, but Manchester United would loom large in my life on numerous subsequent occasions. Incidentally, the cup-tied player whose place I took in the cup final was none other than Harry Hood, who not long afterwards signed for my first love Clyde, and went on to have a great career, notably with Celtic. If my football career did not work out I would have liked to have been a P.E. teacher. I loved school and my mum never had to waken me up. I couldn't wait to get to school. I picked up a bus regularly at 8.10am and I at school for 8.30am. This gave us time for a kickabout before the bell sounded.

After a great holiday in Ireland with my family during which my brothers really put me through my paces, I headed for Leeds by myself in June 1962.

Chapter Two

LEEDS UNITED MY FIRST PROFESSIONAL CLUB

DON REVIE probably thought he was doing me a favour. The Leeds United manager spotted me at the bus stop outside the car park at Elland Road and swung up in his Rover saloon and wound down the window. 'Jump in,' he said. 'I'll give you a lift home.' By the end of that twenty-minute journey, I realised I had no future at Leeds United Football Club.

I acknowledged the offer by the boss and it would have saved me the hassle of two bus journeys home to where the family stayed in a club house in an estate called Carr Manor. However, I politely turned him down. I was never an apple-for-the-teacher sort of guy. I didn't want to appear as a bit of a sook with the manager. Maybe that's my Gorbals upbringing. My mum and dad taught me from a very early age to stand on my own two feet and not to rely on others. 'My bus will be along in a couple of minutes, boss,' I said. 'Thanks, anyway.

Don Revie persisted. He stretched across the passenger seat, released the lock and pushed the door open. 'Come on, get in,' he urged. Actually, he didn't live too far away from me and it was probably on his way home. The club had found a private housing estate where they based a lot of their players and I had other Scots such as Eric Smith, Willie Bell and Jim Storrie as neighbours. I relented and took the manager up on his offer. I thanked him again and jumped in the car.

We made some small talk for a few minutes and then I had to grasp the opportunity. 'How am I doing?' I asked. I thought I might as well cut to the chase. I recall it was nearing the end of the season, around May in 1963, and I was sixteen years old. I was ambitious, but I didn't know if I actually had a career in football. I could only do my best in training, which was something that came naturally to me, anyway, and give it absolutely everything when I was playing for one of the club's youth sides. It seemed a reasonable question to ask the manager of the football team who, as everyone was aware, had a dossier of every player on the club's books.

'You're doing well,' Revie replied. 'We're going to build you up. You'll be graduating to full-time training.'

Music to my young ears. Part of my duties back then consisted of painting walls and doors, mucking out dressing rooms, cleaning boots and doing all sorts of drab chores around the ground. It was something all hopefuls in their apprenticeship encountered and it didn't do me any harm. I wasn't the biggest or the strongest and I accepted some hard work lay ahead. That never fazed me one bit. My ambition was to be a full-time footballer and I would do what it took to achieve that target.

I had another query for the boss. 'Are you going to sign me full-time?' I asked. Again, it seemed a natural question. I was due to celebrate my seventeenth birthday on September 23 and I knew that was the time I could be asked to make the step up. Originally, I had been on amateur forms and the next stage beckoned.

Two years earlier, I had been invited to Leeds at Easter to have a look around the place. I was with my young brother Freddie, who was a talented footballer in his own right, and the club put us up in a five-star hotel. It was wall-to-wall luxury and, obviously, it was not anything we had encountered during our young lives as we were brought up in a tenement flat in Caledonia Road - known locally as Caley Road - in a district of Glasgow that didn't have the best of reputations. Growing up in the Gorbals was an experience, trust me. So, there we were, my brother who was a year younger than me, in the lap of what we considered opulence in a city centre hotel. That was the second time I had met Don Revie. I recall he gave money to me and told us to go and enjoy ourselves.

Where do two kids from Glasgow go in a big, unexplored city? We went to the cinema, of course. The only film being shown at the time was 'The Sound of Music' starring Julie Andrews as an individual tasked with looking after seven young children in Austria during the Nazi occupation. She was prone to bursting into song and the movie, unsurprisingly, would not have been our first choice. However, that was all there was on offer - remember, these were days long before anyone had a clue about multiplex theatres - so we went along, with some cash in our pocket, too. We bought the biggest buckets of popcorn they had on offer and we purchased giant containers of some soft drink called Kia-Ora. I think we might have created a racket with all the munching and slurping Hopefully, it didn't drown out Julie's relentless singing.

Thankfully, though, Leeds liked their first sight of this wee boy from the mean streets of Glasgow. On one of the first days, trainer and coach Les Cocker, one of Don Revie's trusted lieutenants, took Freddie and I to the training ground at Fullerton Park. One of the routines was to attempt to strike the ball off the bar from around twenty yards. We were told we would get six shots each. Les Cocker went first and hit the woodwork once with his attempts. I stood up and thumped the crossbar with my first three shots. Les Cocker just looked skywards, but I could tell he was pleased. The trainer called a halt to the exercise before I could take a fourth. He had seen enough. He moved us onto another exercise. Actually, I think my brother and I really enjoyed it and were excited at being involved in gaining the insight into the workings of a football club. I didn't see a lot of Don Revie on that week-long visit and when we left there were no promises, but I was told the club would keep tabs on me.

However, Don Revie must have heard good things about me and he did keep in touch. At that time I gave him a verbal assurance I would sign for Leeds United when I turned fifteen. My fledgling career moved up a notch when I was selected to play for Scotland Under-16 Schoolboys against Northern Ireland at Windsor Park in 1962. We won 5-1 and I scored the first goal. A further cap followed, this time at Ibrox against England. It was a thrill to play at the home of Rangers where I had seen a few games as a kid. I was football crazy and used to take in games at Shawfield, supporting my favourite team Clyde, Celtic Park, Hampden and Ibrox. I walked practically everywhere and, in fact, on the day of the match against our English counterparts, I walked to and from the game. I'm delighted to say we won 4-3.

By the time I had strolled home, there was a surprise visitor at 42 Caledonia Road. It was Tommy Docherty. I recognised him immediately from my Christmas football annuals. Mr Docherty had just taken over as manager of Chelsea and it was an enormous thrill to actually meet the man I had watched playing for Scotland at the national stadium, a man who won twenty-five caps for Scotland and had played alongside the great Tommy Finney at Preston North End.

Like me, Tommy Docherty had been born and raised in the Gorbals. I was too young to appreciate that perhaps we were kindred spirits. However, I couldn't possibly guess at the influence he would have on my career. Back then, though, he was sitting in the front room of my parents' home and he told me he thought I had performed really well. In fact, he said he thought I had had a great game and he wanted to sign me for the Stamford Bridge club. To be honest, it was all a bit overwhelming for me. It was tempting to think about being with Tommy Docherty at Chelsea, but the values instilled in me by my parents were now part of my character and I informed Mr Docherty that I had given my word to Don Revie that I was going to sign for Leeds.

The football grapevine must have been buzzing because the following day Don Revie and his chief scout Maurice Lindley arrived at the front door of our home. The Leeds boss told me he had received glowing reports of my performance at Ibrox. I thought it only fair to inform him of the visit from Tommy Docherty twenty-four hours earlier. I reassured Mr Revie I would keep my word, but it certainly hastened the matter and about half-an-hour later, the deal was done and I had signed for Leeds United as an amateur.

In hard cash terms, Leeds put £9,000 on the table as a signing-on fee, with half going to my parents and the other half for furniture when they moved with me to a club house in Carr Manor. The entire family shifted with me to Yorkshire. The club arranged for my dad, who was a motor mechanic, to get a job down there and I saw the deal as giving my family security. I agreed £14 per week with £2 going towards the rent of the club property, £2 for buses and £10 for my mum. Everything was going according to plan - until that afternoon when the boss Don Revie considerately offered me a lift home.

When we had originally discussed me going full-time when I reached seventeen, the Leeds United manager had promised me an £11,000 signing-on fee and £35 per week in basic wages. I expected him to be as good as his word. My family and I had done everything that had been asked of us when we uprooted from Glasgow. Maybe Revie thought we wouldn't want to go through the upheaval of flitting again. Possibly he thought I was already as good as his player. Maybe he thought I had forgotten our verbal agreement. He thought wrong.

'Are you going to sign me full-time?' He stared ahead as he guided us through the traffic. He didn't even look round at me. I reminded him of what I had been promised when he had visited my parents' house. Revie shook his head. 'Bobby Collins doesn't even get that kind of money,' he said. Bobby Collins was the captain of the team and the man who had been their inspirational figure on the pitch since arriving from Everton in 1962, saving them from relegation and masterminding their return to the First Division in 1964.

I felt as though I had been hit by a sledgehammer. It was evident Don Revie had no intention of honouring his word. As far as I was concerned, he had made a verbal offer, I had accepted and I believed he would see it through. On that car journey home, I realised that was not going to be the case. There was little point in arguing. My feelings went way beyond disappointment. I sat there lost in thought for the remainder of the journey.

My word is my bond. Ask anyone who knows me. It was the case back then and it still holds good today. If I say I'll do something, I'll follow it through. If not, there will be a good reason. It's a matter of honour. I had kept my end of the bargain when I said no to Tommy Docherty's enticing offer to join Chelsea. So, you will have a good idea of how I felt when it was clear that the Leeds United manager was going to renege on our agreement. His guarantee didn't seem to mean anything. That hurt me. I felt that if the boss had lied to me once he could easily do so again.

We pulled in at the pavement outside our family home and he said: 'Okay, see you tomorrow'. I didn't say anything. I had already made up my mind.

I had no intention of returning to Leeds United.

Chapter Three

JIMMY McGRORY AND THE HONEST TRUTH

I WAS stunned. I froze on the pavement outside our front door of the Leeds United club house, I watched Don Revie's car pull away and I knew I would not be in his company again. Not as a Leeds United player, anyway. In an instant - and on a matter of principle - I realised it was all over for me at Elland Road. He had broken a promise and I found that unacceptable.

Do not think that it was all about finances. Maybe Tommy Docherty would have offered me more money to go to Chelsea. I'll never know because we never even reached that stage in our chat while we sat in my parents' front room in the Gorbals. I had told this charismatic individual I had promised Don Revie I would sign for Leeds United. Remember, Leeds were a Second Division club at the time while Chelsea, as a top London First Division team, always seemed to be in the news. Certainly, they got a lot more media exposure. To be fair, The Doc sensed my feelings and didn't attempt to dissuade me from my convictions. He must have realised it would have been a waste of time.

So, money was not the be all and end all. Maybe that makes me look a little naive. People are welcome to their opinion. Back then, as a fourteen year old, I had been satisfied with what had been on offer from Don Revie and Leeds United. I thought it had been a great deal for myself, my mum and dad and my siblings. It also offered the McCalliog family a secure future they could only have dreamed of in Glasgow. Plus I had been impressed with what Don Revie had to say about his plans for Leeds United. I was getting the opportunity to be in at the start of something good and that was an exciting prospect. I liked a challenge and that represented a huge one for a young kid with ambitions.

My honesty even cost me the opportunity to join Celtic before Leeds came on the scene. I was fourteen years old at Holyrood school on Glasgow's south side when I was called out of class by my PE teacher Mr Murphy - I never got to know his Christian name - who told me Celtic wanted to speak to me. I was aware he had connections with the Parkhead club and, naturally, I was excited. I didn't even get the chance to contact my parents to tell them about the remarkable turn of events. A taxi had been arranged to take me over to Celtic Park for an audience with their manager, Jimmy McGrory.

I was ushered into the manager's office at Celtic Park where Jimmy McGrory sat behind a huge desk and was puffing on a pipe as we were introduced. He informed me Celtic knew all about me and how I was progressing on the football field. Then he asked which team I supported. I suppose the smart thing would have been to reply 'Celtic', but I gave him an honest answer and admitted I was a Clyde fan. Did I notice a change in the manager's demeanour? McGrory sat back on his chair and sucked on his pipe for a moment. He looked me square in the eye and asked: 'Well, Jim, if you had the chance to sign for Clyde or sign for Celtic, which club would you choose?'

The expected answer, of course, would have been 'Celtic'. That must have been the reply Jimmy McGrory anticipated as he once again puffed on his pipe. Yes, I was more than aware, most people would have immediately offered the response that could have opened the way to me joining Celtic. However, having been brought up to tell the truth, that is exactly what I did. I would have been more than delighted to have represented my favourites Clyde or Celtic. I replied: 'Either.'

Jimmy McGrory didn't say a word and simply stared at me for a few seconds. Another puff of his pipe, then he stood up and left the room. I was left sitting by myself for what seemed an age in an empty manager's office at Celtic Park with the stale, pungent aroma of pipe tobacco permeating the confined space. I wondered what was about to happen next. Finally, it dawned on me that the 'interview' had been concluded. Someone came in to inform me there was a taxi at the front door of the stadium to take me home. I admit I was very puzzled by the entire episode.

When I arrived at 42 Caledonia Road, I wondered how my mum and dad would react to the news of my meeting with the great Jimmy McGrory. I gave them chapter and verse, well, what there was of a fairly brief meeting. My parents were fairly displeased at my treatment. My honest reply hadn't been the one Jimmy McGrory had wanted or expected. I have to say, even all these years down the line, I am still not impressed by the actions of the manager to say nothing, simply walk out of the office and leave a fourteen year old kid to twiddle his thumbs. My parents' thoughts were in line with mine.

The following day at school, it got even more baffling. I was called into Mr Murphy's office and I was informed he was really annoyed with me because apparently I had upset Mr McGrory. I replied I had simply told the truth. The Celtic manager had asked me two questions and I had delivered honest answers. I could hardly believe I was being told off by my teacher for being truthful. Would it have been more acceptable if I had lied? Apparently, that was the case. Years later, I discovered my dad had gone to see Mr Murphy and let it be known he was far from satisfied with the treatment of his son from two adults who really should have known better. With the teacher's close relationship with Jimmy McGrory, I'm sure the Celtic manager would have received the message loud and clear.

So, maybe it was written in the stars I would go to Leeds United. In June 1962, I was alone as I took the train journey to Yorkshire . My parents and siblings would follow me down after the club house had been prepared for their arrival. I spent the hours during the trip contemplating on life so far and speculating on my future. I had been happy enough growing up in the familiar surroundings of Glasgow, but now I had to dedicate myself to all the challenges that lay ahead of me. I was determined to succeed as a footballer, but I realised there were many who had embarked upon the identical path and had been left disappointed. There are so many might-have-been stories out there. I had no intention of swelling those particular ranks.

The one thing I knew was that if it didn't work out, it would not be for the lack of dedication, hard work and application on my part. Without being in the least bit conceited, I was aware I had some talent when it came to kicking a football around. Otherwise, why had twenty-plus managers and scouts bothered to knock on my parents' door? Confident? Reasonably so. Complacent? Not a chance. I reasoned if I could dodge injuries and was allowed to get my head down, listen to advice and act upon it, then I had a chance. I had been given the opportunity to enhance whatever ability I had.

I really believed I was on my way. It didn't quite follow the course I had anticipated, though.

Chapter Four

EXCITEMENT OF JOINING LEEDS UNITED

AFTER a holiday in Donegal Ireland with my family during which my brothers really put me through my paces, I headed to Leeds on my own. The train journey gave me time to reflect and speculate on my future.

You may be surprised to discover Leeds United arranged for me to become an apprentice printer when I joined the club in the summer of 1962. Don Revie picked me up along with another young Scottish lad, Peter Lorimer, from Broughty Ferry in Dundee, and drove us over to a large printing works in the city. Peter and I had no idea why we were there.

We were in and out of the place in about five minutes and whisked back to Elland Road. It would be a bit of an understatement to say the boss had two rather mystified passengers in his car that morning.

Later on, all was revealed. Peter and I had signed amateur forms with the club and we joined another nine or ten boys on the ground staff, including future Scotland World Cup goalkeeper David Harvey, who was actually born in Leeds, England international Jimmy Greenhoff, Terry Hibbitt and Mick Bates. At the time, English clubs were not allowed to sign Scottish boys as apprentice professionals, so Leeds, in common with other English teams, bucked the system by supposedly finding youngsters from across the border employment outwith the club.

That's how I became an apprentice printer, but, of course, it was all a front for my football wages. If memory serves me correctly, I visited the printing works once and never went back. It was a method for clubs to get the cream of the teenage crop signed up and was common practice. Strictly speaking, as amateurs, the club were not allowed to pay us. As I have said elsewhere, the law of the land did not prevent Don Revie from offering me a signing-on fee and a weekly wage to persuade my family and I to move en masse to Yorkshire.

Revie may have let me down by reneging on his promise when it came to the full-time professional contract, but you cannot criticise the way he went about restructuring Leeds United who were doing very little of any note until he took over as manager in 1961. He sold the club to me and you had to be impressed by his ambitions for the team. He worked overtime putting together a superb nationwide scouting network that brought in some excellent youth players. In addition to myself and Peter Lorimer, Eddie Gray, a talented winger from the Glasgow housing scheme of Castlemilk, arrived a year after us. In the early sixties, the Leeds manager was putting the bricks together for the great sides of the mid-sixties and seventies. And, of course, Peter, Eddie and I all represented our country at the highest level and David Harvey, who played for Scotland because he had a Scottish grandmother, was the keeper in the 1974 World Cup Finals in West Germany.

When I arrived, the manager made certain Peter and I met the huge Scottish contingent that was already at the club. I suppose he was making us feel at home away from home. The first team boasted seasoned professionals such as former Celtic midfielder Bobby Collins, the team's dynamic captain and a pocket-sized bundle of energy, international goalkeeper Tommy Younger, Jim Storrie, Tommy Henderson, Willie Bell and Eric Smith, who, like Collins, had been at Parkhead before venturing across the border. They all made us welcome and Tommy Younger was a lovely guy who always made time for the new arrivals and went out of his way to pass on the benefits of his experience to the kids.

Unusually for a goalkeeper, Tommy, who won twenty-four caps, had captained Scotland in the 1958 World Cup Finals in Switzerland. He had played for a variety of clubs, including Hibs and Liverpool, before he arrived at Elland Road a year before me. Don Revie signed him when he was searching for tried-and-trusted campaigners to form a solid foundation at Leeds. I found him extremely helpful. In fact, it was Tommy who gave me some advice when I was taking penalty-kicks. He insisted I should aim hard and low and into the corner at the opposite end to the goalkeeper's favoured side. Most people are right-handed, so it stood to reason their left would be their weaker side. Simple, isn't it? If only.

Bobby Collins was Don Revie's onfield lieutenant. Like Tommy Younger, he was thirty-one when he was signed from Everton in 1962. He was an inspired purchase and the manager often acknowledged he had been his best-ever signing. That's some accolade from a guy like Don Revie, believe me. Bobby was a tough little Glaswegian who believed firmly the battle had to be won before the match itself. Bobby was a key figure in Leeds' rise to the top in the mid-sixties and his incredible drive, desire and will-to-win-at-all-costs attitude became catalyst for the club's success.

I also recall Welsh international star John Charles returning to the club. I had only been there a short time when it was announced this legendary figure was coming back after his five-year career in Italy with Juventus. I was just a kid when he was transferred to the Turin club in August 1957 for a-then British transfer record fee of £65,000. Coming from my part of the world back then, I didn't even believe there had been that much money printed. Actually, Don Revie paid out a Leeds all-time high fee of £53,000 for Charles, who, coincidentally, was also thirty-one when he signed for a second time. He rejoined after enhancing his reputation worldwide and he arrived at the club looking like a movie star.

When I was training along with the other apprentices at Fullerton Park all of us couldn't help but look over to where the first team were training for a glimpse of the versatile player who could play centre-half and centre-forward and rejoiced in the moniker 'The Gentle Giant'. So, where did all the money come from to buy back the Leeds icon? Don Revie and the board agreed they should hike the prices for season 1962/63 and the supporters were happy enough to stump up.

There was also a certain Billy Bremner around at the time and he was about nineteen when I arrived. One day, Peter Lorimer and I were talking to Billy and it was obvious his mood was low. He said to us: 'Why are you two here? You could have gone to better clubs.' This gave me a bit of a jolt, but, upon reflection, things under Don Revie had yet to kick off and Billy was probably speaking from frustration. He was struggling for form, clearly suffering from homesickness and there was a proposed move to Hibs on the horizon. I just wonder how different football history might have been if Billy, a Stirlingshire boy, had gone to the Edinburgh club.

In contrast, I was enjoying myself after settling in well. My family had moved down, my dad was working and that was a huge bonus for me. Training was something to look forward to and working with Sid Owen was a joy, as well, The ground staff trained every morning at nine o'clock and you couldn't help but pick up a hint or two from some excellent coaches. It was terrific to work with Sid, from whom I learned so much. Les Cocker and Bob English were also heavily involved, although at this stage I didn't see too much of the boss.

Of course, there was a downside of being on the ground staff at a football club in the early sixties. I'm talking about the jobs were required to carry out throughout the stadium. I accepted it was fair enough that we had to clean the boots of the first-team players and splash some fresh paint around the dressing rooms. Those were chores expected of kids at most football clubs. However, you have to draw a line somewhere. On Mondays, following the weekend home games, we were usually instructed by the head groundsman, a bloke called Cecil, to clean the stadium from top to bottom. This charming gentleman would inevitably find other unwelcome tasks for the young players which we believed might have come under his remit.

Things came to a head one day when youthful rebellion made a long-overdue appearance. Jimmy Greenhoff and I were a two-man revolution when we were told to brush the stand opposite the players' entrance. It wasn't exactly a mutiny. We sneaked down the stairs at the back of the stand and headed for the nearby sweetie shop. In today's world, it would hardly rate a mention and certainly wouldn't have been seen as a transgression. Back in the early sixties, though, things were a little different. Jimmy and I soon discovered that such behaviour could provoke disciplinary action. Honestly! We found ourselves carpeted by a clearly dissatisfied Mr Revie.

The manager tore a strip off Jimmy, telling him he should have known better as he had been at the club longer. The manager then fixed me in his gaze and barked: 'Okay, Jim, what's you excuse?' I thought for a moment, took a deep breath and replied with complete honesty: 'I came to Leeds to play football, not do a groundsman's job.'

With his face expressionless, the boss continued to look at me. My words seem to hang in the air. He paused before saying: 'Okay, I'll leave it for now.' We were told to remove ourselves from his office and I wondered if I had dropped myself in it. However, over the following weeks, I noticed that the jobs with the groundsman were gradually being scaled down and I have to admit I felt vindicated for standing up for myself.

There was another occasion when I had a discussion with the boss which I found fairly rewarding. One major downside as a sixteen year old playing in the Under-19 side was that I felt shattered at the end of the day. I was struggling a bit as I accepted I was not the biggest or strongest. I was counting down the days until my seventeenth birthday when I expected to sign full-time forms which would step up my training routines. Sid Owen was a very astute observer and could see what was going on and he offered me a lot of encouragement. He gave me a lot of hope and I also discussed the problem with the boss who allayed my fears by telling me he was satisfied with reports of my progress while reassuring me everything would fall into place.

The 1962/63 season saw one of the worst winters in living memory and some teams went weeks, if not months, without playing. Conversely, this actually helped me as by the time the weather had relented around March 1963, I was feeling a lot stronger and I now felt I was on a more level playing field. I was now performing with a lot more confidence, playing well and contributing a lot more and, more importantly, I wasn't so knackered at the end of the day. I was standing out in training and junior matches while beginning to feature quite regularly in the reserve side. One day in March 1962, when I was cleaning out the reserve dressing room, I checked the second team line-up for the next day's game at Everton and saw that my name was on it. The boss had a policy of giving young players their reserve debuts away from Elland Road as he felt they wouldn't be under as much pressure. My first game for the reserves went well and I became a fixture in the side until the end of the season.

Another highlight was getting half-an-hour game-time during the Testimonial Match for Tommy Younger. I didn't feel out of place in an international line-up that kicked off with this eleven: Bert Trautmann; Roy Gratix, Ray Wilson; Bobby Robson, Ron Yeats, Peter Swan; Brian Douglas, Pat Quinn, Ian St John, Jimmy Melia and Mike O'Grady. I felt as though my career was moving in the right direction at this stage. That thought hit the buffers the day Don Revie drove me home and I realised he had lied to me.

When I went into the house that afternoon, my mother sensed immediately something was bothering me. She was concerned, so I told her that I would speak to them both when my dad came in from work while I thought about my next move. I went into the back garden and had a kickabout with Freddie my brother while my mind raced. I was in a bit of a whirlwind. Earlier that day, I had set off as usual for training and now, only a few hours later, I knew deep down any thoughts of a career at Leeds United were over. In my mind, it was not about money, it was the principle. Don Revie clearly had no intention of keeping his word and that helped me make up my mind. Later that evening, after my dad had returned from work, we sat down and discussed the rather dire and totally unexpected situation. My parents left the final decision to me. I told them I would not be going back to Leeds United. They respected my wishes and went with my decision.

Uppermost in my mind was the fact that my parents had uprooted the family from Glasgow to come down to Leeds. They had a comfortable life in surroundings they had enjoyed, but now they would have to leave the house and

32

my dad would have to give up his job. All this weighed heavily on me. My parents had been such huge sources of inspiration and encouragement to me and I owed them so much. However, so typical of them, they did not hesitate to support my decision. I felt totally shattered.

The following day, I boarded a train for Glasgow.

Chapter Five

PRESSING MATTERS, CELTIC AGAIN AND CHELSEA

I DIDN'T hang around when I got back to Glasgow. Relatives, Auntie Bridie and Uncle Eddie, had very kindly agreed to let me stay with them and the following day I was on my travels again as I walked from Govanhill on the city's south side into the city centre.

My destinations were Albion Street where the Daily Express was produced and Hope Street where the Daily Record was printed. I was eager to talk to sports journalists I had met and tell them of my predicament. Nowadays, of course, a player would simply phone his agent and let him take care of business, Back in the early sixties, there was no such luxury. It was my problem and I would do my best to sort it out.

Jim Rodger, known as 'Scoop' to a lot of the footballers, met me at the Express building, I outlined what had happened with Don Revie at Leeds United and I insisted I would not be going back to the Yorkshire club under any circumstances. I thought it was only fair to let Jim know I would be going to the Record to tell my story to Ken Gallacher. It turns out Jim and Ken were big friends. Their newspapers may have been bitter rivals in the ongoing circulation war, but these two had become press-box buddies over the years and they enjoyed their daily jousts in print at their respective newspapers. I knew they were well-respected journalists and that's the reason I sought their assistance. If I hadn't made that move, who would ever have heard of a basically unknown sixteen-year-old Scottish hopeful walking out on Leeds United?

I was satisfied to leave the story with the sports scribes and see where they could take it. They both promised to let the situation be known to clubs they thought might be interested. I trusted them and I wasn't surprised they both kept their word. No doubt they would have been working in tandem and I still don't know to this day who made the contacts with Celtic and Chelsea. I later discovered Jim Rodger had contacts in clubs everywhere - and I do mean everywhere, not just in Britain - while Ken Gallacher was a big friend of a certain Tommy Docherty.

There was a little bit of red tape to be sorted, as well. Although I had only signed amateur forms, I was receiving messages Leeds believed I was their player and the contract I had agreed to as a fifteen year old was legally binding. I later discovered this was not the case. I was free to sign for whoever I wanted and there was little Mr Revie and his club could do about it. I arranged with the journalists to phone them at their office in a couple of days to see if there had been any progress.

Things moved very swiftly at this stage. The Express sportswriter contacted me to say Celtic and Chelsea had expressed an interest and, just a few minutes later, the Record reporter got in touch to confirm the interest from The Doc. The London club's manager actually told Jim Rodger to pass on his home phone number while Sean Fallon, who was the Celtic assistant manager, indicated he would make a personal visit to meet me at my auntie's house.

I rang my mum to relay the news and she informed me that Don Revie had been in touch and was coming up to Glasgow along with the club's chairman Harry Reynolds to talk to me. He really should have saved himself and the club's supremo the bother. I was not about to be swayed from my original decision. In any case, I telephoned The Doc and I agreed to fly to London to meet him. Before that, though, Sean Fallon turned up at my auntie's house. We had a meeting in her front room and I have to admit we had a great chat. He was certainly a lot more interested in my future than his boss, Jimmy McGrory, when I had met him at Celtic Park. The Celtic No.2 was very likeable - it must be the Irish charm - as he talked about the possibility of joining the Parkhead team and I promised him I would let him know my decision after I had met Tommy Docherty.

The situation now went into overdrive when Mr Revie and Mr Reynolds, an extremely wealthy individual who had bankrolled his manager's plans for the club, turned up at my auntie's place. If they had been five minutes earlier, they would have bumped into the Celtic assistant boss. Mr Revie had adopted a very different character from the one I had witnessed in his car when he drove me home, the manager who had basically laughed off my question of a full-time contract. He had certainly changed his tune. He could also be very persuasive. Mr Revie even told me he would honour the original terms, but I would not budge. I told him I had no intention of going back to Leeds and I detailed my reasons. Mr Revie had clearly promised me things he had no intention of honouring just to keep me away from other clubs.

I was aware he was ruthlessly ambitious. He made Leeds into a top club that were always challenging for honours. Actually, I take pride in my choice to join them. My feeling was that they would grow into a great team, but, unfortunately, things didn't work out for me with them. Mr Revie, the manager, was very different from Don Revie, the player. He had been a highly-skilled footballer who did not embrace the physical side of the game and I had been informed he would often jump out of tackles.

As Leeds manager, however, he built a team renowned for their uncompromising style of play which made a lot of enemies, on and off the field. Consequently, they didn't always get the credit they deserved for their achievements and at times the way they could actually perform and produce some eye-catching, attractive football. In my opinion, Mr Revie was motivated by money. As I have stated previously, it wasn't all about cash for me. Growing up and living in a deprived area of Glasgow, my family did not have a lot, but we had morals and principles and if Mr Revie had not reneged on his promises, I would never have left Leeds United. Now he was ready to resurrect the original offer, but I felt if he put it on me now, he would do it for the rest of my career while we were together. The official line from the club was that I was homesick which, of course, was far removed from the truth. Yes, I missed some of my pals, but my family was with me in Leeds.

When the penny dropped I would not change my mind, veiled threats were made about Leeds having the authority to hold onto my registration. At that time, I wasn't too sure about the contractual situation, but I wasn't convinced by what turned out to be bluff from Mr Revie, a person I knew had lied to me previously. Once again, I stuck to my word and told Mr Revie and the club chairman I would not be returning to Elland Road. They looked fairly resigned to the situation by the time they left my auntie's house. As it happens, a phone call to Tommy Docherty immediately cleared up the registration situation. 'Did you sign professional forms?' he asked. I reassured him I did not. 'Then you are free to sign for whichever club you want,' he said.

Soon afterwards, I flew to London with my mother to meet The Doc. My fellow-Glaswegian was an impressive character and it was obvious he knew what he was doing as a manager. Chelsea had just won promotion to the First Division with a talented young side and it was clear The Doc, a dynamic, bubbly, effervescent individual, believed in giving youth a chance. He was a breath of fresh air in the game. I signed professional forms for the Stamford Bridge outfit on my seventeenth birthday. A dream come true.

When I returned to Scotland, one of the first things I did was to put a call into Sean Fallon and inform him of my decision. He would have been disappointed, but, ever the gentleman, he wished me well and told me he hoped I would have a great career. I was fated never to play for Celtic and their assistant manager's words meant a lot to me. Remarkably, though, Don Revie refused to give up on me and plainly wasn't a guy who accepted rejection. He sent coach Sid Owen to Glasgow to try to get me to change my mind. As much as I respected and liked Sid, there was no way I would consider going back. In any case, it was too late. I had got my wish and signed full-time professional forms which had been my aim in the first place. If Mr Revie had been as good as his word, the entire event would not have been set in motion.

My family had to give up the club house in Yorkshire, of course. They returned to Glasgow, had an interlude in Ireland and then joined me in London. Under Tommy Docherty, my career as a Chelsea player was about to take off in earnest.

Or so I thought.

Chapter Six

CHELSEA TO THE FORE, VIBRANT LONDON

TOMMY DOCHERTY messed up. Four words I never thought I would write. And these were far removed from my sentiments when I joined Chelsea on my seventeenth birthday on September 23 1963. Just over two years later, I would leave the London side after my third transfer request when Sheffield Wednesday paid £37,500 for me, at that time a UK record transfer fee for a teenager.

To be completely honest, I could never have forecast a return to Yorkshire when I joined The Doc in London. Everything was positive at that point and moving on from Stamford Bridge would never have entered my thinking. I was delighted to be part of the Chelsea revolution, as the media were calling the extraordinary and ambitious transformation of the club under my fellow-Glaswegian, the garrulous Tommy Docherty.

He had, of course, made his pitch to me after watching me play for Scotland Schoolboys against our English counterparts when we won 4-3 at Ibrox in 1962. As I have stated elsewhere, I had to say no to Mr Docherty because I had given my word to Don Revie I would join Leeds United. The situation had somersaulted and now I was a Chelsea player and I couldn't have been more happy. I received a decent signing-on fee spread over a few years at the club moved my family into a lovely semi-detached house in Twickenham.

The previous occupant had been Welsh international midfielder Graham Moore who had just been transferred to Manchester United for £45,000. Eventually, following my promotion to the first-team squad in 1964, my wages had risen to £80 per week plus bonuses. With the incentive scheme designed around winning games and remaining unbeaten, there were some weeks when I was earning between £120 to £200 per week which was considerably more than the average wage and what the man in the street was picking up. It was a simple enough system; the longer we remained undefeated, the more cash went into our bank account. Liverpool, under Bill Shankly, operated a similar system with a low basic wage with fabulous add-ons for success. Didn't do our Anfield rivals any harm, did it?

When I arrived at The Bridge, it was apparent there was so much potential at the club with a host of bright prospects desperate and determined to make an instant impact. Docherty called us his 'Little Diamonds' and you could hear him shouting those words at the top of his voice from the dug-out on match day as he encouraged his players to drive forward. The youth set-up was the envy of most of the clubs in the First Division. The list of players who came through the youth ranks was breathtaking. Jimmy Greaves had initially made his breakthrough at Chelsea before his move to AC Milan in 1961 and his subsequent quickfire return to English football with Spurs for the memorable fee of £99,999 because their manager Bill Nicholson did not want to saddle the prolific hitman with the first £100,000 tag in the UK. I'm sure that quid made all the difference.

Around the same time as the emergence of Greaves, there was a winger by the name of Peter Brabrook who went onto play for England and when I joined there were young talents such as Terry Venables, Ken Shellito, Alan and Ron Harris, Bobby Tambling and John Hollins with others such as John Boyle, Peter Osgood, Peter Houseman and Alan Hudson still to break through. Everywhere you looked, there was wall-to-wall quality. It was a pleasure and honour to be in such company. It was more than just a little reassuring to look around the dressing room and see these guys wearing the same colours as yourself.

So, you may ask, what went wrong? Tommy Docherty is to blame.

Chapter Seven

TREBLE IN CHELSEA'S SIGHTS!

CHELSEA faced Liverpool in the English FA Cup semi-final at Villa Park on March 27 1964 in front of a crowd of 67,686. The average age of our team was just over twenty-three. As we lined up that Saturday afternoon, there was the chance Tommy Docherty's 'young diamonds' could win the glorious treble of domestic honours.

The League Cup was halfway to the Stamford Bridge trophy cabinet following the 3-2 first leg victory over Leicester City in London twelve days before the FA Cup-tie. At the time. we were also involved in a three-way tussle along with Leeds and Manchester United at the top of the First Division and were just one game away from a Wembley Final. These were thrilling times to be part of Chelsea Football Club. Everything was there to be won and so much silverware seemed within touching distance.

The dream began to fade on a grey, still afternoon in the Midlands. I was on the sidelines with Terry Venables in the team. I didn't have a problem with that. He was the club captain and a key component in Tommy Docherty's strategy which, as results emphasised, was clearly working. We played well enough against Bill Shankly's side in the first-half and both keepers - Peter Bonetti for us and Tommy Lawrence for the Anfield outfit - made timely saves to keep it scoreless at the interval.

However, we were caught out shortly after the hour mark when Liverpool's pacy left-winger Peter Thompson got clear to beat our budding England international No.1 at his near post. We rallied, but Willie Stevenson, a former Rangers left-half, struck the killer goal from the penalty spot in the seventy-ninth minute and there was no way back. That put paid to our treble ambitions - incidentally, Liverpool went on to win the Cup when Ian St John got the decisive goal in extra-time against my old club Leeds - although we did secure the League

Cup with a goalless draw at Filbert Street on April 5, so the strikes from Bobby Tambling, Terry Venables and Eddie McCreadie, a future Scotland international team-mate in a small celebration at Wembley, were crucial in Chelsea winning their first major trophy in a decade.

Naturally, though, the First Division title was our main target, that was the Big One for every ambitious club at the start of the season. And we were in with a real chance. Even all these years on, I still insist Chelsea were the best team in the land and should have had the championship to show for their efforts. Somehow, though, Tommy Docherty made an unfathomable decision that derailed the team and, ultimately, cost the club dearly. It was as spectacular an implosion as you could get in football. Meltdown doesn't come close.

Around that time, many astute observers were convinced the club could go all the way. We had such style, we were a swashbuckling unit that was exciting to watch and were the talk of the football world. Our team spirit and camaraderie were second to none, we were a marvellous mix, a real fusion of talents. The boss had a little trick before each game. He held us back to the last possible moment. He made sure our opponents were out on the pitch before us and then he released us down the tunnel with the orders to run full-pelt onto the playing surface. We positively raced out, each of us sprinting as fast as our legs would carry us. Everything seemed to be coming together.

And then came the Blackpool incident. With three games to go, we were two points adrift of Manchester United and level on points with Leeds. With two points for a win, no-one would dare to write us off. Our remaining outings were all in the north west and were due to be played within the space of seven days. Tight? It was suffocating. As was the boss's custom, we were based at a hotel in Blackpool for the encounters with Liverpool at Anfield, Burnley at Turf Moor and Blackpool at Bloomfield Road. It was an unfortunate sequence with all the meetings scheduled to take place away from The Bridge, but it's just the way the cards had fallen as we played catch-up following a savage winter.

We travelled to Merseyside for the first match on Monday April 19 and, unfortunately, they repeated the Cup semi-final scoreline of 2-0 which left us with the burden of winning the remaining two encounters and attempting to rack up massive victories with goal average - and not goal difference as it is today - likely to be vitally important. We were due to play Burnley five days later and the manager realised his young players required some relaxation.

Following training on Wednesday, The Doc told the players there would be an 11pm curfew as we prepared for the trip to Burnley on the Saturday. We went out on Blackpool town and returned at the appointed hour. I was sharing a room with fellow-Scot John Boyle and we both got our heads down and made sure we had a good night's sleep. Naturally, we hadn't a clue at the events that were about to unfold. Ignorance is bliss, they say. The following morning, John and I went down for breakfast and you didn't require Sherlock Holmes qualities to detect something wasn't quite right. The mood, the atmosphere, everything just didn't click. Little did we know, but we were in the middle of a sensational situation that was to blow Chelsea off course. What happened next destroyed that special team spirit that was evident in our dressing room. There was a genuine one-for-all-and-all for-one feel among the squad. That was obliterated overnight. Quite literally.

It was clear something was certainly not right when we entered the dining room. For a start, there was hardly anyone there. There were only a few players dotted about, so I asked the trainer Harry Medhurst what was going on. I was also aware there were a few cameras clicking away from press photographers, but I was still none the wiser about the happenings overnight. Harry thought I was taking the piss and must have believed I was well up to speed with what had occurred. Trust me, when I put my head on the pillow the previous evening, I thought Chelsea could win the First Division title. Hours after wakening up, I was beginning to have a dramatic change of mind.

I was informed the bus was leaving for the training ground at 10am sharp after breakfast. John and I ate in silence and wondered where the rest of our team-mates were. I was at a loss to understand what was going on and no-one seemed prepared to clue me in. When the team bus arrived at the training HQ, Tommy Docherty took us into one of the changing rooms and locked the door behind him. It was all very mystifying.

He told us he had sent eight players home for breaking the curfew. He named the team-mates involved: Terry Venables, the club captain, Eddie McCreadie. John Hollins, George Graham, Marvin Hinton, Bert Murray, Barry Bridges and Joe Fascoine. I was stunned. I didn't have to ask the question about their availability for the so-important game at Turf Moor only two days away. What had they done to incur the wrath of the manager?

It transpired the players had sneaked down the fire escape and left the door open. They had gone out on the town and hadn't returned until the early hours of the morning. The Doc had been tipped off by a hotel porter and he waited for them coming back. Basically, he then told them to make themselves scarce. The manager warned us not to speak to the press when we returned after training.

The news, of course, had spread like wildfire. The national newspapers in London sent what seemed like platoons of news journalists and photographers to our location. It wasn't the usual sports reporters, but newshounds not one bit interested in football. They were there for the dirt as they sniffed front page headlines. And, yes, the sensational story hit the front and back pages of the journals.

As the game against Burnley approached, the players who were left did not have a clue to the boss's next move. Had they been suspended for twenty-four hours? Would they return for the vital game? Would he bring in reinforcements? So many questions and so little time. By the Friday, it was evident we would be playing at Turf Moor with a severely-depleted side. Venables and Co would not be involved. It was a preposterous situation and it played right into the hands of our title rivals Manchester United and Leeds.

I was one of the players who was brought in for the Burnley match. The line-up also included two untried youngsters from Scotland, Billy Sinclair and Jim Smart. It's extraordinary to look back and note this was their solitary first-team appearance for either of my compatriots. The atmosphere, if you can call it that, in the dressing room before kick-off was almost funereal. The team who took to the field did their best to make the best of a bad job. Astonishingly, the excluded players were also in the changing area before the kick-off. It was simply surreal. They sat down beside us, but no words were spoken. Let's face it, nothing could be said to repair the damage that had already been inflicted upon the squad.

We were three goals down inside nineteen minutes as our championship hopes were torpedoed. Fellow-Scot Andy Lochhead, a big, burly old-fashioned centre-forward, scored two and Northern Ireland international Willie Irvine added a third. Ron Harris pulled one back, but Lochhead completed his hat-trick just on half-time. Alas, he wasn't finished torturing us. He thumped in two more to hoist his personal total to five and our only reply after the turnaround was an effort from Peter Houseman four minutes from the end. It was a disaster from start to finish. Trounced 6-2, our last chance of the championship was buried in the Lancashire mud.

To this day, I have never mentioned the Blackpool incident to any of the players who broke the curfew. So, who was to blame for ruining the prospects of an unbelievable group of players? Was it the manager or the players? So many people offered opinions at the time and Tommy Docherty received a lot of support and praise from different sources, including club chairman Joe Mears. However, the facts were that, despite faltering slightly with two games to play, we still stood a good chance of winning the First Division. Had we faced Burnley, who finished twelfth in a twenty-two team league, with a full-strength side we would have fancied our chances.

As it turned out, Manchester United lifted the championship on goal average after finishing level with Leeds on sixty-one points. We lost 3-2 in our last game against Blackpool to complete the campaign on fifty-six points. So, the history books show us we could have taken a maximum four points from the matches against Burnley and Blackpool and still have come up one point short. But that is with the benefit of hindsight. When you are in the thick of the action. you have to remain positive and do your best to win your games and hope your nearest challengers slip up along the way.

My opinion is that things would never be the same again at Stamford Bridge. The trust between the manager and players had been irretrievably shattered. I am not ashamed to admit that I shed tears at the realisation that our dream as a team was over. The newspapers and the media, in general, had a field day and my God how it hurt. The future had seemed so bright at one stage and then it had been engulfed by a dirty black cloud. I wished we could put it right, get it back to the way it had been, but I knew better.

Football is an emotional game and feelings matter. It's more than just physical challenges. For me, it's a more mental game. Contrary to popular opinion, footballers are sensitive to criticism and, naturally, it is vital to be in the right frame of mind. That is why I contend the harmony and team spirit at Chelsea couldn't be the same after Blackpool. Discipline at a football club is paramount, but there is a fine line to be drawn. Indiscipline is not acceptable and the club and the players paid a heavy price for that night out in Blackpool.

It has long been my opinion that Tommy Docherty over-reacted to the situation. It should have been dealt with in-house. Tackling the situation the way he did resulted in the story being splashed all over the newspapers and fatally undermined the morale and team spirit at the club. Of course, the players who transgressed should have been disciplined. There is no argument or debate about that. However, I know they did not get drunk, make a fool of themselves or embarrass the club on the night in question.

They ended up being publicly humiliated with their indiscretions, such as they may have been, splashed all over the television and newspapers. That was the end of the dream. A couple of weeks later, I knew it was time to move on.

Chapter Eight

DOC AND THE DILEMMA

I READILY admit I had set the bar high when I embarked on my playing career. Why not? Why restrict your ambitions? Why narrow your options? I wanted to make a success of my chosen profession and that included playing for Scotland against England at Wembley. That had to be my ultimate goal.

I was young and I was confident. Never complacent, I hasten to add. I was prepared to work hard, put myself through all sort of agonies, deprive myself and maintain a professional outlook away from training and playing in order to hit my targets.

I wanted regular first-team football and in the awful aftermath of the Blackpool incident, with all the banner and sensational headlines in the newspapers and the intense coverage on TV and radio with all the attendant innuendo, I just knew instinctively it would not be at Chelsea. I felt as though I had stepped onto a rollercoaster. One minute there were genuine thoughts of an extraordinary treble of Championship, English FA Cup and League Cup at a club where it had been an absolute joy to turn up each day and go to training with a fabulous bunch of guys. The next, the dreams are in rubble, lost in mayhem and turmoil with events off the pitch.

Life, never mind football, rarely goes to plan, but, at the age of eighteen, it had all been fairly incomprehensible. I couldn't fathom the unnecessary upheaval, in my opinion, of the events that led to the First Division trophy heading to Old Trafford rather than Stamford Bridge. In the immediate fall-out of the banning of eight players that led to us being thrashed 6-2 by mid-table Burnley, I had turned everything over in my mind that weekend. It didn't get much better when we lost 3-2 to Blackpool on the Monday. The curtain came down on a campaign that had promised so much with three straight defeats with eleven goals conceded into the bargain. None of this had been in the script.

The atmosphere in the dressing room when I turned up for training was dreadful. There was none of the usual piss-taking or banter. In the space of just over a week, my football world had turned on its head. The previous Monday, we had been preparing to take on Liverpool at Anfield. At that stage, we had genuine ambitions of claiming the title. We suffered the setback of a two-goal loss and then came the Blackpool blow-up, the six-goal hammering from Burnley and a defeat by Blackpool who completed the season just five points off the relegation zone and were twenty-one adrift of us. Yet they were still good enough to beat us 3-2. Tommy Docherty had relented and brought back the likes of Terry Venables, John Hollins and George Graham among six of the banished eight players. It wasn't just a case of being too late to close the barn door, the horse had long since bolted and was well out of sight.

So, it was make-your-mind-up-time for myself again. I had made a monumental decision for me and the rest of my family to leave Leeds United after Don Revie had broken a promise. Now I realised things were not working out at Chelsea. The first time I went to see Tommy Docherty about the situation, he was as nice and ninepence. His demeanour changed rather dramatically when I told him I wanted a transfer. He chased me out of his office and informed me in his usual blunt fashion he wouldn't even bother telling the directors about my request.

The second time I asked to leave, The Doc softened slightly. At least, on this occasion, he did listen although he did inform me he would be recommending to the directors that they reject my request. In between, I had told my parents of my dilemma and, as ever, they were very supportive. At this time, I had no idea if any clubs were interested in me, but I realised that when the news reached the newspapers that I wanted a move, I would have an inkling as to which clubs had shown any notice and how much Chelsea would demand in a transfer fee.

Following the decision to ask for a transfer, I pushed myself even harder in training and in matches. I was learning, improving and getting stronger all the time. However, I have to admit it was incredibly frustrating not playing regular first-team football. Chelsea were involved in a lot of friendlies and I recall travelling up to Scotland to play against a Glasgow Select in a charity match at Hampden in August 1965. Our opponents that day included Celtic's Billy McNeill and Tommy Gemmell and Rangers' John Greig, all of whom I would get to know well in the near future. The game was noteworthy for the relaxation of the offside law, with the 18-yard line being extended to the touchlines with offside being given only in these areas. That, though, was not a contributing factor in our 3-0 win with second-half goals from the unfortunate John Grieg who diverted one away from keeper Tommy McCulloch, George Graham and Bobby Tambling.

For the record, The Doc sent out a strong line-up which read: Bonetti; Shellito, Harris; Hollins, Hinton, Boyle; Bridges, McCalliog, Graham, Venables and Tambling. The Glasgow Select read: McCulloch (Clyde); Johansen (Rangers), Gemmell (Celtic); Murdoch (Celtic), McNeill (Celtic), Greig (Rangers); Hughes (Celtic), Forrest (Rangers), Jim McLean (Clyde), George McLean (Rangers) and McParland (Partick Thistle). Incidentally, Davie McParland was my first professional coach when I was fourteen.

That game was part of a pre-season tour that also took in West Germany, Sweden and Denmark. I was involved in most of the eight matches, scoring a hat-trick against Swedish side Orebro SK while we also played a match against the West German international team in Essen. Our opponents were preparing for the World Cup Finals in England the following year where, of course, they reached the Finals before losing 4-2 in extra-time to the host nation at Wembley. Barry Bridges and I scored, but we lost 3-2 against a very accomplished team.

I reckoned I had done well in the friendly encounters and, thankfully, the manager agreed and selected me in midfield along with Terry Venables for the league opener against, ironically, Burnley at Stamford Bridge on August 21 where the club captain scored our goal in a 1-1 draw.

Chapter Nine

CHELSEA IN MY PATH TO WEMBLEY

I MAY have left Chelsea on October 1 1965 to embark upon a new career with Sheffield Wednesday, but Tommy Docherty was still to play a part in my future. Six months after my £37,500 exit from The Bridge, we were rivals in the English FA Cup semi-final at Villa Park on the Saturday afternoon of April 23. It seemed fated that our paths would cross.

The previous season, of course, I had been at Chelsea when they met Liverpool at the same stage of the competition. Unfortunately, I didn't play that particular day, but it was a sore one to take when the team lost 2-0 to Bill Shankly's side. They say it's worse to lose in a semi-final than a final. At least, if you go all the way to Wembley there is the glamour, glitz and kudos that come your way for that achievement in itself. All I can say is that the atmosphere in the Chelsea dressing room after the loss to the Merseyside outfit was dreadful. I felt for the lads that day.

And yet here I was, at the same venue just twelve months down the line, and I was desperate to play my part in making certain they were just as dejected. My focus was totally on Sheffield Wednesday. That had been the case as soon as I agreed to sign on the dotted line for Alan Brown. I had done my homework on the manager, his ambitions and the players who would become my new team-mates. Football, as I've said, can be an emotional game, but there are occasions when you have to detach yourself from personal feelings. Wednesday had shelled out a record fee for a teenager to sign me, they paid my wages, my family had now joined me in a club house in Yorkshire and they deserved every ounce of effort I could possibly engender on the field for the good of the club.

I was totally concentrated on what this semi-final meant to Wednesday, the manager, the players, the club as a whole and, of course, their superb supporters who had made me welcome from the moment I stepped in the front door. On the day of the game, winning and getting a place at Wembley was all that mattered. In the opposition would be my Scottish pal Johnny Boyle as well as the likes of Terry Venables, George Graham and goalkeeper Peter Bonetti. Our past friendships were of no concern at that moment. On the same afternoon, Everton were due to play , but that game meant nothing to me. There was absolutely no point in thinking about a massive encounter at Wembley with the world and its auntie looking on if we didn't do the business against Chelsea. Only then - if we were victorious, of course - would I show any interest on opponents on the most prestigious and colourful confrontation in the football calendar.

It's a long and winding road to that grand finale. On that FA Cup run we never played a solitary tie at Hillsborough. My first goal in the competition came away to Reading in the third round when I grabbed our winner in a 3-2 triumph after Johnny Fantham had struck a double. Next up was a meeting with Newcastle United at St James's Park which I recognised as being a lucky ground for me during my career. And so it proved again. Joe Harvey, the opposing manager, had pinpointed me in the press as the danger to his side. I can't recall if I lived up to that assessment, but we did manage to win 2-1 on Tyneside to move into the fifth round.

Once more the draw was unkind and we were on our travels again, this time to Huddersfield Town. Once again, it was a tough scrap and we managed to do enough with a second successive 2-1 win. We were building momentum in the tournament and we were delighted because we were not giving our supporters an awful lot to smile about with our league form. In the end, we finished in seventeenth position, just three points clear of Northampton who finished second bottom.

No-one at Wednesday was surprised to hear the ballot had paired us with Blackburn Rovers at Ewood Park for the FA Cup quarter-final. We weren't exactly getting an easy route to Wembley, were we? I wasn't one hundred per cent fit for that match and had sustained a knee injury. I was asked to play and I reassured the manager I would give it my best shot. The heavy pitch that afternoon was a real drain and a monumental test for everyone, but we once again battled to a 2-1 success with David Ford our hero with two excellent goals. Chelsea - and Tommy Docherty - barred our path to the final.

I was asked my thoughts by the newspapermen about the prospects of playing against my former team-mates. I answered that my only focus was on winning the tie for Sheffield Wednesday. My solitary target was to play in the final. I'm sure my old Chelsea pals would have given an identical answer, their only aim would be to reach Wembley. I'm sure they would get over my disappointment as I would I knew they were an ambitious bunch, but, by the same token, they would have known of my desire and determination to be a winner. Why else would I have left Stamford Bridge the previous year? I was eager to go somewhere where I could succeed and I believed I had more of a chance at Wednesday. Tunnel vision? You better believe it.

So, on a Saturday afternoon in April 1966. I wasn't interested in any old pal's acts or sentimentality. And I was fully aware every single player in the opposition would take to the Villa Park pitch with precisely the same thoughts. As we warmed up for the game, I shook the hands with some of the Chelsea lads. That was only good manners. However, something strange occurred as I went through a kickabout routine with Don Megson, our captain, prior to the kick-off. Tommy Docherty appeared on the touchline and intimated he wanted to talk to me. Highly irregular, of course, but it is The Doc we're talking about. You could say my fellow-Glaswegian was a one-off.

I still don't have a clue as to the Chelsea manager's intentions that day. He was great at kidology, I was aware of that. He might just have been about to wish me good luck. He might have wanted to talk about the state of the Villa Park which was just a sea of mud even before a ball was kicked in anger. Maybe he wanted to get my new address to send me a Christmas card. Unlikely, I suppose. I'll never know. Don, who was our club captain, intervened. He was a big lad. I didn't hear the exchange of words between the two, but, suffice to say, we resumed knocking the ball around and The Doc trudged off to the dug-out.

In the build-up up to the semi-final, Chelsea v Sheffield Wednesday at Villa Park, Laurie Pignon, sports reporter in London with the Daily Sketch, posed the question: 'Who is the greatest teenage centre-forward of them all – Jim McCalliog, the one that Tommy Docherty sold for £37,5000 or Peter Osgood, the one he kept for keeps?' No pressure on myself or Ossie. After the match reports from Maurice Smith in the Sunday People read: 'Chelsea couldn't say manager Tommy Docherty hadn't warned them…Jim McCalliog is their danger man.' Donald Saunders in the Sunday Telegraph reported: 'It was left to McCalliog, on this day so much more effective than Osgood, the lad who was preferred to him at Stamford Bridge, to ensure victory by heading in a centre from Ford.'

It was a great victory, we were a young team and Wembley beckoned.

Chapter Ten

FIRST FA CUP FINAL - AND A PROMISE TO MYSELF

IT was FA Cup Final Day, Saturday May 14 1966, Everton v Sheffield Wednesday. I woke up about 9.30am to watch the build-up to the game. I had FA Cup Day Fever as usual every year I would sit and watch from afar in Glasgow. Looking to learn and pick up what information I could in my ambition to be a footballer. I wouldn't move from the television. I loved all the pomp and ceremony and seeing some of my football heroes.

I remember watching two of my Scottish football heroes, Denis Law and Pat Crerand play for Manchester United against Leicester City when United won 3-1. I was delighted to see them doing a lap of honour at Wembley with the FA Cup going back to Manchester. My room-mate Wilf Smith woke up and said: 'What time is it?' I said: '9.30, and did you sleep well?' 'Yes, okay, how about you?' he replied. I had a great sleep. I was nineteen years of age and Wilf was twenty years old and it would be a long day for us both.

I started to get ready so I could watch the build-up to the FA Cup Final. Myself and Wilf wouldn't be watching the game. We would be playing for Sheffield Wednesday and hopefully take the FA Cup back to Sheffield as winners for our wonderful supporters who had generously got behind me since I had arrived in Sheffield as Britain's costliest teenager, a title I cherished and still do. For our manager Allan Brown to pay that big fee and for Tommy Docherty to demand such a big fee for myself filled me with confidence as I made my way in my football career.

Watching the television with Wilf my team-mate was so surreal. Our eyes were glued to the television. It was fantastic and we were not due downstairs for our pre-match meal until 12pm. The time went very quickly and soon we were ready to go downstairs with a big grin on our faces and couldn't wait to see the other lads. The pre-match meal was very enjoyable as always. I always had scrambled eggs on toast and tea to drink, nice and light and not hard to digest as I wanted to be able to get up and down the pitch. All the team were excited and ready for a difficult game against the Bank of England team Everton that had cost £340,000 (a lot of money in 1966). Everton's owners were the Moores family who owned Littlewoods and Vernons Pools. Everton's manager was Harry Catterick who had managed Sheffield Wednesday earlier in his career.

As we got on the coach, the hotel staff came out to give us a wave. And then we saw the police escort at the front of the bus, it was getting serious. I couldn't wait to get moving on our way to Wembley. I think we all knew what was coming next. There was a great atmosphere on the coach. We were a young side, six players under twenty-two years of age. Everton were an experienced side with seven international players in their ranks and they left out Fred Pickering, an £80,000 signing from Blackburn Rovers. There were four Scottish internationals in their team, Alex Parker, Jimmy Gabriel, Alex Scott and Alex Young, players I knew of but never met. I was the only Scot in our team.

As we got closer to the twin towers, we could see the fans. It was difficult to identify some as both teams wore blue and white. We had to change our strip to all-white for the final. All through the rounds to the final we were drawn away from home and in the final we were in the visitors' dressing room a Wembley. It was fantastic to see all the fans, the colours were amazing. Driving up Wembley Way was special. We the players were looking out hoping to see family or friends and waving to our fans. Once the bus stopped, we were cheered into the dressing room by our fans. Inside the dressing room, I checked to see if there were any telegrams for myself. There was from my family and friends. It was good to read their best wishes for the game. Then the boss took over: 'Let's go out onto the pitch and check your studs are correct for the state of the pitch.' I decided short studs. As we walked up the tunnel and onto the pitch, it was perfect. Our fans were at the tunnel end and the atmosphere was everything I hoped it would be.

As time moved on towards kick-off, the boss had a word. He said: 'Go out and enjoy yourselves. We have done our preparation and we are ready. All the best.' Time to go in the tunnel and wait for the referee to take the teams forward and onto the hallowed Wembley turf. I was buzzing. We were introduced to Princess Margaret and it was a great thrill meeting royalty. Up until now, I was fine and taking everything in my stride. I had a quick look around and took in the occasion. What a moment to treasure. Lots of players have never played in an FA Cup Final at Wembley. How sad for them. Jack Taylor, the referee, got the game underway and we were kicking into the tunnel end behind the goal where our supporters were. We pushed Everton to defend. After four minutes I moved onto a throw from our left-hand side and I hit a half-volley with my left foot goalwards. It beat the keeper, Gordon West. He got a touch and Ray Wilson, England's full-back, could only help the ball into the roof of the net. What a start for myself and my team. We had Everton on the rack, but we couldn't get another so went in at half time one-nil up.

The boss said: 'Same again second-half.' And we did. John Fantham made a great run with the ball and fired a shot at goal which Gordon West fumbled and David Ford slotted in our second goal. For an hour, we were the better team and then Everton got back in the game. Mike Trebilcock scored and shortly afterwards scored again. We kept battling away, but the momentum was with Everton and they scored the winner through Derek Temple. It was heartbreaking, but it was a great final. We didn't let anyone down, but we should have won. We dominated Everton for long periods of the game. We needed another goal. Their first two goals knocked us sideways. We lost our way for too long, we needed to pressure Everton more when they came back to 2-2.

Our manager made us do a lap of honour, it seemed strange for the losers normally just walk off. When we got to our supporters, the result had sunk in. They had followed us to all the away ties. I felt desperate for them, but it wasn't to be. Our manager had total respect from all the players throughout the Cup run. Our league position wasn't great, but we had found a style of pay in my opinion that suited most of the team. It will be interesting to see what the boss does because of the Cup run. When he signed me he tried to spend more money on Wyn Davies, supposedly £70,000, so if he had that sort of money to spend plus the money the club made for the Cup run, I couldn't wait to see if there would be more new players.

The Sunday after the final, we got the train back to Sheffield. There was an open-top bus at the station to take us back to the Town Hall. There were so many people alongside the route it was packed with our supporters to welcome us back home. Reports said: 'There were 100,000 people lining the streets.' It was an astonishing turn-out by Wednesday fans. It really got to me sitting in the Town Hall. It was really special, we the players were really taken aback. I remember reading the paper and Don Megson, our captain, had said: 'We will bring the Cup back to Sheffield.' Don was a great man, a great captain, the best I played under in my football career. He deserved to lift the Cup and give it to the Wednesday fans.

That summer myself and Peter Eustace went to Palma Nova in Majorca for a two-week holiday. We had a great time, we didn't talk about the Cup Final. But Peter, being a Sheffield man, was shattered. We just needed to recharge our batteries and get ready for a new season. The Press were already backing Wednesday for honours in 1966/67 season after our Cup Final display and tipping myself, Peter Eustace, Wilf Smith and David Ford for international honours. Reporting for pre-season training was exciting. There had been no signings so far. I went to see the boss and it was good to talk to him after all that had happened. I said we needed two or three players of quality to go with the players who played in the Cup Final. He asked me if I had any players in mind. I said there were two players in Scotlad who would cost £70,000 for them both. I recommended Pat Stanton, of Hibs, and Tommy McLean, of Kilmarnock, who I had played with and I knew their quality. They were two exciting players. Tommy went to Rangers and Pat played for Celtic. They both played for Scotland and they had great careers at the top in Scotland.

We went to Bulgaria pre-season and played some matches out there and it went well. The boys were in good spirits and ready for the new season. While we were in Bulgaria they were selling bottles of sexy water as there had been a population boom I the country and the water was made out to be responsible. More like there was no television or distractions, so family life was getting bigger. So for a laugh I brought a bottle back and gave it to my dad. He said" 'Thanks, but no thanks. Me and your mum have five children already.'

Chapter Eleven

AN AIR OF OPTIMISM AT SHEFFIELD WEDNESDAY

A COUPLE of months after we lost 3-2 in the FA Cup Final to Everton, one Sheffield Wednesday team-mate at least had the satisfaction of leaving Wembley as a winner. Ron Springett was back-up goalkeeper to the great Gordon Banks in the England international squad for the 1966 World Cup Finals.

There were no substitutes during games back in those unenlightened times, so Ron, who had picked up thirty-three caps by the time he reached thirty years of age, was in the stand that afternoon on July 30 1966. Coincidentally, the other stand-by shotstopper in Alf Ramsey's 22-man pool of players was my old Chelsea team-mate Peter Bonetti, who, at twenty-four, had made one appearance for his country.

England overcame West Germany 4-2 in extra-time courtesy of a hat-trick from Geoff Hurst and a single from Martin Peters. Everyone at Wednesday was delighted for Ron, a thoroughly likeable guy and a solid professional. I appeared to be the lone Scot in a sea of Englishmen at Hillsborough and I got the drift of just how much that historic triumph meant to them and, of course, the entire nation. It cast a giant smile across England and I had no way of knowing that I would play a role in wiping that beaming expression from their faces the following year.

However, before I could even dare to dream of such a momentous occurrence, there was the matter of taking care of business as I prepared for my first full season at Wednesday. As you would expect, the nation was on an exhilarating high after Bobby Moore and Co had claimed the Jules Rimet trophy, to give the global prize its proper title back then. Brazil were awarded the honour of keeping the trophy when they followed up their 1958 and 1962 successes to conquer the world for a third time in Mexico in 1970 when they samba-danced their way to an unforgettable 4-1 triumph over Italy.

There was an air of optimism around Hillsborough, too, as we prepared for the 1966/67 campaign. Rather than allow the crushing disappointment of losing the previous season's FA Cup Final in such heartbreaking circumstances, there was a general feeling around the club that our Cup run could act as an inspiration and propel the team to even better and sustained performances in the new campaign. Certainly, I had been very happy with my form at the conclusion of the previous term and couldn't wait for the kick-off and all the fresh challenges that lay ahead.

My first seven months at the Yorkshire club had been very much a learning curve for me and quite a few of my new team-mates. Alan Brown had obviously decided youth was the way to go, as I have said elsewhere, and once again he built the nucleus of the team around young players. I would not be twenty until September and Graham Pugh was eighteen. Sam Ellis and Wilf Smith had both yet to blow out the candles on their twentieth birthday cakes while Peter Eustace and David Ford were pushing for places in the England Under-23 squad. We also had the backbone of players such as Ron Springett, captain Don Megson and Gerry Young who was determined to atone for his slip against Everton. We reflected on what-might-have-been in the previous season and acknowledged it had been a tremendous achievement to reach the FA Cup Final with such a youthful squad. We reckoned we could only benefit from the experience and build on it.

Initially, that's how it seemed to be going as we got off to a whirlwind start in the league and were undefeated after the first seven matches which included a 2-2 draw at Anfield against reigning champions Liverpool. We even reached the First Division pinnacle for a couple of weeks, but, as we sailed on, we hit the undetected iceberg. We went out of the League Cup, beaten 1-0 at home by Second Division Rotherham, and we floundered for a spell after that shocker. We stumbled to just two wins in the following fourteen games and we were unrecognisable from the team that had begun the season in such swashbuckling style. The swagger became a stagger as we attempted to regain our composure.

Christmas came early, though, in the shape of two back-to-back successes when we defeated Manchester City 1-0 and then romped to a 6-1 victory over Chelsea, of all teams. I was delighted to open the scoring and the triumph was made even more enjoyable following Tommy Docherty's moans about the state of the Villa Park pitch when we had deservedly beaten them 2-0 in FA Cup semi-final the previous season. There was no room for excuses after this display. Of course, it's only natural to think of opponents when they are on the receiving end of a landslide defeat and I made a point of commiserating with their young keeper, a Scottish lad by the name of Tommy Hughes.

Actually, I knew him from our days together at Stamford Bridge and I made a point of going straight for him at full-time. It was a rare outing for Tommy because of the consistency of Peter Bonetti and there was nothing he could have done to prevent us from racking up an impressive scoreline on that form. We were unstoppable as we dominated proceedings and the annoying thing was the fact we could hit these heights. We had the ability and we possessed the quality, but we just didn't show it often enough on a consistent basis.

After the festive period, we rallied a bit and hovered around mid-table. The 1967 programme started with our second game against Manchester City in six days and this one finished in a scoreless stalemate. After beating Leicester City 1-0 with a goal from John Ritchie, we lost by the same scoreline to Liverpool with Peter Thompson netting the winner. We lost to West Ham (3-0) and Sheffield United (1-0) before we defeated Southampton 4-1 at home where I scored and Johnny Fantham claimed a hat-trick. We see-sawed our way through the fixtures without any consistency and we thumped Sunderland 5-0 on March 28 where the visitors had a bloke by the name of Jim Baxter playing at left-half. We would share a pitch again the following month on a rather special occasion. I'll cover that performance in a bit more detail in another chapter!

Following the FA Cup loss to Chelsea, we were back on league business when we faced Manchester United at Hillsborough on Wednesday, April 12 - just three days before my Scotland international debut at Wembley against the world champions. The meeting against the Old Trafford side, with a crowd of 50,315 looking on, gave me the opportunity to meet my idol Denis Law. I still treasure the photograph I have of us shaking hands before kick-off. Neither of us scored in a rousing 2-2 draw. We were leading with goals from Johnny Fantham and John Ritchie, but Bobby Charlton hammered in two efforts to give the champions-elect a point. I hoped those goals were not an omen for Wembley. Nowadays people talk about burning young players out when they play two games in a week. At the age of twenty and in the space of eight days, I would play a crucial FA Cup quarter-final, a vital league game against Law, Charlton, George Best etc and then make my international debut against the reigning world champions who hadn't lost a game in nineteen.

As far as the league was concerned, we eventually finished eleventh which, if we are being positive, was an improvement on the previous season when we limped in seventeenth. So, for the second successive campaign, it looked as though our best chance of silverware would be the FA Cup. Could we go one stage better than the previous year? Could we move up from second best? Wins over Queens Park Rangers (3-0), Mansfield (4-0) and Norwich City (3-1) took us through to the quarter-final against, almost inevitably, Tommy Doc and Chelsea at Stamford Bridge. Could we repeat the result from our last head-to-head confrontation in the trophy?

My goodness, we gave it our best shot. We outplayed them for lengthy spells in the tie, but we just could not get the ball behind Bonetti. As the clock ticked down, we thought at least we could get them back to our place for the replay and finish the business then. Then your hopes are obliterated in a split-second when the ball bounces loose in your penalty box in the dying seconds and an opponent, this time Tommy Baldwin, is on to it in a flash and he leaves Ron Springett without a hope. Your heart sinks and, seconds later, the referee blows for full-time. The Chelsea players dance around, hugging each other and you realise any thoughts of Cup success have been buried for another year. That's football.

It was the Sunday morning I received **THAT** phone call from Tommy Docherty.

By the way, I wished the Chelsea lads all the best after they had defeated us and they went on to beat Leeds United 1-0 in the semi-final to overcome their so-called Villa Park jinx at the third time of asking and I supported them in the Cup Final against Spurs at Wembley. Unfortunately, for The Doc and my former colleagues, they lost 2-1 to a White Hart Lane team that was driven by Scotland international powerhouse Dave Mackay, they had former St Mirren winger Jimmy Robertson opening the scoring and had Alan Gilzean leading the attack. My mate John Boyle played that day, but the best Chelsea could manage was a consolation goal from Bobby Tambling five minutes from the end.

After my international debut at Wembley, it was back to collecting league points for Wednesday and once again we displayed our unpredictable nature when we hit another soaring peak when we beat a good Burnley side 7-0. It might even have been eight if hadn't contrived to miss a penalty-kick. I did score one, though. Just over a month beforehand, we had lost 2-0 to the same side at their place. Jack Whitham, our promising young centre-forward, scored a double against the Turf Moor side while David Ford claimed a hat-trick. John Quinn got the other. That performance represented us at our best. Burnley had some excellent players such as Willie Morgan, who would later become a good pal, Brian O'Neill and Ralph Coates.

And there was Big Andy Lochhead, the guy who demolished Chelsea after the Blackpool fiasco. He was a burly Scottish centre-forward who would scare the life out of centre-halves. In an era where defenders habitually kicked lumps out of forwards, Big Andy turned it around and he would batter centre-halves. In fact, I reckon he could terrorise them just by looking at them, although I have to say he was a good footballer, as well. Bringing down the curtain on the First Division programme, we drew 1-1 at home to Arsenal and lost 1-0 to Leeds United at Elland Road.

So, despite a niggling feeling of underachievement at club level, my first full season at Hillsborough had gone well on a personal basis. I hit a good run of form and missed just three games all season, all due to me being away on international duty. Hard to believe that even as recently as the 1960s there was sometimes a full league programme north and south of the border when Scotland and England were playing the same day. When I made my full Scotland debut on a fateful afternoon on April 15 1967, Wednesday were playing Spurs at the same time.

I confess my full focus was on helping Scotland beat England at Wembley that day.

Chapter Twelve

CELEBRATING A DOUBLE OVER ENGLAND

IN THE space of only forty-five remarkable days in 1967, I played against England twice, scored in each game and celebrated triumphs on both occasions. Making the memories even sweeter, the games were in England.

The first encounter was watched by an attendance of 21,860 spectators on a wet, windy and grey Wednesday evening at Newcastle's ground of St James's Park. No surprise in my admission that the second outing was the one that hit the headlines with a capacity crowd of 100,000 cramming into Wembley on a gloriously sunny Saturday afternoon for my full international debut. Slightly contrasting atmospheres, I must say. I was informed after the game that the amount of football scouts unprecedented for an Under-23 game, Scotland v England.

I made my first appearance for Scotland at Under-23 level on November 30 1966 at the Racecourse Ground in Wrexham when we took on Wales. Around 5,000 spectators bothered to turn out that bitterly cold night, but I was just so excited and anxious to get into the dark blue shirt and get out there to represent my country. That had been my aim since I kicked the ball about the streets in the Gorbals with my mates. I saw it as a stepping stone to attracting attention from the Scottish Football Association selectors when they got around to recommending players for the full squad.

It was one-way traffic against the Welsh lads and we won 6-0. I was fortunate enough to continue the habit of scoring on my first appearances for clubs and country when I netted two. My former Leeds United pal Eddie Gray played in that game, as well, and he also netted a double. Alex Edwards, a tricky winger at Dunfermline, and Ian Mitchell, a direct wide player at Dundee United, were the other marksmen. I was happy enough with my international baptism, but I wasn't kidding myself - there would be far greater tests ahead.

Under-23 matches were few and far between back then and I had to wait until March 1 1967 to get another chance to don the dark blue of my country. I was selected along with Eddie Gray once again and there were also players such as Bobby Clark, the Aberdeen keeper who would go on and have a fine career at international level, Pat Stanton, an absolute hero at Hibs, and Tommy McLean, who was at Kilmarnock, but would shortly join Rangers with the unenviable task of replacing wee Willie Henderson. It was a strong line-up and it had to be for England had chosen a formidable formation and I would be facing two of my former team-mates in Chelsea midfielder John Hollins, Leeds United right-back Paul Reaney.

Liverpool's Tommy Smith, known as 'The Iron Man', was playing, too, and you knew you had been tackled when you were hit by the Anfield star. He was as tough as they come and the joke was that he shaved with a blow-torch. Making the encounter even more intriguing for myself was the fact my Sheffield Wednesday colleague David Ford was in the opposition's attack.

It had all the ingredients of a 'proper' game. With no disrespect to Wales, we were rarely asked to get out of second gear in the previous encounter. Scotland and England clashes were always tasty affairs and we acknowledged no quarter would be asked or given on Tyneside. And that's the way it turned out. It was goalless until the sixteenth minute when I turned an effort beyond Sunderland keeper Jim Montgomery. That stung our hosts and they did everything to get back on level terms as swiftly as possible. We played really well on a murky night on a heavy pitch and it looked as though my strike was going to give us victory.

However, as luck would have it, the English were awarded a penalty-kick with only ten minutes to go. Tommy Smith stepped up to take it and fairly smashed the ball behind the helpless Bobby Clark. At that point, we might have settled for a draw, but I'm delighted to say we were hell-bent on winning the match. Okay, it was only billed as a friendly, but you try telling that to anyone on the pitch that evening. Three minutes after their equaliser, we were back in front courtesy of a goal from Peter Cormack, the elegant Hibs forward. Ironically, Peter would end up a team-mate of Tommy Smith at Liverpool. Just to make certain, Jimmy Smith, another ball-playing inside-forward, claimed our third as we triumphed 3-1.

I came off my 'lucky' pitch at St James's Park feeling very positive. We had performed really well against strong opposition and won deservedly. I had played twice for my country at Under-23 level and had scored three goals and featured in two winning teams. Naturally, I hoped they would be the perfect launch pad for my career with Scotland. I saw it as encouraging steps in my development at this level. I could only wonder what the future held in store.

In just over six weeks I would get my answer.

Chapter Thirteen

MY INTERNATIONAL DREAM

ON April 8, 1967, I picked up a copy of the Green 'Un, Sheffield's Saturday evening sports paper. I had just returned from London with my team-mates after our 1-0 loss to Chelsea in the FA Cup quarter-final. Naturally, I wasn't in the best of moods, but my spirits were immediately lifted with what I read in the journal.

The newspaper notified its readers - and myself - that a member of the Scottish Football Association had been in attendance at Stamford Bridge to watch a certain Jim McCalliog. Scotland, of course, were due to play England at Wembley the forthcoming Saturday. It was the game every red-blooded Scot wanted to play in and I thought I might just be in with a chance. I wasn't getting too far ahead of myself, though.

I was aware other selectors had looked at me on several occasions and I have to admit my form had been good. I was always one of my biggest critics and I didn't need anyone to tell me when I hadn't played well. At the same time, I knew I had been performing consistently at a reasonable standard and, of course, there were my three goals at two winning appearances for the nation's Under-23 side against Wales in Wrexham and England in Newcastle. Now I was being tipped as a possible for Wembley. I was beginning to wonder if I would ever get the opportunity to play for my country at Hampden!

According to one famous national newspaper sportswriter, Hugh Taylor, of the Daily Record, I might have been given a chance the previous year when Scotland were due to play Brazil at the national stadium. The South Americans were preparing for the World Cup Finals in England in the summer of 1966 and they were acclimatising themselves to the conditions. They had won the trophy in Chile four years earlier and they were determined to keep a firm grasp on their property. It was great to get a mention and Taylor actually compared me to the famous Hibs and Scotland centre-forward Lawrie Reilly as he pushed my claims for inclusion. Apparently, the soccer scribe had been impressed with my performance in Sheffield Wednesday's 3-2 FA Cup Final defeat against Everton. The Wembley game was on May 14 and Scotland were scheduled to play the so-called samba superstars, with Pele, Jairzinho and Gerson in the line-up, on June 25.

John Prentice was Scotland boss at the time and I hoped he was a Daily Record reader or, at least, an admirer of the football knowledge of that newspaper's chief sportswriter. Alas, I never got the call-up and I missed out on what I'm sure would have been an unforgettable experience. I didn't find out for quite a while later that Alan Brown, my manager at Hillsborough, had asked for me not to be considered for the match. He felt that, at nineteen, I had come a long way in a short space of time and was wary of me getting too much too soon. I suppose I understand that attitude now. He was protecting me, but if I had known at the time, I would have been hammering on his door.

A crowd of 74,933 rolled up to Hampden that Saturday afternoon to see Stevie Chalmers scoring in the first minute for the Scots. What an unbelievable start against the country that had dominated global football since lifting the World Cup in Sweden in 1958, successfully defended it in Chile in 1962 and were going for the incredible hat-trick in England. The Brazilians grabbed an equaliser shortly afterwards and the match ended 1-1.

Had I been given the nod to play on that occasion, I would have been teaming up with Rangers pair John Greig and Ronnie McKinnon, Sunderland's strolling genius Jim Baxter and my old Leeds United pal Billy Bremner, that bundle of energy in midfield. The story goes that Pele refused to swap his jersey at the final whistle with Billy because he did not like the attention he had been receiving throughout the game from the fiery little red head from Stirling. The player acknowledged as the best in the world at the time exchanged shirts instead with Celtic's Chalmers. I would have to be patient for another year before I could line up alongside Greig, McKinnon, Baxter and Bremner, but it was well worth the wait.

So, on the Saturday evening, seven days prior to Scotland's game against England at Wembley, I was in a bit of a quandary. Had I done enough to make my first appearance for my country? Bobby Brown had taken over as the first full-time manager of the Scots and I was more than aware he had an embarrassment of riches from which to choose his team on his international debut. The former Rangers and Scotland goalkeeper had made the step up from club management at St Johnstone to replace John Prentice. Would he gamble on a twenty-year-old player untested at full international level? Although I thought I had been playing well, I could never be sure until it had been verified 100 per cent.

At that point, Celtic, the country's champions, were going well in the European Cup and were due to play their semi-final first leg against the Czechoslovakians of Dukla Prague in Glasgow in midweek, three days before the Wembley encounter. They had natural goalscorers in their team such as Stevie Chalmers, John Hughes and Bobby Lennox. There were others in the frame and there was little I could do but wait and wonder. I would know for certain on the Monday when I returned for training with Sheffield Wednesday. The way things were done back then was that the club would know before the individual and they would pass on the information.

Tommy Docherty beat Allan Brown to the punch with his phone call that fateful Sunday morning. But I still could not be certain.

Chapter Fourteen

CONGRATULATIONS – MY DREAM IS COMING TRUE

I REALLY didn't know what to expect when I turned up for training on the Monday at Sheffield Wednesday. My old Chelsea boss Tommy Docherty had phoned to tell me I was in the Scotland team to play England at Wembley on Saturday, April 15 - only five days away.

I had spent the remaining hours of Sunday in a quandary. I didn't know who I could phone for confirmation, so I just had to be patient. I did my utmost to keep my emotions in check and I did not want my imagination running away with my thoughts or hopes.

Could you blame me for my slightly distracted state? Playing for Scotland at the highest level had been my ambition since I had been a kid kicking a scuffed football around the streets of Glasgow. And now I was being mentioned as a possible to represent my country against England. And at Wembley, too. The same venue where our fiercest footballing foes had picked up the World Cup the previous summer.

As I said right at the beginning, Wednesday manager Allan Brown put me out of my misery. I was summoned to his office. The walk from the dressing room was hardly any distance at all, but it appeared to have been extended by a mile or so that morning. I was invited into the office and the boss's warm north east burr never sounded more welcoming than when he said the words I will never forget: 'Congratulations, Jim, you have been selected for Scotland against England at Wembley on Saturday.'

He came round his desk, extended his hand and shook mine with genuine affection. He was obviously aware I was about to realise my dream. 'You deserve the honour,' he added. 'You go out there and show them how you can play.' Then he led me back to the dressing room and made the announcement to my team-mates. To a man, they were delighted for me. The handshakes came quick and fast and I would have needed plastic surgery to remove the grin from my face. I was the lone Scottish accent at Wednesday at the time. We had a squad of around twenty players and the rest of my colleagues were English. At that moment, I had a feeling of how Custer must have felt at the Battle of the Little Big Horn!

There was some good-natured ribbing as we went through the motions of a light training session in preparation for our match against Manchester United in midweek. Everything passed in a whirl. I was bursting with pride. I couldn't wait to get home to tell my mum the wonderful news. I realised my dad would still be at work. Tommy Docherty's call had caught us all on the hop. Like me, they were desperate for official confirmation. There was a warm glow around a little piece of Yorkshire that afternoon.

I drove as swiftly as I could - observing speed limits, of course - to relay the news of my elevation to full international status. I didn't get the opportunity to break the news. The press had already got wind of the information and were camped on our doorstep. My mother was beaming. She had a lovely smile and I had witnessed that emotion so often as I was growing up. My mum had already phoned my dad and he cried tears of joy. I'm sure his work-mates understood. There wasn't much time to celebrate as I had to get back to Hillsborough to get ready for the visit of Matt Busby's Old Trafford side who were heading for the First Division title.

Modern-day football fans may be forgiven for being just a little bewildered at all the commotion, publicity and importance attached to Scotland v England matches over five decades ago. For many of my fellow-countrymen, including not a few players, it was the most important game in the football calendar. Everyone was eager to get involved, play their part. It is the oldest international fixture in world football and it certainly stirred the emotions. In the weeks leading up to the showpiece showdown, newspapers would be full of speculation as to which players would or should be playing for Scotland. The countdown to kick-off seemed to begin about a fortnight or so before the actual match. Sports pages were bursting with opinions from managers and footballers, past and present, the newspaper's writers and the fans. Everyone wanted to have a say in the team formation. Poor Bobby Brown, preparing for his first match in charge of the nation, was being avalanched with advice from every conceivable angle.

The match at Wembley had been a 100,000 sell-out months in advance. There were Scottish supporters who started saving in their Wembley Funds as soon as one game had finished and they began preparations for the next one in two years' time. There were pubs in Glasgow who operated these unusual 'banks'. The fans would chip in when they were flush. Maybe they had a win on the horses, dogs, the fixed odds or whatever. Or they might just chip in their change. They obviously trusted the bar owners to keep a tally and make sure they got every penny back on the big day. The punters were not allowed to touch it for two years. they were ordered to forget it was even there. That was an unwritten rule. Two years down the line, all would be revealed. They could get to see their balance. A few Scottish followers, surprised at how much they had amassed over twenty-four months, would stay overnight at a top London hotel and be driven to Wembley in stretch limos. Some might even have spent more in a weekend in England's capital than they did on their annual family holiday!

When I came into the set-up in 1967, the line-up was known six or seven days before the match. Two or three travelling reserves would be taken with the team in case of an injury in training or a late reaction to a bump received during a game. In an emergency, additional replacements could be drafted in. That's exactly what happened as Bobby Brown put his thoughts together for the meeting with the world champions. Jimmy Johnstone' Celtic's mesmerising outside-right, had taken a knock as Jock Stein's team had beaten Dukla Prague 3-1 in the first leg of their European Cup semi-final at Parkhead in midweek. Wee Jinky had to withdraw on the Thursday and Bobby Brown had no hesitation in calling in Willie Wallace who had scored a double against the Czechs. Coincidentally, Johnstone hit the other goal. It wasn't quite a like-for-like replacement. Willie had played wide right for previous clubs Stenhousemuir, Raith Rovers and Hearts, but no-one had any recollection of him playing on the wing since he had joined up at the Glasgow giants the previous December. Clearly, though, he was the man in form and he got the nod.

No doubt today's fans will raise an eyebrow when they are informed the players only met up a couple of days before the game. We would have a kickabout in training on the Friday, visit the venue and that was all of the preparatory work taken care of. Nowadays, of course, it is quite different. A pool of about twenty players is named about a fortnight before the match and they meet up almost a week ahead of the fixture for training and team bonding. The manager rarely announces his selection much before two hours until kick-off. In normal circumstances, the league programme will be postponed or curtailed to give the country every possible advantage in their quest for success at the highest level.

On the day we met England at Wembley with myself in the Scotland side and Spurs' Jimmy Greaves in the opposition's line-up, our clubs played a First

Division game at White Hart Lane. Wednesday lost 2-1 to a London side that had only four Englishmen - my old Chelsea mate Terry Venables, Cyril Knowles, Alan Mullery and Frank Saul - in their team. They also contained three Scots, Dave Mackay, Jimmy Robertson and Alan Gilzean.

These days, with so many varied nationalities playing at the top sides in Scotland and England, some teams would be hard pushed to put out a five-a-sides formation if they were forced to play on international match days. The squads are festooned with so many imports and there really is no alternative to scrap league fixtures with players flying all over the world to represent their countries. There was no such luxury of club sides getting the day off in such circumstances back in the sixties.

And that is why my idol Denis Law was both an enemy and an ally within the space of three special days in April 1967.

Chapter Fifteen

MEETING UP WITH THE LAWMAN

WHEN I was a kid, I used to walk to Hampden on the south side of Glasgow from my parents' home in Caley Road in the Gorbals to watch the Scotland international team. It was always a thrill to see all the big-name players in action. But there was an extra dimension when Denis Law was in the line-up.

The Lawman was an absolute favourite of mine. I would stand on the slopes at the old ground and marvel at this guy's skills. He was a dynamic presence on the pitch. He lit up the place when he was on the ball and everyone knew he was something special, the real deal. I admit I was spellbound when I saw him perform in the dark blue of my country. I was far from alone in my admiration of his extraordinary skills.

Denis was awarded the prestigious European Footballer of the Year honour in 1964, the only Scot to have been selected for the ultimate tribute. The Lawman was following in the footsteps of greats such as Real Madrid's Alfredo di Stefano, France's Raymond Kopa, Czechoslovakia's Josef Masopust and the man acclaimed as the world's greatest-ever goalkeeper, Russia's Lev Yashin. England icon Stanley Matthews picked up the inaugural accolade in 1956. Outstanding individuals such as Holland's Johan Cruyff, Germany's Franz Beckenbauer, Portugal's Eusebio and French genius Michel Platini, among a glittering array of the finest exponents of the art of football, would follow the Scot. The boy from Aberdeen was mixing in exalted company - and deservedly so.

I had played against my schoolboy idol before, but I had never actually met him. We had never been introduced. On the night of April 121967 at Hillsborough that situation was about to be rectified. Before Sheffield Wednesday's First Division encounter against Manchester United, with future winners of the European Player of the Year award, Bobby Charlton and George Best, in the team, the press guys were not slow to spot a photo opportunity. They arranged for a picture to be taken of myself and 'The King', as the adoring Reds legions had termed him, before the kick-off to the Wednesday evening match. A photographer asked me if I was up for a snap with Denis. Try and stop me!

We met in a corridor between the home and away dressing rooms. I was in my blue and white Wednesday strip and Denis was in the famous red top of United. I hadn't a clue I would someday play for the Old Trafford club and wear their colours. On this night, though, as far as the newspaper snappers were concerned, it was all about Denis and I, the two forwards who would be teaming up for the first time against England at Wembley the forthcoming Saturday. I admit it was a special moment to actually shake the hand of this gifted individual. I liked him immediately. It would have been impossible not to. Despite all the fame and the glamour, Denis Law proved to be a genuine down-to-earth character without any airs or graces. They say you should never meet your heroes for the fear of being disappointed. That certainly was not the case with Denis. We posed happily for the image and I still have a couple of framed copies at home to this day, treasured mementoes of a special moment with a special man.

In terms of the upcoming international at Wembley, it prepared me perfectly. It put me at ease and filled me with so much confidence and anticipation. Denis just had an aura about him that seemed to reassure you. With this character around, what could go wrong? He was twenty-seven-years-old - seven years older than me - when we teamed up against England, who, remember, had gone nineteen games unbeaten before they faced us. Denis just presumed an authority that needed to be respected. He had spent some time in Italy with Torino only five years after his initial breakthrough at Huddersfield Town, the team, then in the English Second Division, he had joined as a sixteen-year-old straight from his native Aberdeen. That must have taken some courage and conviction. Without being immodest, I could identify with that to a certain extent. However, at Leeds, I had my family around me; Denis was on his own.

At the age of twenty, he joined Manchester City for a British transfer record fee of £55,000. Amazingly, Denis was only one year at Maine Road for one year before Torino came in with an extraordinary offer of £110,000. City doubled their money in only twelve months. These were massive figures at the time and underlined the player's worth. Denis played in the ultra-defensive Serie A, Italy's top flight, and scored ten goals in twenty-seven appearances. That was a phenomenal strike rate in that country. The good news for Manchester United supporters was that Denis couldn't settle and it was another year before he returned to Britain in yet another record deal of £115,000. Is it any wonder I was more than just a little excited at the prospect of lining up alongside Denis at Wembley?

First things first, though, there was a league game to be won at Hillsborough and hero worship would have to go on the back-burner for at least ninety minutes as I attempted to help Wednesday to two points, as was the case back then. I lined up against former Celtic player Pat Crerand, who, coincidentally, also hailed from the Gorbals. Bobby Charlton was in the visitors' line-up and he fired in two drives inside three first-half minutes to give United the interval advantage. In the dressing room, manager Allan Brown told us we were affording them far too much time and space, we had to play to our strengths and take the game to them. It worked. Johnny Fantham pulled one back four minutes after the turnaround and big John Ritchie netted in the fifty-seventh minute to give us a deserved 2-2 draw.

I confess I had been a wee bit concerned I would pick up an injury of some sort and that could put the kybosh on my appearance at Wembley. Having said that, I didn't hold back during a frantic ninety minutes. Neither, for that matter, did Denis which was no surprise to anyone. He was a terrier of a player who hunted everything down and was willing to go into places where only the brave would venture in packed penalty areas. He was absolutely fearless. The best and most rugged Italian rearguards had tried to nullify this guy's goal threat and had failed. I felt sorry for any defender who was in direct opposition to him.

At the end of the 2-2 stalemate, I saw Denis briefly and told him I was looking forward to playing alongside him on Saturday. He flashed that charismatic Lawman smile and said: 'Me, too, Jim. Aye, me, too.'

Chapter Sixteen

HERE WE GO...HERE WE GO

I TRAVELLED on my own by train from Sheffield to London to meet up with my new Scotland international team-mates at the Hendon Hall Hotel on Thursday April 13, only two days before my full debut against world champions England at Wembley. My dad was working and couldn't get the time off, but there was no way he wouldn't be in the stand by the time the three o'clock kick-off rolled around.

Travelling solo gave me a lot of time to look ahead to the biggest match of my career. To a lot of English players, the pinnacle would probably be an appearance in the FA Cup Final at the national stadium. I had already sampled the glamour and glitz of that occasion and, alas, the bitter disappointment when the result does not go your way. However, playing for Scotland against England was as good as the showpiece confrontation against Everton. What was uppermost in my mind as the train rattled its way to its destination? The first one, as always with me, was to give a good account of myself. Winning the game was the absolute priority and I wanted to make sure I played my part. I did not want to disappoint anyone and I knew if I failed it would not be from the lack of giving every ounce of energy I possessed.

I had no intention of letting anyone down and that included my colleagues, manager Bobby Brown who had awarded an eager and ambitious twenty-year-old kid with his first full cap, and, naturally, my family. Not forgetting the entire nation of Scotland, of course. I suppose I was going into the unknown, to a certain extent. But, as I think I had already proved as a teenager, that didn't necessarily scare me. I had known Billy Bremner and Eddie McCreadie from my days at Leeds United and Chelsea, but I had never played alongside any other of the lads. I would be lining up with in a couple of days' time. So, that preoccupied some of my three hours or so of my rail journey.

I also made some mental notes on our opponents. They had gone nineteen games unbeaten before, during and after the World Cup triumph in the summer of 1966. Their previous best sequence without a loss was twenty and guess who ended that run? Scotland! Could lightning strike twice? We could always hope. For the statistically minded, the remarkable English run kicked off in March 1890 and came to a halt in April 1896 when the Scots won 2-1 at Celtic Park.

I was interested to note that Alf Ramsey, the England manager, had made one change from the line-up that had beaten West Germany 4-2 after extra-time to lift the ultimate global prize. Jimmy Greaves, Spurs' nippy and gifted goalscorer, was in and Liverpool's Roger Hunt, a more hard-working type of forward, was out. To many neutral fans it looked like the switch in personnel actually strengthened our rivals. In the previous game before our visit, England had trounced Wales 5-1 at Wembley with the same team that had beaten Franz Beckenbauer and Co. Geoff Hurst, who scored a hat-trick in the World Cup Final and has yet to convince any Scot I have ever met that his second goal was over the line, netted a double against the Welsh. The Charlton brothers, Bobby and Big Jack, also got on the scoresheet while the other goal came from a misdirected effort from Terry Hennesey. It had been a strong Welsh selection, too, with Wyn and Ron Davies, not related, leading the attack with the speedy Cliff Jones on the left flank and his Spurs colleague Mike England the captain of the side and their rock in the middle of the rearguard.

The British Championships doubled up as European Championship qualifiers in 1966 and the following year with the Finals due in Italy in June 1968. So, it was doubly important that we got a good result in London if we hoped to mix with football's creme de la creme the following summer. There were two points for a win back then and it was Denis Law who rescued the Scots when he netted the equaliser with only four minutes to go in our opening game against Wales at Ninian Park in October 1966, a dour game played on a mudpatch which ended 1-1. The following month, the Scots overcame Northern Ireland, minus George Best, at Hampden with strikes from Celtic pair Bobby Murdoch and Bobby Lennox. They had to come back from the shock of losing a ninth-minute goal to Jimmy Nicholson.

Five months later, a lot had changed on the Scotland international front - including the introduction of myself. We had a new full-time manager in the aforementioned Bobby Brown and only five players who played against the Irish would be on the Wembley pitch, Rangers duo John Greig and Ronnie McKinnon, Celtic pair Tommy Gemmell and Bobby Lennox and Leeds' Billy Bremner.

Interestingly, five of the six players who had been overlooked played for the Old Firm, Celtic's John Clark, Bobby Murdoch, Stevie Chalmers and Joe McBride, who was injured, and Rangers winger Willie Henderson. The other change was in goal where Kilmarnock's Bobby Ferguson was dropped. Ironically, he would become the highest-priced keeper in British football a year later when West Ham boss Ron Greenwood paid a record £65,000 to take him to Upton Park.

The popular public perception of the England manager, Alf Ramsey, was that of a reserved sort of man with those clipped tones of his and the very proper English. However, Norman Hunter, my former team-mate at Leeds United, told me an interesting little anecdote about 'Gentleman Alf'. Norman played three times for the England Under-23 side - as it was then - and one was against their Scottish counterparts at Pittodrie on a cold evening on February 24 1965. Alf's pep talk to my old chum was sharp, short and to the point. 'Norman, dear boy,' he said, 'I want you to kick the shit out of these Scottish bastards.' Well, at least, Alf's elocution lessons weren't in vain. In the Scotland team on that occasion was Billy Bremner, so that would have been an interesting coming-together. For the statistically-minded, it ended 0-0.

So, there was a lot to ponder as I made the trip south. Another thing I was determined to do was not to allow the game to flash past me. That's what had happened in the FA Cup Final. The ninety minutes that afternoon just appeared to zoom by. On this occasion, I was going to make sure I was relaxed, enjoy the atmosphere created by a 100,000 boisterous crowd and this time I made a mental note to actually enjoy the moment. Let's face it, I couldn't be sure if I would ever sample the experience again. So, I was out to make the most of it. If only I knew what lay ahead.

I jumped into a taxi at the railway station and headed over to the Scotland HQ at Hendon. I was excited, but fairly cool at the same time. The friendly, laidback vibe of the Scotland squad immediately eased me into the scheme of things. Right away, I felt relaxed. Jim Baxter saw me entering the room and came straight toward me and threw an arm around my shoulder. 'I'll look after you, son,' he said in his cheery Fife accent. 'Don't worry about a thing.'

Denis Law, who enjoyed a pot of tea, also saw me and put down his cup on its saucer and got up from his comfy chair to welcome me, too. He shook my hand and then gave me a huge hug. 'Everything will be fine, young man,' he grinned as he reassured me. At once, I felt at home. Denis, in fact, had been saying some wonderful things about me in the press in the lead-up to the play. Did his praise put extra pressure on me? Are you joking? I lapped up every word and I kept those words in my head as we prepared for the game. According to The Lawman, I was one of the best prospects around and I was a big-game player who thrived on momentous occasions. Well, who was I to argue with a genuine football legend?

Usually on a Thursday before a weekend fixture, I would be concentrating on the game. However, on that particular evening, thanks to the warmth and friendliness of the players, not to mention the hilarious banter flying to and fro, I didn't give England a second thought. That really is testimony to the comradeship that was in that bunch of individuals. The following morning, there was a light training session and everything was so relaxed. The players strutted around, looked very much at ease and comfortable and, for me, confirmed the feeling of authentic confidence that flowed through the squad.

In the afternoon, we visited Wembley. I know I had been there the previous year, but somehow this was different. I had to pinch myself as I walked with Law and Baxter on the lush and perfect playing surface. I remembered my promise to myself following the FA Cup Final loss to Everton that I would be back. But this situation was far removed from my wildest dreams. The jokes and good-humoured wisecracks continued in the hotel on Friday evening and then it was off to bed for an early night. I slept surprisingly well. I rose about nine o'clock, had a light breakfast and watched some television. We had a light lunch at noon and then prepared to be taken by coach, under police escort, across London to Wembley about fifteen minutes past one.

The clock was ticking and I had a date with destiny.

Chapter Seventeen

WRITTEN OFF AT WEMBLEY: DON'T TELL THE SCOTTISH TEAM!

A SPECTACULAR riot of colour, Saltires, tartan mixing with Union Jacks, welcomed us as our driver nudged the coach up Wembley Way. It was quite breathtaking, a marvellous experience as hundreds of fans, resplendent in their respective country's favours, thronged around the bus on the way to the match. Scarves were waved, flags fluttered and the sun shone. It was simply a perfect setting for a game of football.

And it was to get better. A whole lot better.

The players made their way to the away dressing room and awaiting us were bundles of telegrams wishing us good luck and offering their congratulations. I sifted through mine. Mum, dad and the family never let me down and there was a card from them wishing me all the best. There were several from relations and friends. I was delighted to get one from my old Holyrood Physical Education teacher Jimmy Murphy. I was intrigued to discover one from Don Revie, my old boss at Leeds United. There was also one from my ex-Chelsea team-mate Terry Venables who, of course, would go on and manage England someday. I still have every telegram and card with good wishes I have ever been sent and they are all treasured mementos of my career.

After the players had read their individual cards of congratulations, it was time to go out and inspect the Wembley pitch and have a quick look around. There was still a fair way to go to the three o'clock kick-off, but I was astounded by the sheer volume of the noise generated, mainly by the Scotland supporters. The Lion Rampant fluttered in the midst of our travelling fans. The official number of our followers in the national stadium that afternoon was 40,000, the amount of tickets allocated by the English Football Association to their Scottish counterparts. I have absolutely no doubt the briefs that made their way across the border were snapped up.

As I stepped onto the playing surface, I looked around at the mesmerising and shimmering kaleidoscope of reds, yellows, blues and whites. Name any tartan you wish and it was on display, swaying to and fro in the light breeze. It was an extraordinary spectacle and we hadn't even got out of our civvies. What, I wondered, will it be like when we come out in our strips? The sheer optimism and fervour of our fans hit me and it really sunk in that I was about to achieve my dream of playing for Scotland. I can still see in my mind's eye our followers, so eager for the game to get underway.

When we returned to our dressing room, I thought about our opponents for probably the first time. Naturally, I realised we faced a monumental task. We had been written off before one rotation of the ball. Someone forgot to tell the guys in the Scotland dressing room that day. If they were terrified at the prospect of facing the world champions who had gone nineteen games without defeat, then I must say their disguise was perfect. I had never seen such a confident bunch of players. Okay, we were about to go on the park and square up to peerless footballers in Bobby Moore and Bobby Charlton, a fantastic goalkeeper in Gordon Banks and a consummate goalscorer in Jimmy Greaves. The other seven wearing white shirts that afternoon weren't too bad, either.

And then I looked around the Scotland dressing room. There was the remarkable Ronnie Simpson, who, at the age of thirty-six, was making his debut for his country. There were two players making their first appearances that day - me, at twenty, and our goalkeeper, sixteen years my senior. Ronnie was by the far the oldest player to take his bow for Scotland and that may have raised a few eyebrows. There were two defining factors to take into consideration, though. Jock Stein thought he was good enough to be Number One at Celtic and, at that stage, the legendary manager was on the brink of leading his team to the historic feat of becoming the first British team to win the European Cup. Up until the Wembley game, Ronnie had played in every game, including the 3-1 triumph over Dukla Prague in the first leg of the elite competition only three evenings beforehand. And Bobby Brown, our new manager, had been a goalkeeper in a glorious career with Rangers that spanned a decade from 1946. You would have to reckon he knew a thing or two about being a last line of defence.

At full-back, as I've already said, we had the swashbuckling Tommy Gemmell on the right and my old Chelsea pal Eddie McCreadie, hard as nails, on the left. The Rangers double-act of Ronnie McKinnon and John Greig, the nation's captain, were at the back. Billy Bremner would be to the right of me and Jim Baxter to my left in midfield. I was to play a free role between these two great footballers. Up front, the roving, intelligent Willie Wallace and speed merchant Bobby Lennox, a fantastic player and a born goalscorer. And to top it off we had Denis Law as our spearhead, a performer who had so many facets to his game. His goals, his passing, his determination, his electric bursts of pace, his guile. Did I mention he was brilliant in the air, too?

With five Anglos in the line-up, motivation was not a problem. No-one wanted to go back to their club side on the back of a defeat and face a ribbing from their team-mates, a massive percentage of whom would have been cheering on England in the game. We had just about been written off by bookies on both sides of the border. The English press portrayed us as being lambs to the slaughter, another country to be swept aside by their all-conquering, invincible heroes. Not one of them gave us a sporting chance. We were mere cannon fodder for Alf Ramsey's side.

Folk seemed to be overlooking the fact Simpson, Gemmell, Wallace and Lennox were ninety minutes away from playing in a European Cup Final - where, of course, they would beat Inter Milan 2-1 in Lisbon on May 25 - Greig and McKinnon were in a similar position in the Cup-Winners' Cup and would only lose out to Bayern Munich to an extra-time goal in Nuremberg, hardly a neutral venue. Plus we had genuine world-class talents in Bremner, Baxter and Law. What on earth did we have to be afraid of? Not one of that Scotland eleven, including me, had any intention of coming off that Wembley pitch as second best.

Bobby Brown didn't actually give a team talk before the kick-off. Hard to believe these days with all the tactical jargon that is fired around by so many so-called experts. He spoke to us all individually and I recall him telling me just to go out, enjoy myself and continue doing what I did for Sheffield Wednesday. I have no memory of the manager talking about complicated strategies and suchlike. I just remember all the players wishing each other well. Jim Baxter, an extrovert and complete one-off, was holding court, as you might expect, and his attitude was very much: 'Just give the ball to me, boys, and it'll be nae bother'.

Denis was quieter, very focused. To Jim, it was just another game, whereas Denis knew better. Of course, both had enjoyed success in the past in this fixture. The irrepressible Baxter scored two, one a majestic penalty-kick, in a 2-1 victory in 1963. Four years down the line and they were the only survivors from that game. Denis, of course, had been involved in the 9-3 loss at the same venue in 1961 and it's not a ninety minutes he has ever spent too much time talking about. A year later, Denis played when Scotland gained revenge with a 2-0 success at

Hampden. And, after Baxter's two-goal display at Wembley, a header from Alan Gilzean made it three consecutive wins against the English in 1964. There was a 2-2 draw in London the following year - with Denis scoring one of the goals - and Ramsey's men just squeezed a 4-3 victory in Glasgow before they went onto win the World Cup a couple of months later. If memory serves correctly, Willie Wallace had an effort headed off the line by Nobby Stiles in the closing stages at Hampden otherwise it would have ended with the nations sharing eight goals. So, if anything, Scotland had been the form team in this particular fixture over the past five years with three wins, a draw and one loss. However, the record book had been dismissed by the critics, experts and bookies. We were there for the taking, apparently. Oh, yeah?

Try telling that to my new team-mates. John Greig, the wholehearted onfield leader and quietly authorative, Tommy Gemmell, bubbling with confidence. As we lined up to go out, Bobby Brown began to speak and with that Baxter started bouncing a ball, headed for the door and said: 'Great, boss. Come on, boys, let's go.' I wasn't sure what to do, but some of the players began to follow Jim and I did likewise. And, of course, Baxter wasn't even captain! It was probably the first and only time in my life I followed a crowd. Bobby Brown shouted ‘good luck’ as we entered the tunnel.

The air of confidence and the nonchalance displayed by Baxter probably summed up the mood of the players. Arrogant? Possibly. Self-assured? Definitely. Lining up between Tommy Gemmell and Willie Wallace, I looked over at the English players, nodded and said hello to a few of them and shook hands with a couple. In fact, most of the players were very friendly wishing their opponents well. Denis Law excepted. The Lawman was so single-minded and such a patriot, he totally ignored his own Manchester United team-mates Bobby Charlton and Nobby Stiles. Wee Nobby later admitted he knew Denis was ready for a battle because he noted he was wearing shinguards and he rarely bothered with them.

I was totally focused, no nerves at all. I was thinking: 'This is it. Everything you've wanted since you were a kid.' Uppermost in my thoughts was to make my parents, my family and club boss Alan Brown proud of me. I also wanted to take something out of the match in terms of my development. At the age of twenty, this would be my second match at Wembley in the space of a year. I had learned so much in a short space of time and I knew this match in this sort of company could only benefit me as a footballer. My only negative thought was: 'Am I ready?' I was about to find out.

Chapter Eighteen

WEMBLEY WONDERLAND

AT precisely three o' clock on the gloriously sunny afternoon of April 15 1967 at Wembley, West German referee Gerhard Schulenburg blew his whistle to signal the commencement of the annual international meeting between England and Scotland. I had the honour of setting the game in motion as I kicked off and, naturally, my first-ever touch of a ball at this level was to pass it in front of Denis Law. (Not like today's football, the first pass is back.)

So far, so good!

We settled very quickly, pressing England all over the pitch. Even that early on in the encounter, the challenges were flying in. I remember two particular tackles early on from big Tommy Gemmell that set the tone. The first was on Jimmy Greaves as the elusive frontman tried to take our full-back on his left-hand side. Tommy's timing was perfection and he took the ball cleanly and started a swift counter-attack. Only a few minutes later, the Celtic cavalier full-back, better known for his awesome shooting power, repeated the feat when he took the ball off the toes of Alan Ball. We had put down a marker early in proceedings.

In the thick of the action in midfield, I was loving it. I was linking up well and getting plenty of touches. My job was to keep our game flowing and stitch the play together. So I resolved not to dwell on the ball and there would be no attempts at gold medal passes, unless, of course, they were clearly on. I started steadily and my confidence began to build. There was an interesting flashpoint moment when Jack Charlton flew into a tackle on the pacy Bobby Lennox. Both went down and, for a moment, it looked serious. Wee Bobby, obviously made of good stuff, was the first to get back to his feet although he had been on the receiving end of a full-blooded challenge from the no-nonsense centre-half. Big Jack got up and, fairly gingerly, moved back to his post in the middle of his country's rearguard.

A few moments later, the England defender went off for sustained treatment and was on the sidelines for about ten minutes. He was reintroduced and Alf Ramsey threw him up front as a nuisance-value striker. Some English critics displayed vast quantities of sour grapes and tried to say England had been effectively reduced to ten men after Charlton's switch from his normal beat at the back. I doubt if any of them would care to watch the ninety minutes again, but, if they could be bothered, they would see that Big Jack became a real pest to the Scottish defenders. He threw himself at every high ball, tried to block passes out of defence and, basically, attempted to unsettle John Greig and Ronnie McKinnon. Remember, too, Big Jack even scored a goal. He wasn't exactly a passenger, as some have insisted over the years.

Irrespective of what was happening to Jack Charlton or what he was contributing, Scotland were playing with great confidence and had been clicking through the gears from the first minute. We were on top and Denis Law had the opportunity to give us the advantage in the twentieth minute. To be fair to The Lawman, he had to stretch every sinew in an attempt to reach a cross from the right whipped in by Willie Wallace as he capitalised in some uncharacteristic hesitancy from Gordon Banks. The keeper and left-back Ray Wilson got into a tangle at a short goal-kick and Wallace forced a mistake. The goal gaped for a split-second and Denis lunged full-length for the ball. He got his left foot to it, but, unfortunately, his effort rattled the sidenet. Scottish fans on the opposite end of the pitch saw the rigging ripple and believed the ball had hit its target. Their ecstatic cries of 'Goal!' were quickly stifled.

Seven minutes later, their larynxes were given another opportunity to go full throttle and this time there was no illusion. The ball was in the England net, placed there neatly by Denis. The Lawman, displaying his trademark lightning reactions, stabbed the ball home after Banks had spilled a low angled drive from Wallace. The ball bounced free for a split-second and that was all Denis needed to pounce and drill in the rebound. He celebrated with his iconic one-armed salute as the travelling support went crazy with joy. We were on our way.

England were stung, but we stayed on top to remain in the lead until the interval. After the break, there was a spell when our opponents just couldn't get the ball off us, although Ronnie Simpson had to maintain his concentration to make a couple of good saves. In the main, though, our passing was crisp and accurate and when we lost possession we immediately piled in to regain the ball. With twelve minutes to go, we deservedly doubled our advantage. Tommy Gemmell tried to unleash one of his specials from long-range, but his effort was blocked and spun into the air. The Celtic man was not to be denied, though. He continued his charge forward and managed to get his head to the ball to knock it down to Bobby Lennox. That was all our little predator needed. He swivelled quickly to catch the ball as it landed in front of him and he sent a whiplash first-timer from just inside the penalty box low past the despairing Gordon Banks.

Chants of 'Easy! Easy!' immediately sprung up from all corners of the ground. The Scottish fans were in fine voice and they were here to enjoy themselves. Who could blame them after all the hype before the game that we were there merely to make up the numbers? The outcome was a foregone conclusion, apparently. It's marvellous proving people wrong, isn't it? If it was party-time on the terracings, it was contagious as far as a couple of my team-mates were concerned. Gemmell, Bremner and Baxter, in particular, began to take the rise out of the England players. They were knocking the ball around with nonchalant ease and at one stage Alan Ball was racing around with smoke coming out his ears as Gemmell, Bremner and Wallace continued to play a triangle around him. Wee Bally would race to Gemmell who would knock it down the line to Wallace and the Englishman would race to him. Then Willie would touch it inside to Bremner and he would roll it back to Gemmell. All the time the determined little opponent chased after the ball.

Remember, this was Scotland playing the undefeated world champions on their own ground. What a wonderful day to be Scottish! What can I say about Baxter? He was in his element. He was going through his full repertoire, including his famous keepy-uppy sequence. At that point the game had slowed and it really looked as England had given up the ghost. I must plead guilty to my part in the mickey-taking as it was my back-heel that created the opening for our cheeky Fifer to indulge in his ball-playing routine. I flicked it to Denis who nudged it in front of Jim. Genuinely, I didn't mean any disrespect and I don't believe Jim did, either. It was simply in his DNA, he was a flamboyant, cocky character and he seized on an opening. The ball arrived at the right pace for him to take the first caress and loft it into the air and keep it there with a couple of perfect touches. He was a Fifer, but he had been around Glasgow long enough during his years at Rangers to know what the word gallus meant. He was also a proud Scot and he was clearly relishing the moment. As a matter of fact, it was only four touches, but it has now entered Scottish folklore. Time lends enchantment and some fans now insist it was four minutes.

Let me debunk the myth that Baxter actually sat on the ball during play. Good story, but it didn't happen. Sorry for being a killjoy, Scottish fans! I can categorically deny Baxter did not tease our rivals to that extent, however, I have to admit he did rattle wee Bally's cage by calling him Jimmy Clitheroe. For those of you who have never been acquainted with the name Jimmy Clithroe I can tell you he was a diminutive English comedian who was just over four feet tall in his adult years. He usually played a schoolboy with a high, squeaky voice. Bally, of course, was no skyscraper and did have a somewhat high-pitched voice. That may be seen as being a wee bit cruel, but it was just so comical at the time, I have to confess. Thankfully, the England player saw the funny side. Much later, of course. Probably after he retired!

While we knocked the ball about, Denis was still screaming for us to get forward. He smelled blood. No doubt he saw this as the moment he could obliterate the memory of the 9-3 debacle once and for all. In fact, before the grand finale, Denis almost scored a stunning goal when he skilfully and expertly lobbed the ball over the seemingly-stranded Banks who had strayed off his line. The effort looked to be sailing serenely towards its intended target, but somehow the England keeper managed to swiftly get back, take off in an incredible backwards somersault, get his right hand to the ball and paw it away for a corner-kick. It was a truly inspired piece of goalkeeping. Denis almost applauded. I did say 'almost'. That moment arrived in the eighty-sixth minute, only two minutes after Jack Charlton had scrambled in a low cross from the left by Ball. (Nuisance value from Big Jack? You can say that again. But he did have plenty of practice!)

Sixty seconds after working miracles to deny Denis, my special moment arrived and Banks was helpless. We didn't even have time to panic after Big Jack's goal when the ball was worked forward. Billy Bremner brilliantly broke up an England attack and scuttled forward deep into enemy territory on our left-hand side, seemingly in an attempt to run down the clock. Billy passed the ball back to Bobby Lennox on the left wing and I seized my opportunity, motoring forward in support of Bobby who passed inside to me. Taking the ball in my stride, I headed for the English penalty area and spotted Willie Wallace just inside the penalty area. I passed to Willie and continued my run. Willie played it straight back to me and, steadying myself as Bobby Moore came across, I slammed the ball with my right foot from eight yards and a slight angle past Banks.

The sight of the World Cup-winning captain and one of the world's top keepers on their backsides and the ball nestling in the net was a sweet moment for me. The first team-mate to embrace me was my idol Denis Law. What a moment!

In a heartbeat I was mobbed by my other team-mates. The one-two with

Wallace was the old-fashioned wall pass that I had practised so often outside my tenement in the Gorbals as a child. Willie's part in the goal may have looked simple, but, for me, the way he cushioned the ball into my path was a thing of beauty. I have read since that Banks blamed himself for my goal, but, forgive me for saying this, I knew exactly what I was doing. I hit the ball swiftly before he had time to set himself and probably took him a little by surprise.

More cries of 'Easy! Easy!' began to ring around Wembley. Scottish flags flew everywhere and there was hardly a murmur when Geoff Hurst headed a long cross from Moore past the helpless Simpson. There was no way back for England on this occasion. We weren't going to be knocked out of our stride

Wembley belonged to Scotland.

Chapter Nineteen

THANK YOU, TEAM-MATES

IT was all a little surreal as I sat alone on the train taking me back to Sheffield the following morning. Twenty-four hours earlier, I was primed and ready to go for the biggest game in my career. Just under 100,000 supporters were at Wembley and there were millions watching worldwide on television. The cheers from the ecstatic Scotland supporters had bounced around the stadium in joyous echoes. But sadly not live on English or Scottish TV.

Now I was in a railway carriage with just the constant rattle of the metal wheels grinding on the track to accompany me on my way home.

It had been a bit of a party the previous evening. Just file that under: Great Understatements of our Time. The supporters were obviously in no rush to bring a halt to the carnival atmosphere at England's shrine to football and there were hundreds still waiting to applaud us onto our team coach when he we left the stadium for the journey back to Hendon Hall Hotel. I still smile at the recollection of the raucous celebrations of my team-mates on the bus. The hard work had been done, world champions England had been beaten and it was time to let our hair down.

We had to maintain some sort of decorum, of course, when we had a reception to attend alongside the vanquished opponents later in the evening at the swish Savoy Hotel. It was all very sociable and players of both countries mixed reasonably amicably. Of course, it was made all the more convivial because we had actually won the match. I think Denis Law, Jim Baxter and Billy Bremner may have made that point a couple of times during the function. After that, it was off to a party at the Shaftsbury Theatre and, following that, there was a visit to a nightclub. I steadfastly refused all offers to sample the delights of champagne. I declined them all, but you may not be surprised when I reveal a few of my colleagues did not follow my abstemious example!

Eventually, we made our way back to our hotel, I was still high on adrenalin - who needs alcohol? - and couldn't sleep. A bunch of us sat around the lounge chatting until the wee sma' hours. I was lucky if I managed to get three hours' sleep before I was up and getting dressed for the journey to the railways station and then the train trek home. It should have been a time to wind down from the excitement of the past few days. I wanted the celebrations to continue, but, alas, it didn't work out like that. At breakfast, I had a light meal, the taxi arrived, I bade a final farewell to my team-mates, collected my luggage, headed for the Georgian-style hotel's massive front doors and, in that moment as I stepped out onto the front concourse and eased into my waiting transport, the unforgettable experience was despatched to the memory banks.

When I was a kid, my pals and I used to sneak onto the lush and immaculately manicured lawns of the bowling green at Glasgow Green and I would imagine I was playing for Scotland at Wembley or Hampden until the greenkeeper came running and blew his whistle, shouting at us to get off the green. Now I had achieved my dream and I couldn't wait for the next time. On that lonely train ride, I was given time to reflect on my Scotland debut and I felt vindicated in the decisions I had made in my short career.

I had left Leeds United on a point of principle just when they were on the brink of becoming one of the most successful club sides in England. Equally, I had moved on from Chelsea at the age of nineteen to further my career, two huge decisions that had potentially life-changing implications for my family. My honesty and principles, along with the unstinting support of my parents, had helped win this day for me. And there to meet me at the station when the train rolled towards into its final destination was my dad. He gave me a massive hug and said: 'Jim, you've made a great start to your Scotland career. We're all very proud of you.'

My one regret about that fabulous Scotland performance is the fact that those eleven players never played together again. I suppose that fact alone is enough to immortalise the team in Scottish football history. If we had lined up again and lost, then perhaps some of the shine would have been taken off the day we took on the world champions in their own backyard and gave them a football lesson. Bobby Brown picked the perfect team to beat England as Alf Ramsey said: ‘It took a great team to beat us.’

However, it would have been marvellous to have lined up just one more time with Ronnie Simpson, Tommy Gemmell, Eddie McCreadie, John Greig, Ronnie McKinnon, Jim Baxter, Willie Wallace, Billy Bremner, Denis Law and Bobby

Lennox. I have a heartfelt message for those guys.

'Thank you. The pleasure of playing with you and helping make my dream come true was all mine.'

My second Scotland appearance was a friendly against Russia at Hampden on May 10, which we lost 2-0. While travelling back to Sheffield, I had time to think and when I arrived home I talked to my mum and dad and told them I had been tapped up by another club – Manchester United. It would have been a fantastic opportunity for myself as they had just won the First Division title. The following day, my manager Allan Brown was not very happy when I told him I wanted to leave. I went into the dressing room and changed into my training gear. I trained with the first team. After training, I wasn't expecting to be in the first team against the manager's old club, Burnley, at Hillsborough. The next morning, my transfer request was all over the local and national newspapers. Fans were even at my house with banners saying: **DON'T GO**. In the dressing room before the game, I was focusing on the match to make sure I would give 100 per cent, as usual. When I went onto the pitch the fans were shouting 'Don't go' and that continued throughout the game. What a game it turned out to be. We beat Burnley 7-0 and I scored one and missed a penalty. It hit the post.

After the game, I was sitting in the dressing room when Allan Brown walked over to me and whispered: 'You can go.' I said: 'Thank you.' It was going to be a long weekend. I was also mobbed outside in the car park while trying to get to my car. When I eventually got home, there were fans outside the house shouting the same message, 'Don't go'. It was an emotional time for myself. The papers next day were full of me going to me going to Manchster United sooner rather than later. There were other clubs interested, but no-one knew how much Wednesday wanted for me. The season had finished and I was selected for the Scotland squad for the round-the-world tour. The papers were saying the deal was imminent as Manchester United were going on a six-week tour of Australia the following Monday.

I waited in vain and checked with my manager until I went on tour. While I was away, I was hoping something might happen. Tony Waddington, the Stoke City manager, was interested, depending on the price. He commented if Wednesday paid £70,000 for John Ritchie, how much would they want for McCalliog? And if Matt Busby was in, he usually got his man. In seemed that no-one knew what Wednesday wanted for me. If Allan Brown said to me I could go, then what was holding it up from clubs making bids, anyway? I knew there was a lot of interest.

On the international front, next up was a game against Northern Ireland at Windsor Park, Belfast, on October 21. It was also a European Championship qualifier. I was delighted Willie Morgan was getting his first game for Scotland. I struck up a friendship with Willie on the Scotland B tour and we are still friends to this day.

Willie started well on his debut and Tommy Gemmell and myself had good efforts saved by Pat Jennings. We were well in the game and could have been ahead. A certain George Best started to play in the second-half and we lost our grip on the game. Ronnie Simpson kept us in the game as Bestie weaved his magic. Ronnie Simpson saved a penalty-kick from Johnny Crossan and David Clements scored for Ireland with a header. Our goalkeeper had a fantastic game, but George Best was exceptional. He tormented our defenders all over the pitch. What a display he gave to his home fans. 'Unforgettable.' I am a big fan of Nat King Cole and when he sings 'Unforgettable' it reminds me of George at his best.

On the plane back to Manchester with Denis Law and Willie Morgan, we were despondent because we needed points to qualify for the European Championship and losing to Ireland could cost us dearly. Denis remarked: 'Don't get tomorrow's papers. As we, as Anglo Scots, will be blamed.' Maybe I had lived a lucky life so far with the media, up till now outside interference wasn't on my agenda. I knew when I had a bad game and I did not need the media or anyone else's opinion unless I asked for it. A big part of myself was to be honest with myself and that way I could do something about it in the future.

When I first started in my football career at Leeds, a big part of Don Revie's philosophy about the game was good and bad habits. As my ex-boss was a former international player with England, I listened intently to him and Sid Owen, his coach, both Footballers of the Year in England, Revie in 1955 and Sid in 1959.

Chapter Twenty

LEAVING MY BELOVED OWLS

YOU may have caught my drift that I was more just a shade delighted with my introduction to top-level international football. Alas, all was not so well on the club front at Sheffield Wednesday. Manager Allan Brown had changed the style of the team and I have to confess I felt it was detrimental to the way we played.

Don't label me a troublemaker. Nothing could be further from the truth. In my first season at Hillsborough, we had Johnny Fantham and David Ford up front and they provided a perfect combination. They both worked hard, made good runs, they knew when to come for the ball to feet or when to run into space. They were an ideal double-act for a midfielder such as myself.

In a way they reminded me of Denis Law and Bobby Lennox when they teamed up with Scotland. They sparked off each other and there was a lot of instinctive interaction between the pair. I would have loved to have played in the same team as Denis and Bobby every week. I reckon I would have found them more often than not with the kind of pass they would have thrived on. I wouldn't have fancied being a defender with these two dovetailing in the opposition's attack.

Our normal midfield at Wednesday consisted of Peter Eustace, Johnny Quinn, Graham Pugh and myself. Other than Peter, we were flexible, we could go where we wanted and someone would fit in and cover. So, it was a fluid 4-4-2 formation with the entire team on the move, a formula that had worked pretty well thus far. For whatever reasons, though, the manager decided to change the pattern of our play and bring in a big targetman. Possibly, Alan Brown believed he had to react to a run of poor form from the team. I think the idea was that David Ford and myself could benefit playing with a tall and powerful centre-forward. It would be a departure from the style to which we had grown accustomed.

Nevertheless, the team boss was obviously looking at a fairly dramatic change in how he would set up Wednesday. Earlier, he had tried to sign Wyn Davies from Bolton Wanderers. It would be fair to say the Welsh international forward did most of his good work in the air, hence the nickname 'Wyn the Leap'. He had been prolific at Burnden Park and had scored sixty-six goals from one-hundred and fifty-five appearances I wonder how many he scored with his head! Instead, Davies went to Newcastle United and, later on, Alan Brown turned his attention to John Ritchie who was banging them in at Stoke City, Like Davies, he provided a genuine aerial threat and his main strength invited players to bypass intricate lead-up play to fire the ball high into the box. Ritchie, to be fair, was prolific and had netted eighty-one goals in one-hundred-and-thirty-five appearances in the First Division, including four in one game against us. That feat just may have flagged up his goalscoring capabilities to our manager.

Anyway, John arrived in a £70,000 transfer in November 1966 and that was a lot of money back then. Allan Brown was unlikely to make that financial outlay and then leave the player out of the team. At a stroke, the formula that had us to within thirty minutes or so of an FA Cup Final victory and also steady, if unspectacular, progress in the league had been binned. The manager hadn't been getting on too well with Johnny Fantham, who was a lovely touch player, so perhaps that could have been another reason for the drastic change. Our crisp, one-touch football had been replaced for a far more direct style. This is not a criticism of John Ritchie. He was a hard-working player who ended up with a decent scoring record of forty-five strikes from one-hundred-and-six First Division outings. He had a great career in two spells at Stoke City where he is regarded as a legend. However, John was no better than we already had at our club and was not what we needed at the time.

To me, the differing styles to what we were used to did not do the team any favours. For instance, you could be getting ready to thread a ball through for someone to run onto, but they are more comfortable getting to the back post to get on the end of a cross and the danger vanishes in an instant, the pattern is interrupted. I went to see Alan Brown to tell him I wasn't happy with the way we were playing. He asked me to elaborate and I explained that I thought that, after the great football we had been playing to reach the FA Cup Final, we were now just hitting the ball up to a big target man. Consequently, it wasn't sticking and, as often as not, we didn't have control of the ball. If you don't have possession of that ball it stands to reason you're not in charge of the game.

You may think that for a young player to talk to his manager like that may have demonstrated some balls - and I admit part of me felt I shouldn't have been saying it - but, in my defence, I think it showed my depth of feelings for the club and our supporters. The easy thing would have been to shut up and keep collecting my wages, but I thought I should at least tell the manager of my thoughts. Eleventh position in the First Division and a place in the English FA Cup quarter-finals may look not too bad on paper, but I was convinced we were capable of so much more. It was my contention that if we had strengthened the squad with a couple of quality players, we could have put in a more sustained challenge for honours that season.

In the 1967/68 season, we really struggled in the league and, ultimately, we finished in nineteenth position, just two points clear of relegation. That was far too close for comfort. Like the previous league campaign, we had made an excellent start and, despite my reservations over our style of play, we looked a force. So much so, in fact, we led the table in October after thirteen games. As we all know, the race for the title is a marathon and not a sprint. We endured an inexplicable loss of form and plummeted down the ratings and were sitting in mid-table when Alan Brown suddenly quit. No-one saw it coming, but at the start of February 1968. he walked away to take over at Sunderland. Former Scotland manager Ian McColl had been sacked after three years at Roker Park and our boss, who had previously been in charge of the Wearside outfit in the late fifties and early sixties, quickly answered the SOS to return.

To say I was annoyed by this development would have been an understatement. Brown had steadfastly knocked back any suggestions about a transfer from me. He knew I wanted to further my career and, as I have emphasised, I didn't see that happening at Hillsborough. He played the loyalty card time and again, but he was off to Sunderland as soon as they came calling. Double standards? Football is crammed with such stories. Okay, I understand there may have been an emotional attachment to the Roker club, but he made the move with around four crucial months to be played.

I had to bite my tongue. He blocked any chance I had to go at every turn. There were reports Manchester United liked the look of me. I had played well alongside Denis Law in the 3-2 win at Wembley and it would have been reasonable to assume we could replicate our country form at club level. Word reached my ears that Matt Busby, the manager of the Old Trafford club, was interested. Obviously, any move for a player registered with another club would have to go through the proper channels. Making direct contact with a footballer outwith your own club was known as 'tapping' and would lead to FA fines or worse. Of course, it went on. Who would be so naive to think for a moment that it doesn't? An interested club could simply drop the information in the ear of a willing and trusted newspaperman and leave it there. Back then, journalists could simply phone you for an interview. These days they have to go through most top clubs to gain permission and the teams monitor what their players are saying. They don't want anything appearing in big, bold print in the media the following morning. Makes sense, of course, but it was different back then.

There weren't too many agents in the game in the sixties or seventies before there was an explosion of them coming from all corners of the globe. Had I an inkling United were watching my progress? I'm not going to lie. I had been informed it had gone beyond the initial interested stage. It appeared the ball was now in Matt Busby's court. It was all down to the Old Trafford manager. Did he take the legal route and make a firm bid? Had an offer been rejected by Wednesday? I'll never know. At that stage, though, it really would have been a dream move. I loved the way United played and, naturally, who wouldn't want to play alongside the likes of Denis Law, George Best and Bobby Charlton in their prime? While I was left in football's version of limbo, Alan Brown cleared his desk and made a hasty exit. It was all done almost overnight with barely a farewell to the players.

Jack Marshall, who had been Brown's assistant, took over, but couldn't arrest the slump as we drifted towards the relegation zone. After just two defeats in our first thirteen games of the campaign, we only won four of the remaining twenty-nine. That's the sort of form that gets you demoted. Ironically, it was our city neighbours Sheffield United who went down as we completed the schedule a mere two points better off. Remarkably, we had been drawn against Chelsea in the FA Cup for the third consecutive season, this time in the Fifth Round. We had home advantage, but couldn't benefit from it. Actually, it ended 2-2 and had been a thrilling game for the 50,000 fans. We lost 2-0 in the replay at Stamford Bridge and any thoughts of Wembley were obliterated.

It was a similar story in the English League Cup. In the fourth round at Hillsborough on November 1 we had to settle for a scoreless stalemate with Stoke City and crashed 2-1 in replay at the Victoria Ground a fortnight later. At this stage, I was convinced my career had stalled somewhat as Wednesday's performances had declined on the pitch. I was still giving everything I had out on the pitch and in training, but we just could not turn things around and we limped to the end of an uneventful campaign. On the international front, I had kept my place for a match against Russia at Hampden where we lost 2-0. It was the team's homecoming after beating England, but it was a night that definitely lived up to its 'friendly' billing. It was an end-of-season affair and it felt like it, too. The game was on a Wednesday night, May 10 - just fifteen days before Celtic were due to play Inter Milan in the European Cup Final in Lisbon. Six of Jock Stein's side that would become the first UK team to conquer Europe were selected to start the game - Ronnie Simpson, Tommy Gemmell, Billy McNeill, John Clark, Jimmy Johnstone and Bobby Lennox. Their team-mate Willie Wallace came on for Denis Law at the interval. There was no chance of any of the Parkhead seven suffering a serious injury before the most crucial game of their careers in Portugal's capital.

I lined up alongside the Lawman against Northern Ireland at Windsor Park in Belfast on October 21 1967 where we were still searching for European Championship points to build on what we had achieved at Wembley. The confrontation became known as The George Best Match where the Irish genius ran amok. He was unstoppable as he dismantled our defence. He teased and tormented us for ninety minutes and we just didn't have an answer to the Manchester United maestro in this irresistible mood. Coventry City's Dave Clements got the only goal of the game just before the seventieth-minute mark and it could have been even worse but for a superb Ronnie Simpson save from a Johnny Crossan penalty-kick. No excuses, Bestie stole the show and we had to hold our hands up.

I was injured and missed the next game against Wales at Hampden the following month and I was delighted when we won 3-2 with Spurs' Alan Gilzean notching a double and Rangers centre-half Ronnie McKinnon thumping in the winner twelve minutes from time. I hadn't been selected for the game against England at Hampden on February 24 where we had to settle for a 1-1 draw with an equalising goal from Celtic's John Hughes after Martin Peters had put the visitors ahead. It had been a must-win match for the Scots who missed out on qualification for the Euro Finals. I desperately wanted to get my place back in the Scotland squad, but it would be a full year - minus five days - before I was chosen for my country again following Bestie's extravaganza in Belfast. I got the nod to play in a friendly against Denmark in Copenhagen where a late goal from Bobby Lennox proved to be the only strike of the game.

I came off three minutes from the end of the match against the Danes with Hibs' Peter Cormack coming on in my place. I didn't realise it at the time, but I would only wear the dark blue of Scotland on one more occasion.

Chapter Twenty-One

ERIC TAYLOR – INTERFERING AS USUAL

I WAS overlooked by Scotland boss Bobby Brown when the World Cup 1970 campaign kicked off with a game against Austria at Hampden on November 6 1968. It was a massive game and obviously I had been desperate to be involved. The international manager kept faith with the same defence of Ronnie Simpson, Tommy Gemmell, Ronnie McKinnon, John Greig and Eddie McCreadie who had played in the 3-2 win over England the previous year.

However, he elected to make changes elsewhere and I was not included. Billy Bremner, Denis Law and Bobby Lennox were still strutting their stuff for their country while Celtic pair Jimmy Johnstone and John Hughes had been introduced. Chelsea's ball-playing Charlie Cooke also had a role to play. I was out along with Jim Baxter and Willie Wallace. Despite my disappointment, I was delighted Scotland got off to a winning start with goals from The Lawman and Bremner giving the team a 2-1 triumph in front of a crowd of over 80,000.

A slightly more modest attendance of under 6,000 saw the Scots win their second qualifier 5-0 over Malta in Nicosia the following month and Bobby Brown took the opportunity to bring in players such as Birmingham City keeper Jim Herriot, West Brom right-back Doug Fraser, Celtic midfielder Bobby Murdoch, Kilmarnock winger Tommy McLean and strikers Alan Gilzean, of Spurs, and Rangers' Colin Stein. Alas, there was no sign of the name Jim McCalliog. I felt as though I had come out the international traps at one hundred miles per hour and hit a brick wall.

In season 1968/69, I was growing increasingly disillusioned at Sheffield Wednesday. It was obvious my Scotland chances were diminishing while I remained at Hillsborough and the team toiled to make an impression. We finished an unremarkable fifteenth in the First Division and the highlight of the league campaign had to be an extraordinary game against Denis Law and his Manchester

United mates in Yorkshire on August 31. In football parlance, it had been a real humdinger. These games come along every now and again and, thankfully, we had over 50,000 fans in the ground that day to witness some fabulous entertainment from two teams having a real go. We might have guessed something special was about to happen when Jack Whitham gave us the lead inside two minutes. George Best equalised and my pal Denis put United ahead. We came back and John Ritchie levelled by the fifteenth minute.

The Lawman netted again, followed by Bobby Charlton before Whitham replied. It was 4-3 at half-time for the visitors and everyone wondered what was in store in the second period of a rip-roaring confrontation. Although seven goals had been scored in the opening forty-five minutes, neither of the keepers, our own Peter Springett or United's Alex Stepney, could be blamed. Two minutes after the turnaround, we levelled when the unfortunate Nobby Stiles turned the ball into his own net. It was all set up for a dramatic winner and Whitham duly provided the effort to complete a superb hat-trick in the seventy-second minute. It was exhilarating stuff, but it was hardly indicative of how our league campaign progressed.

Likewise, we had a fabulous high in the FA Cup before that also came to a halt. We were drawn against my old club Leeds United, the bookmakers' favourites to win the trophy, and we had to be content with a credible 1-1 draw at Hillsborough on January 4 1969. Peter Lorimer thumped the visitors into the lead via the penalty spot, but I was fortunate enough to glance down a high ball to John Ritchie and he did the necessary. Of course, the smart money was on Don Revie, Billy Bremner and Co finishing the job at Elland Road four nights later. And it looked as though everything was going according to plan when Albert Johanneson gave them the early advantage. They had been unbeaten at home up until that point, but we got the equaliser through Brian Woodall, a twenty-year-old forward who was playing one of his first games. Remarkably, he repeated the feat three minutes after the interval and we weathered the storm before John Ritchie made certain with a third goal five minutes from time. Leeds would go on to win the title, but we made sure there would be no league and Cup double.

Suddenly, the critics were sitting up and taking notice of us, but, typical of Wednesday at the time, Birmingham City knocked us in the next round, beating us 2-1 at St Andrews after a 2-2 draw at our place. There was no shame in that loss against dangerous opponents on their own pitch in the Midlands, but the same could not be said for our exit from the League Cup. We lost 3-1 at Fourth

Division Exeter City on September 4 1968 and my frustration was building. Spurs walloped our conquerors 6-3 at the next stage. It was clear to see all was not right behind the scenes at Hillsborough and one of the problems was the influence of Eric Taylor who had been secretary/manager in the 1940s and 50s. He was a great administrator, but had never played the game and was very much an office-based manager.

During his tenure in charge, Wednesday were very much the yo-yo club between the First and Second Divisions and it was only with the appointment of forward-thinking team bosses such as Vic Buckingham, Harry Catterick and Alan Brown that the club became established as a rightful member of the top flight. Taylor was then able to get on with his forte, the administrative side of the game and he was responsible for establishing Hillsborough as one of the top grounds in the country. The downside to spending a lot of money on the ground was that the product on the pitch was neglected, hence the decline in the club's playing fortunes.

With Allan Brown's departure, Taylor was able to exert his influence again and in May 1969 paid Aberdeen £100,000 for eighteen-year-old Tommy Craig making him Britain's costliest teenager. I couldn't miss the irony in that. Had Wednesday bought Tommy to replace me? Was I, at last, going to get the move I had craved for so long? Tommy and I played one match together at the end of the season, so I couldn't form an opinion on his abilities and by that time the club were looking for a new manager. Jack Marshall was a lovely man, but it must be admitted it had been a rather uninspiring appointment by the board,

The team needed a more dynamic choice to get the best from our talented but under-performing side. Marshall stepped down at the completion of the 1968/69 season and was replaced by Danny Williams who had just won the League Cup with Swindon Town. In one of the greatest upsets of all time, the Third Division team beat Arsenal 3-1 on a Wembley mudheap with mercurial winger Don Rodgers netting a double in extra-time. Naturally, Williams' stock was high when he arrived at Hillsborough. Not long after he had taken over, I had the opportunity to discuss my situation and I listened to what he had to say about his plans for the future.

The new manager told me he wanted me to stay, but the meeting concluded with me telling him I didn't think I could work with him. He agreed to listen to offers for me. After two years of unrest at Hillsborough, I was finally going to be granted my wish to move elsewhere in an attempt to further my career on the club and country front.

With Eric Taylor calling the shots, his appointment of Danny Williams as manager, Tommy Craig's expensive outlay it all ended up with Sheffield Wednesday getting relegated to the Second Division and further decline of the club. Eric Taylor, Mr Sheffield Wednesday? I love Sheffield Wednesday, his decisions were to the detriment of the club, so why would he be called Mr Sheffield Wednesday? He and the board have a lot to answer for in the sixties and seventies. I feel vindicated in gong against him in most situations. I remember we were in Ireland for a pre-season game. Jack Marshall was caretaker manager and after training he said: 'Casual dress for dinner tonight.'

Myself and Wilf Smith were going downstairs for dinner and the other players were coming back up upstairs. As we got further down the stairs, Eric Taylor was at the bottom of the stairs telling the players to go and dress up. I said to Eric Taylor: 'Why are you giving the players instructions? The boss has already said casual dress for dinner. Why are you interfering?' I went into dinner casual. After a while Jack Marshall came to me and told me to change. I told him to shove his dinner and I wouldn't be taking any orders from a secretary (Eric Taylor). I left the dining room and the chef must have heard the noise as when I went outside he told me to come into the kitchen and he would give me my dinner on a small table in the kitchen

Chapter Twenty-Two

SIGNING FOR WOLVES – ANOTHER DREAM COMES TRUE

I SIGNED for Wolves on Thursday July 29, nine days before the new season started. Birmingham City were also interested in me when it became obvious I would be allowed to leave Sheffield Wednesday. I was well aware I had to get my decision spot on. I was twenty-two years old and had already been at Leeds United, Chelsea and Sheffield Wednesday. I wanted to put down roots, but I was determined to do it a club that matched my ambition

I decided it was only right and proper - due diligence, I believe it's called these days - to talk to both clubs to weigh up what was on offer. The St Andrews outfit were managed by the great Stan Cullis, who, ironically, had been sacked by Wolves in 1964 before taking up his post at Birmingham a year later. He was such a Molineux legend and I believe he actually said he was finished with football on the day he left the club. Naturally, he changed his mind and it was an experience to meet and talk to such an icon. He was an impressive man, but the major problem was that City were in the old Second Division. At my age, I thought that would have represented a step backward, although Stan Cullis clearly had grand ideas for the team.

I also had talks with Bill McGarry, the Wolves manager. Like Cullis, he had been a very accomplished footballer. Cullis won twelve England international caps and McGarry picked up four honours for his country, so I was mixing in good company. McGarry had established himself as a tough, no-nonsense manager. He had taken over at Wanderers the previous season after winning the Second Division championship with Ipswich Town and he was now in the process of revitalising the fortunes of the Black Country club. The Molineux team, under the leadership of Cullis, had been one of the most successful sides in the fifties, winning three league titles plus the FA Cup in 1960 when they beat Blackburn Rovers 3-0. They also became famous for their glamorous floodlit friendlies against Spain's legendary Real Madrid and the marvellous Hungarians of Honved.

Their star had dipped somewhat in the sixties and now McGarry had been charged with bringing back the glory days to a proud old club eager to return among the elite. Could I play my part? McGarry certainly thought so and was willing to pay a club record fee of £70,000 for my services. It was a helluva compliment from an individual I later discovered didn't over-indulge in such magnanimous gestures. What really sold me on the shift to Wolves was the opportunity to perform alongside talented and top-quality players such as Mike Bailey, Derek Parkin, David Wagstaffe and Derek Dougan. I especially looked forward to lining up with Peter Knowles, a supremely-gifted midfielder who was making a massive name for himself. If I am brutally frank, Wednesday just did not have this calibre of player at their disposal at the time of my departure. I met McGarry in a hotel in Chesterfield in July 1969 and he impressed me with his ideas on football and his plans for Wolves.

I signed on the Thursday and the transfer fee - quite a lot of money back then - made certain the move got a lot of big, bold headlines in the press. Two days later. I made my first appearance against Kilmarnock in a friendly. My competitive debut came on a hot August day at home against Stoke City in the first league match of the 1969/70 season. I wore the No.7 jersey in front of 32,000 fans and I played my part in a 3-1 victory. Big Derek Dougan - a real character known as 'The Doog' - scored two goals and Knowles hit the other. Little did I know that there wouldn't be too many more matches to come alongside that lavishly-skilled individual. A 2-1 midweek triumph over Southampton - again in front of our own support - followed our opening-day success and on this occasion Big Frank Munro, one of three Scots in the team alongside Hughie Curran and myself, scored and Knowles emphasised his importance to the team by claiming the winner.

Then, as so often happens in football, the next match took me back to Hillsborough to face my old Sheffield Wednesday side. Some of the home fans gave me a good reception which was appreciated, but most of them booed my every touch. I accepted that, too. It's part of football and I understood their reaction. Would you believe I opened the scoring in the first-half as Wolves won 3-2? When I was at the Sheffield club, the supporters had been great to me and had welcomed me from day one. But I was now a Wolves player, they paid my wages and, as you would expect, I was doing my damndest to make sure they won. As I had done when I scored for Wednesday against Chelsea in the FA Cup semi-final three years earlier, I celebrated. All this stuff we're seeing these days with players not showing emotion after they have scored against a former club. What a load of rubbish! It would have been an insult to the travelling support if I hadn't expressed joy at netting for our team. You have to show the fans you care and are passionate about the club. You have to display your dedication and commitment to your new team-mates. I've usually come back and haunted my old clubs. If you are fortunate enough to score a goal that may be the difference between victory and a loss, why on earth would you not want to express your emotions?

Bill McGarry was quite specific about how he wanted me to fit in to his team structure. He told me he was looking for me to play my natural game, quite a free role, but within the constraints of how the team was set up. So, when we lost the ball, the manager was looking for me to back track on the left-hand side of our midfield three. However, not too long after I signed, McGarry moved me more towards the centre of midfield, reasoning that I had an eye for goal and the team could profit from this, especially with targetmen up front in Derek Dougan, Hughie Curran and, later on, Bobby Gould, three big guys from whom I could pick up the scraps.

We began the season really well and won four and drew one of our opening five matches to hover near the top of the league. We also had an excellent 1-0 victory in the League Cup against Spurs where I grabbed the encounter's solitary strike. It was one of my better efforts as I recall. Winger Dave Wagstaffe put a cross into the penalty area and I caught the ball on the volley as I was running away at an angle from the left-hand side of the goal. It was a blur as it left my boot and thundered high past Pat Jennings. Not exactly Marco van Basten against the Soviet Union in the 1988 European Championship Final, but quite similar, even if I do say so myself.

McGarry didn't talk much to the press or even the players. As a matter of fact you would struggle to get a 'good morning' out of him. He was not going out of his way to win a first prize in any personality contests, but he knew football. He was quite innovative as a manager, ahead of his time on players' diets and so on, but his character was dour and brusque. His man-management skills were severely lacking. His captain, Mike Bailey, was the serious sort, as well. So, it was guys such as The Doog and Danny Hegan who created the atmosphere in the dressing room.

I'm glad to say I settled in reasonably quickly at Wolves and at the season's end I felt really happy with the way things had gone on a personal level. I hadn't missed a match and my form had been good. However, in an echo of previous seasons at Wednesday, Wolves hadn't managed to sustain our fine start to the league campaign, eventually finishing a disappointing thirteenth after an awful sequence of thirteen games in the run-in without a win. We exited the League Cup at the third round stage to Second Division Queens Park Rangers and lost in the FA Cup at the same stage to Burnley. So, after our positive and excellent start to the season, it hadn't quite gone as I had hoped or envisaged.

The loss of Peter Knowles after just eight league games with his premature retirement from football to become a Jehovah's Witness undoubtedly had a detrimental effect on the team and, consequently, how we performed throughout the campaign. He was a key man for us, a tremendous footballer who was central to so much of our play. He would certainly have played for England before too long. When he turned his back on the game, it was not only a massive loss to Wolves, but also to the English game in general. Ironically, Knowles was introduced to the Jehovah's Witness belief when he was with the club in Kansas the previous summer. They had agreed to play in The States and had to adopt the name Kansas City.

I well recall there were a lot of rumours flying about Peter Knowles who had seemingly become a Jehovah's Witness. The Doog would pull Peter's leg. We didn't think it was serious. We played Nottingham Forest on a Saturday at Molineux. It would be a tough game and I was looking forward to it. It was a marvellous match. We went 3-0 up and we turned on the style, but later we got sloppy and Forest got back in the game. The match ended 3-3. I was so disappointed, but it got worse! At the end of the match, Peter Knowles went behind the goal and threw his shirt into the crowd before heading for the dressing room. The bad news travelled fast and we now knew what Peter had done. I wanted to speak to him, but that was for the boss to sort out. It didn't look good. The Doog was shaken and was later to say: 'I have been in football a long time and thought I had seen a lot and now this.'

We had Sunday off, but I went to Molineux as the physio would be there and some of the other players would pop in. We were all wondering what the boss would do. Was Peter really finished with football? We came into training on Monday and the boss never said a word about Peter. The players asked coach Sammy Chung what was going on. He just shrugged his shoulders. On a personal note, I was thinking what would the manager do. He had just spent £140,000 on myself and Hughie Curran. Would the board make more money available or would the boss promote one of the young players, either Paul Walker or Kenny

Hibbitt? What a decision. It didn't seem to upset him, but how do you replace Peter Knowles? I couldn't believe what was happening, so I decided just to keep my head down and get on with my career at Wolves.

Peter Knowles was a young man, aged just twenty-three, with the football world at his feet and with four English Under-23 caps already won. He was coveted by such a shrewd judge as Bill Shankly who had recently attempted to buy him for Liverpool. Peter would be mobbed by girls wherever he went, drove a sleek sports car and was the last person you would think would turn to religion. The general consensus was that it was just a fad and he would return to the game. But he never did, despite the club's best efforts. Wolves retained his player registration and would annually send a new contract to his address in the hope he would reconsider. This carried on until it was terminated in 1982. The player was thirty-six by then and it seemed a reasonable bet that he was not about to embark upon a sensational comeback.

Knowles just could not reconcile his beliefs with what he saw as the nasty side of football when you had to show a ruthlessness and disregard for your opponent on the football field. He could have had it all, the fame, the glamour, the money, but rejected the lot. In his years away from the game, he worked as a milkman, a window cleaner and in the warehouse at his local Marks and Spencer. Even today, in his mid-seventies, he still has the faith, has no regrets and has never wavered from his chosen path. I salute him.

Chapter Twenty-Three

GREAT TIMES AT MOLINEUX – GREAT TEAM, GREAT FANS

I DON'T think I could be accused of overstating the fact, but Wolves' start to the 1970/71 season could only be termed absolutely wretched. Three games, three defeats, ten goals conceded and anchored at the foot of the English First Division. We couldn't buy a win, as they say nowadays. It was not the way anyone at Molineux envisaged our launch into a new campaign panning out.

Football, though, is a funny old game, as I keep hearing. Wolves completed the programme in fourth place, earned a place in the UEFA Cup and finished the forty-two game marathon looking down on the likes of Liverpool and Chelsea, who beat Real Madrid 2-0 to lift the European Cup-Winners' Cup in a replay. In fact, we finished up with fifty-two points, the same as Spurs, but the London outfit had a better goal difference that us of twenty-one to our ten. Arsenal won the title with sixty-five points and my old club Leeds United were second, a point adrift.

We were fairly satisfied with our final position, especially considering our form at the kick-off. In quick and painful succession, we lost to Newcastle 3-2, Derby County 4-2 and Spurs 3-0. You wouldn't need to be gifted with the intelligence of Socrates, the Greek philosopher and not the guy who played for Brazil in the 1986 World Cup Finals, to fathom where the team's problems lay. We were leaking far too many goals and I am not just pointing at the defence when I say that. I have always insisted football is a team game, but the statistics emphasised the opposition were finding it far too easy to put the ball in our net. We scored sixty-four goals and conceded fifty-four. You won't win too many championships with those figures.

However, after a mere three outings, it looked grim. Coincidentally, the two teams directly above us in the division at the time were Manchester United and Southampton, my next two clubs. They had a point apiece and we all had got off to a false start. Wolves had planned for a sprint into a fresh term, but had stumbled big-time right from the off. Still, we stuck at it and at least stopped the rot with a 1-0 victory over Coventry City at the fourth hurdle. Then we were thumped 4-1 by Nottingham Forest, beat Ipswich 3-2 and drew 1-1 with Stoke City.

Although we were hardly playing spectacular or breathtaking football, I sensed there was a lot more to come from us as the season unfolded. As ever, I had hoped for a Cup run, but any thoughts of achieving anything in the League Cup were obliterated in the opening run when we lost 1-0 to Oxford at the Manor Ground on September 9. The Second Division team had a player in their ranks nicknamed 'The Tank'. He was a run-of-the-mill, hard-working performer who went on to make a bit of a name for himself in management. You'll know him better by his real name of Ron Atkinson, who actually tried to sign me when he was in charge at Cambridge United in 1978.

We were shocking that evening and I have to confess the better team won. Back then, the League Cup was a prized piece of silverware, possibly not judged that highly by managers in this day and age where they often play their second string in the tournament. Our team on that occasion consisted of experienced players such as keeper Phil Parkes, Derek Parkin, a very under-rated defender I believe should have played for England, skipper Mike Bailley in the middle of the park, winger Dave Wagstaffe while two prolific strikers in Bobby Gould and Hugh Curran were leading the attack. A certain Jim McCalliog was in midfield. The way I looked at it, any team I was involved with had three domestic honours to aim at each season, the championship, the FA Cup and the League Cup. So, just after the first week in September, we were out of one of them and, after our fairly awful start, it would have taken one hell of an effort for us to be in there battling for the title.

Speaking of Gould and Curran, they were two big blokes who were extremely powerful in the air. Completing our main three up front was Northern Ireland international centre-forward Derek Dougan. 'The Doog' was as much an extrovert as our manager, Bill McGarry, was an introvert. Chalk and cheese? Absolutely. I have always thought McGarry bought Gould from Arsenal for £55,000 in the summer of 1970 to replace the Irishman. However, 'The Doog', who would have been thirty-two at the time, had no intention of moving aside for anyone. As it happened, Gould moved on after only fifteen months to West Brom for over £60,000. I have to say I was a fan of Big Derek. He wasn't the greatest on the deck and you would never see him attempt to embark on mazy, solo runs, but he was brave and his ability in the air was exceptional. In fact, the following year he teamed up with young John Richards and Derek Parkin was quoted in the national press as saying they were the 'best partnership in Europe'. Maybe just a wee bit over the top from Derek, but they did click and had a highly-profitable understanding.

Before Richards came on the scene, Gould hit twenty-four goals in season 1970/71 to end fourth highest scorer in the division. The top spot went to West Brom midfielder Tony Brown who had an absolutely phenomenal year with thirty-four goals. Hugh Curran claimed twenty goals, Dougan hit thirteen and I chipped in with seven. One of our best scoring performances of the campaign came in the opening round of the FA Cup and, naturally enough, you can't help but dream of another Final appearance at Wembley. That was always my target in the competition, to go all the way to English football mecca.

We were drawn at home on January 2 1971 against Norwich City who were then mid-table of the Second Division. Their goalkeeper was a chap by the name of Kevin Keelan and he really fancied himself as a top-quality custodian. He was a bit flash with a hint of arrogance. He didn't like getting a bump or two and, as far as I'm concerned, that's all part and parcel of the game. Remember, it is a contact sport, after all. They scored first that afternoon, but I'm delighted to say we equalised shortly afterwards when we were awarded a stonewall penalty-kick. I had my own method of taking spot-kicks and, after coming in slightly from the left, I liked to plant my left foot firmly on the ground before hitting with my right foot. If a keeper elected to go early and choose a corner, I would aim in the opposite direction. There was a bit of banter between the goalie and me as I placed the ball. It was all the usual stuff I had heard before. It never bothered me. I didn't take a lengthy run up, either. I didn't need to because I would get a solid strike of the ball with a shorter approach.

Sure enough, Keelan took off for his left and I rolled the ball in at the other corner. I savoured the moment, but I'm sure he didn't see the funny side. He wouldn't have been smiling, either, after I claimed another while Bobby Gould, with a double, and Kenny Hibbitt made it 5-1. The actual date of January 2 1971 is one of the blackest in football history, unfortunately because that was the day of the Ibrox Disaster when sixty-six fans lost their lives following a 1-1 Old Firm draw. Moments like that put everything in perspective.

Our FA Cup run - if you can call it that - ended at the next stage when we lost 2-1 to Derby County on their gluepot of a pitch at the Baseball Ground. The pitch must have had drainage problems for years because it always seemed uneven, rutted and swampy. And that was on a good day. January 23 1971 was not a good day. Both teams were covered in mud after about twenty minutes or so. They scored first when the referee adjudged Frank Munro, our Scottish international defender, had handled the ball. Big Frank's protestations fell on deaf ears. Alan Hinton took all the penalty-kicks for Brian Clough's team and he favoured a straight run and then a ferocious belt at the ball. He did so again and the effort thundered straight down the middle as our keeper Phil Parkes took off to the left.

I played a role in our late equaliser that we thought would have been enough to earn a replay back at our place. Mike Bailey was the possessor of a mighty throw-in and he propelled a meteor-like shy in from the left. Derek Dougan got up at the near post to flick it into the mix and I got there first to head over the goalie. I think he got the merest of touches to push the ball onto the bar, but, thankfully, John Richards was lurking right on the goal-line to turn in the leveller.

Deep into the fading moments of the game, with both sets of players just about out on their feet, Derby worked the ball down their right and a cross was flung into our box. John O'Hare, another Scotland international player, was a big, burly guy and he threw himself at the ball in front of our defence and forced it over his line. I have no idea which part of his anatomy the ball came off before trundling over the line, but it was enough to knock out us out of the competition.

Thankfully, there had been moments to savour in the league campaign to act as compensation.

Chapter Twenty-Four

CRESCENDO WITH DON REVIE'S DOUBLE-CHASING LEEDS

I WAS looking forward to my third full year at Wolves in season 1971/72 particularly as the club had such a successful run last season by finishing fourth in the First Division and to qualify for a place in the UEFA Cup - and also becoming the first winners of the Texaco Cup!

The fixtures came out and we were handed a tough start, Spurs, Liverpool, Leeds United, Manchester United and Manchester City. So, we started with three draws, one win and one loss. And then two wins and a loss to Manchester City at Maine Road, 4-3. We beat last season's double winners Arsenal 5-1 at Molineux. It was a great win for Wolves. We were absolutely 'on it', as they say now. I scored two, a penalty-kick and header.

We lost four games out of twenty-four from November 13 1971 to April 1 1972. I got my first goal against Spurs in the opening fixture of the new season with a penalty to put us 2-0 up, but we let them back in with two goals from Martin Chivers and Alan Gilzean. I was quoted in the Sunday People saying: 'All Tottenham's birthdays came at once.'

We got our first win of the season against Manchester City, 2-1 at Molineux. Kenny Hibbitt hit a spectacular shot for our first goal in twenty minutes. We should have increased our lead, but in the 73rd minute, I received a pass, went past a defender and curled a right-foot shot into the top left-hand corner of Joe Corrigan's net away from his grasp. Frannie Lee scored from the penalty spot for City. Meanwhile, in the Sunday People, I was linked with a move to Leicester City for £100,000. Jimmy Bloomfield, the manager, was reportedly going to talk to our boss. He never told me about an offer. He must have said 'no', but I knew there had been an offer.

I hurt my knee ligaments and I missed six matches. What a time to be injured! I came back against Nottingham Forest at Molineux and the boss put me up front with The Doog and we ran riot. We hammered Forest 4-2. The Doog got three and I scored the other one. The local paper, The Express and Star, said: 'Jim's back – all's well with Wolves.' Unfortunately, we lost to Chelsea at Stamford Bridge 3-1 where I scored our goal. On October 4, 1971, myself and Frank Munro got picked for Scotland's Nations Cup squad against Portugal on Wednesday October 13. The next game on November 20 against Arsenal at Molineux would be a big test as the Gunners had won the league and Cup double the previous season. We buried them in the second-half after Ray Kennedy had given them a first-half lead. Waggy equalised with a brilliantly-taken goal, Kenny Hibbitt scored our second, The Doog got the third, I got the fourth and The Doog rounded it off with the fifth.

The newspapers were drooling over our performance. Headlines such as the one from The Express and Star, 'Molineux Massacre'. It was a great time with the UEFA Cup coming up in four days' time, but I will discuss the European adventure in more detail in forthcoming chapters. Myself and Waggy had injuries, but the boss thought a couple of days could make all the difference. We had a derby match with West Brom coming up, so Waggy and myself were keen to play at The Hawthorns. Derby matches in football add spice to the season as fans claim bragging rights and love putting one over on their nearest rivals.

We were at full strength for our visit to West Brom and looking forward to catch up with former Wolves team-mate Bobby Gould. The match started well and I also started well, scoring in thirty-one seconds. Waggy made it 2-0 and we went 3-0 up through John Richards. The Baggies pulled two goals back, but we saw the game out. Three domestic wins in a row and ten goals in the process. Our form was amazing. Even the boss, who didn't deal in pipedreams, said: 'Wolves are ready to challenge for the title.' The papers stated: 'The First Division pacesetters should take notice. Not even the nine points that separate Wolves and the leaders can shake McGarry's confidence for the future.' The boss said: 'I refuse to believe we have too much ground on the leaders…nothing is impossible. Arsenal proved that last season and there is still more than half the programme to go. We are only four points away from the top three at the moment and our confidence is running high. The team is going out believing we can win every game these days and if we keep our form we will be up there when it matters.'

Mike Bailey was playing the best football of his career at this moment. If he had been up to speed early in the season, he would have been in contention for an international call-up for England. Kenny Hibbitt was also playing well and chipping in with goals. We had a nice break in Jersey and played against Jersey Wanderers in a friendly. We ran out 9-0 winners and I scored four. I have a lot of friends in Jersey and had been holidaying there for the past few years. On a serious note, I was looking forward to playing Manchester United at Old Trafford. My best friend Willie Morgan would be playing for Manchester United and I was looking forward to spending a bit of time with him after the match.

We were at full strength, but United were minus George Best. We fancied our chances and beat United easily 3-1. The Doog got the first, John Richards got the second and I scored a penalty-kick for our third. The reports on the game were very flattering. 'Leaders Completely Outplayed'. With sixteen points from nine games we were on a high. Sadly, The Doog had to go off at Old Trafford with a hamstring problem and was missing against Leicester City in the FA Cup at Molineux. I scored at the near post, beating Peter Shilton. We lost our skipper Mike Bailey eight minutes later and Leicester scored to make it 1-1 and that's how it finished. We lost the replay 2-0 at Filbert Street. The Doog was back against Ipswich Town in a league match at Molineux, but Mike Bailey was still out. We were second best to Ipswich all over the park and we nearly lost our unbeaten home record. We hadn't lost a game at Molineux all season, but we were 2-1 down with a minute to go when we received a penalty-kick. I placed the ball on the penalty spot and put the kick into the corner of the net, turned away to celebrate, but the referee disallowed it. He ordered a retake and I placed it in the same corner. Another tip taking penalties is to make up your mind and never change.

We lost to Derby County at The Baseball Ground 2-1 after I had scored from an eighth-minute penalty-kick. When we were awarded the penalty, I picked up the ball to put it on the spot. I couldn't find the spot, the rain had rubbed the spot away. So, I had to wait until the groundsman had come on to the pitch and plastered a new spot. I placed the ball to the side of the newly-painted spot. The referee told me to place the ball on the spot. I explained as the spot had just been painted, the ball could stick. So, he allowed me to place the ball to the side. I sent the keeper the wrong way as the ball nestled in the corner of the net.

Next up in the league were Southampton at The Dell. To say I had a mixed day in our 2-1 win would be an understatement. Here's how the Daily Express reporter saw the match: 'Lucky Southampton, lucky Wolves. That's my cockeyed view on Wolves' 2-1 win which made superb entertainment for the fans, but most have driven the managers into a frenzy of frustration. Mick Channon, Southampton's brilliant England Under-23 striker, summed it all up by saying:

"Sure, we had one of two good chances, but they must have had about ninety."' That's a big exaggeration, of course, but we get your drift Mick.

Southampton, crushed 7-0 by Leeds United the previous Saturday, would have been on the wrong end of an even bigger hammering if we had taken all our chances, including myself. In this extraordinary match at The Dell, my opinion is that it is no exaggeration is that we could have scored a dozen. We had five glaring misses in the first ten minutes and after that I missed a penalty-kick which I took twice – and missed twice. I made amends by scoring our first goal two minutes after my second spot-kick miss. Mick Channon equalised, but Gerry Taylor scored a lucky winner for us.

I had scored four goals in the last four games and we were growing in stature as a team. The games were coming thick and fast, but injuries could be a problem. We beat Crystal Palace 2-0 at Selhurst Park and pushed them into the relegation mire. The Doog scored out first goal in twenty-two minutes and I scored the other goal in seventy-eight minutes, making it five in five games. We suffered another injury when Gerry Taylor had to have seven stitches inserted in a cut above an eye. Our next two league games, against Everton away, we drew 2-2 and Leicester City at home we lost 1-0.

The way the boss had brought in young players to the first team squad was very impressive. John McAlle, Kenny Hibbitt, John Richards, Alan Sunderland, Steven Daley, Barry Powell and a young full-back Geoff Palmer, so great credit must go to the boss's backroom staff, Sammy Chung, Norman Bodell and Brian Owen. We had four domestic games to go, included in that sequence would be Leeds United. We beat Huddersfield Town away 1-0, Nottingham Forest away 3-1, but lost 2-1 to Sheffield United at Molineux where I suffered an eye injury. The skin on my eye had been pierced by a thumbnail. I was walking about like some movie star with dark glasses. I got a bit of a ribbing off the players. I was so frustrated and couldn't believe my luck.

We brought down the curtain on the league season against Leeds United at Molineux only two days after they had played and beaten Arsenal 1-0 in the FA Cup Final. Leeds could do the double, all they needed was one point. Derby, their nearest contenders, and Brian Clough were on holiday enjoying the sunshine and hoping we would beat Leeds. The Cup Final would take a lot out of Leeds. Could they lift themselves one last time? Clough must have fancied his and Derby's chances to win his first title.

On the weekend before the Leeds game, there was a story in the Sunday People accusing Leeds of trying to bribe three Wolves players, Bernard Shaw,

Frank Munro and Danny Hegan. Don Revie, the Leeds manager, stood accused of attempted bribery allegations. Leeds captain Billy Bremner eventually won a High Court battle to clear his name of the allegations with evidence provided by Derek Dougan, who was also the chairman of the Professional Footballers' Association. I was shocked to read the story, it was never talked about in my presence in the Wolves dressing room.

What a distraction for Leeds. Could they do the double? The odds were stacked against them. Playing Leeds on the Monday was a sell-out at Molineux. What an atmosphere with such a lot at stake. Leeds going for the double and Wolves playing for pride. I felt sorry for my ex-boss Don Revie because he had dragged Leeds up from nearly being relegated to the Third Division to the pinnacle of English football, one game away from achieving an unforgettable legacy for his club. The game wasn't a classic. Frank Munro scored our first goal with a shot, The Doog scored in the second-half to make it 2-0. We should have increased our lead. Leeds were desperate to get a goal, they kept going and were eventually rewarded when their captain Billy Bremner pulled a goal back. Sadly for Leeds, that's how the match ended.

Shaking hands with the distraught Leeds players after the game, I could feel their pain. Leeds divided supporters of other clubs. On their day, they played great football and were a joy to watch, but because supporters of other clubs didn't like the hard stuff they could dish out it made them unpopular. To play an FA Cup Final and a title decider in two days was just too much even for Leeds United, my first professional club.

With all the excitement going on with games every three days, there was a rumour that Wolves were going to Australia on an end-of-season tour. I had put it to the back of my mind as there had been no confirmation from the boss. Eventually, it was confirmed we would be touring Australia for five weeks. I went to see the boss to ask him to leave me out of the tour. I explained to him my reasons. I had been to Australia for six weeks with Chelsea when I was eighteen years old, at Sheffield Wednesday a six-week tour of the Far East when I was nineteen and then the Scotland B tour of Israel, Hong Kong, Australia, New Zealand and Canada when I was twenty.

The air travel back then was not like it is now. I didn't want to go as I had had enough of long-haul travel. I think it hampered my development when I was younger. I didn't get enough time to recover. When you play a lot of games as I did, it's a long season. I needed time to recover and get stronger. The boss said he would get back to me as soon as possible. I didn't hold my breath. When he

1

2

3

4

5

6

7

8

9

10

11

12

13

14

15

16

17

18

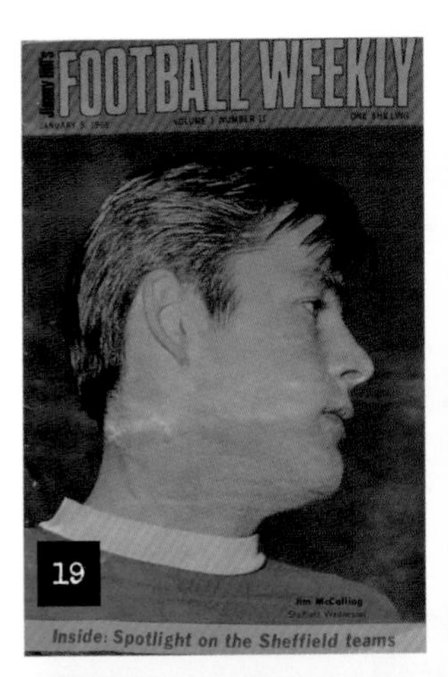
FOOTBALL WEEKLY
Jim McCalliog
Inside: Spotlight on the Sheffield teams
19

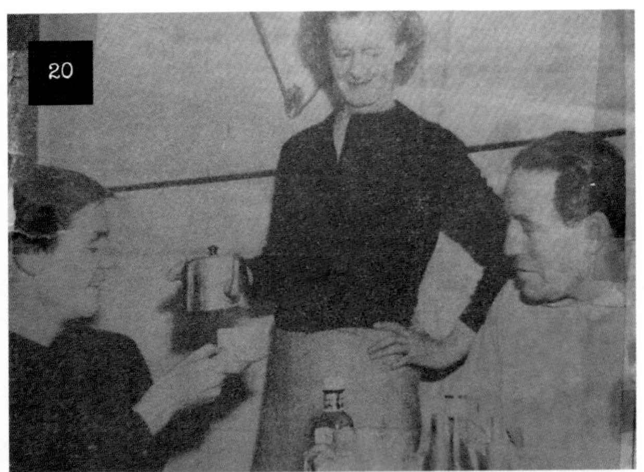
20

21

22

23

24

25

26

27

28

29

30

31

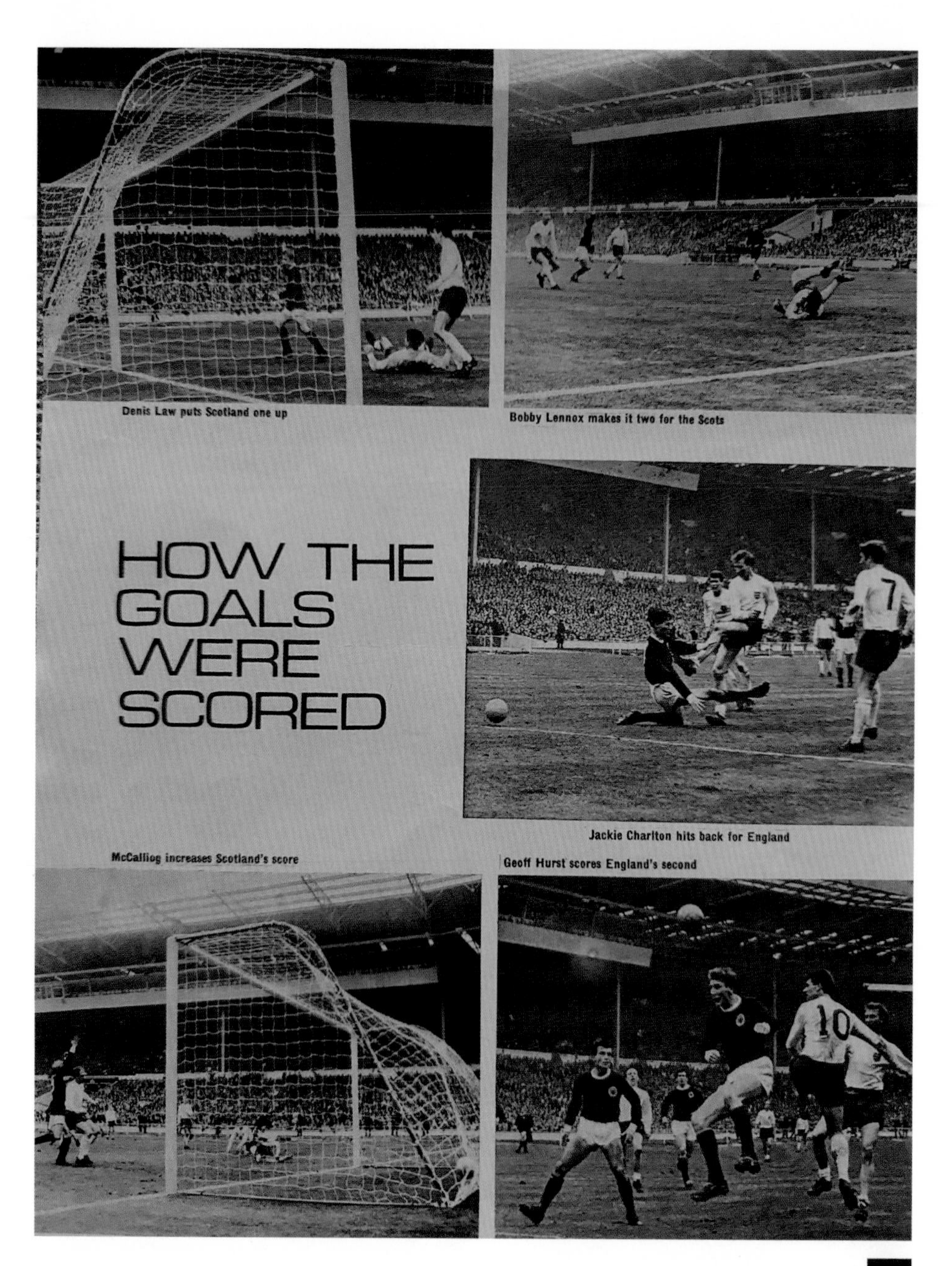

Denis Law puts Scotland one up

Bobby Lennox makes it two for the Scots

HOW THE GOALS WERE SCORED

Jackie Charlton hits back for England

McCalliog increases Scotland's score

Geoff Hurst scores England's second

32

33

dotted line for Wolves
watched by manager
Bill McGary.
34

35

36

JIMMY HILL'S
FOOTBALL
WEEKLY
October 3, 1969 Vol 2 No 50 1s 6d
Jim McCalliog
Wolves
Inside:
President of FIFA,
SIR STANLEY ROUS,
writes in PLATFORM
37

38

39
MEET THE
WOLVES TEAM
MARCH 30TH
40

41

42

43

44

45

46

47

48

49

50

51

52

53

54

55

56

57

Jim McCalliog and Bobby Stokes at a post-match dinner

58

59

60

got back to me, he said the contract to the tour stipulated certain players had to play and I was one of them.

Before the tour was finalised, America was added to the list. I found myself heading out with my Wolves team-mates on another exhausting trip. Our manager actually left the tour when we reached the States to go on a family holiday, leaving coach Sammy Chung in charge. He lost my respect with that decision.

Chapter Twenty-Five

WOLVES' AMAZING EUROPEAN ADVENTURE

SEASON 1971/72 offered Wolves the opportunity to make history. We reached the two-legged UEFA Cup Final, nowadays known as the Europa League, after overcoming strong opposition such as Italian cracks Juventus and Ferencvaros, the very capable Hungarians.

As luck would have it, we would play Spurs in the showpiece showdown. It was the first time two English clubs would match up in a European grand finale and we faced them after failing to beat them in our First Division encounters, drawing 2-2 at our place and losing 4-1 at White Hart Lane. Now we had our chance of revenge with a gleaming trophy thrown in as a special reward. Alas, after the two games, we were still waiting for our first victory.

European football was, of course, nothing new to Wolves. On December 13, 1954, Wolves were hailed as the Club Champions of Europe after beating the famed Hungarians of Honved under the Molineux floodlights. It is true that Wolves outpaced and outpowered the Hungarians and gave English soccer a tremendous boost, but the claim that the Molineux side was the best in Europe was fiercely contested on the continent. As a kid growing up in Glasgow, I knew of Honved and my first football hero Ferenc Puskas, captain of the magical Magyars, as they were known after beating England 6-3 at Wembley. The Hungarian national team was littered with great players besides Puskas. Another football hero, Alfredo di Stefano, of Real Madrid, played against Wolves on Thursday, October 17 1957. They had won the European Cup in each of the previous two seasons and were also current holders of the Latin Cup.

I was part of Wolves' wonderful UEFA Cup run which went all the way to the two-legged final. Our first game in the competition was in Portugal against Academica Coimbra and we won 7-1 on aggregate. We were drawn against ADO from the Netherlands in round two. We gave them a good hiding in both games.

In the first game away from home, we played great, winning 3-1. We controlled the game and scored in sixty-one minutes through The Doog and I scored in seventy-six minutes before being forced to limp off. Substitute Kenny Hibbitt scored in eighty-one minutes and our opponents scored from the penalty spot in eighty-two minutes.

A great result and we hammered them 4-0 at Molineux. We scored with THREE own goals and one from The Doog. I had never heard or played in a game with three own goals. So far so good in the tournament. In round three, we were drawn with East German opponents Carl Zeiss Jena, a well-known team in the Eastern Bloc. I had never been to East Germany, so it would be a new experience. We played in sub-zero temperatures and managed to come away with a 1-0 win. I broke down the right wing and crossed for young John Richards to head in our goal. We beat our East German opponents 3-0 at Molineux where The Doog scored two and Kenny Hibbitt got the other goal.

In the quarter-final, we were drawn against Juventus with the first leg at the Stadio Communale in Turin. They were the current Italian league leaders. When I heard the draw all sorts of thoughts were going through my head. It was a great feeling. I loved everything Italian, football, clothes, food, they were a stylish nation. I had played in Italy before with Wolves, so we were ready. When you say Juventus it is another ball game. Their tradition, like Wolves, was very impressive. At training on Monday morning, the boss was calm, no nervousness just optimism. Sadly, Mike Bailey and Derek Parkin were injured and wouldn't be available. Gerry Taylor and Danny Hegan would replace them. When we arrived at East Midlands airport, there was a huge surprise waiting for us. The boss, with a flash of inspiration, had contacted John Charles to invite him as a guest of Wolves to accompany the team to Italy. It was a masterstroke. I had met John Charles as a young player at Leeds when I was fifteen years old. When I was introduced, he remembered who I was. I was thrilled. John Charles was a Leeds, Juventus and Welsh legend who could play centre-forward or centre-half.

As we had to be in the country a day before the match (or to be precise twenty-four hours before the kick-off), so we left for Italy on Tuesday. There was a great atmosphere and a buzz about the players. They were also curious about Big John. I was glad to tell them all about this legend. Big John volunteered to take us shopping in Turin and I went along. There were about four or five of the lads. It was amazing what happened as we were walking in Turin word must have got out that John Charles was back. People in the streets were chanting: 'Charlo... Charlo...' and all the windows were opening and people were waving. It was great to see how much the Juve fans appreciated Big John. We told the other lads when we got back at what had happened. I was looking forward to leading the team out as captain against Juventus. I was just soaking up the atmosphere until kick-off. The boss was cool. Leading the team out, I felt honoured and privileged. Two big clubs, Juventus and Wolves.

We didn't have a lot of fans in the stadium, three hundred to be exact. They were drowned out by Juve's fans. A couple of minutes later, the boss and John Charles walked to the dug-out and the fans gave John an amazing welcome. We were under the cosh as Juve tried to get an early goal, but we held out until the thirty-seventh minute when Pierto Anastasi scored. At half-time, the boss thought we had done well, but didn't want us to fall back and defend. We pushed Juve and got our reward in the sixty-sixth minute. A Gerry Taylor free-kick was headed back by Derek Dougan into my path outside the penalty area. I was ready and I hit a left-foot volley into the bottom corner of the net and went off to celebrate with our small band of supporters. It was a special moment for myself. I looked to the heavens. The game finished 1-1, it was a great result.

The boss Bill McGarry said after the match: 'This was our best, a splendid team performance, certainly the best in our seven games in the UEFA Cup this season.' Jeff Farmer, in the Daily Mail, said: 'Super Wolves Set Up Kill'. Peter Ingall, in the Daily Mirror, said: 'Wolves Just Great.' Hugh Jamieson, from The Sun, said: 'Euro Glory For Wolves'. From A Special Correspondent: 'McCalliog Goal Keeps Wolves All-Square With Juventus.' It had been a great night's work, but anyone who thought Juve were out needed to think properly. It was only half-time. The boss had been banished from the touchline by the referee twenty minutes from the end. He said afterwards to the media: 'All I was doing was shouting the instructions from the touchline. I suppose I was wrong.' The media were much more convinced we would go through with a home tie to follow.

The second leg in Molineux would be interesting. Our away goal in Turin could prove vital. It was funny watching Danny Hegan jumping on big Frank Munro when we scored our first goal in the return leg and we went in 1-0 ahead at half-time. I was unlucky with a couple of headers. The boss was calm. It must have been a great game to watch and I was loving playing in it. As I led the team out for the second-half, I was confident we would give everything and we had a great chance to go through. Both teams battled away, but we had the important goal. Other managers might now be more cautious and defend. Not the boss and he was rewarded big style. Waggy took a corner on our right-hand side The Doog glanced the ball with his head into Juve's net. Surely we could see out leg out.

Helmut Haller, the West German, scored for Juve in the last ten minutes. Game on, could we hold on? It was frantic. I don't think I could watch like the fans. I was in the right place, especially when the ref blew for full-time. All the money that had been thrown at Juventus couldn't stop us from deservedly beating them over two legs. It was a football night to remember.

When I signed for Wolves in 1969, I knew they had tremendous potential. Peter Knowles and Mike Bailey were missing and new players, John McAlle, Kenny Hibbitt and John Richards, had come through the club system. The boss must have enjoyed a drink, feeling very satisfied. Onto Budapest, Ferencvaros and Florian Albert. As a kid growing up in Glasgow, my mum sourced me a book about Ferenc Puskas, the Magical Magyar, as he was known. Although his club team was Honved, he played in Budapest and we would be going there in the semis.

I hadn't been to Hungary on my football travels and Budapest was a football hotbed in the fifties, sixties and seventies. On April 5 in the Hungarian capital in the Stadion Albert Florian, in the first leg we were venturing into the unknown because I don't think we knew anything about our opponents. I knew the boss wouldn't change our style, so we would be looking for away goals. And I didn't think Ferencvaros would be better than Juventus who we had just knocked out. I was surprised how good technically the Hungarians were. Their control of the ball was first class. We competed well in the game and 2-2 was a great score. Our goalscorers were John Richards, in eighteen minutes, and Frank Munro, eighty minutes. Great result with two away goals.

A fortnight later, on an emotional night at Molineux, we had to bring in two young players, Steve Daley and Alan Sunderland. We were down to the bare bones near enough. Seven of us had played in every game and our squad was thin, but we had a good crop of young players coming through. No sooner had the game started, than we were one up. A long cross from the right was badly misjudged by their goalkeeper and Steve Daley coolly sidefooted the ball into the net. What a moment for young Steve's first European goal. We had some anxious moments. They had nothing to lose and went on the attack. What a game! It was end to end. We attacked the ball on the right-hand side and I chased after it and crossed the ball back into the six-yard box where big Frank Munro headed us 2-0 up.

In the dressing room at half-time, we were buzzing. The outcome was in our hands, but it could change easily. They were a good side and we had to battle until the final whistle. They gave us a lot of problems. They scored to make it 2-

1 and Phil Parkes saved a penalty with his foot. I honestly think the whistle came at the right time as we were under the cosh big-time. In the communal bath, it was a wonderful feeling. My first European final. The last six years were amazing. FA Cup Final, international debut and now UEFA Cup Final.

Chapter Twenty-Six

EUROPEAN GLORY – BEST TEAM OVER TWO-LEGGED FINAL

FOOTBALL is packed with 'what if' stories, isn't it? I look back at the two confrontations in the UEFA Cup Final against Spurs and still wonder how we relinquished the opportunity to get our hands on that trophy.

Both ties were played in May 1972 with the first match at Molineux on the fifth. Normally, the surfaces can show a fair bit of wear and tear nearing the conclusion of a hectic campaign, but I must say both surfaces were in good nick. So there are no excuses for failure on that front. The weather was mild on both occasions, too, so Wolves and Spurs were afforded the ideal setting to put on a show over the two duels. There hadn't been too much to separate the teams after forty-two league games. They finished in sixth position on fifty-one points and we were three places behind and only four points adrift.

They had some superb players in goalkeeper Pat Jennings, the Northern Ireland legend, Mike England, the Welsh international colossus in central defence, the industrious Alan Mullery in the middle of the park, Alan Gilzean, my fellow-Scot who was a clever, crafty and experienced campaigner, and the powerful six foot-plus Martin Chivers leading their line. He had cost a massive £125,000 when he joined from Southampton in January 1968 which made him the most expensive player in British football. He had a good goalscoring pedigree of which we were to be on the receiving end to our cost.

I had the honour of captaining Wolves in both games with regular skipper Mike Bailey on the substitutes' bench. We reckoned we could win the silverware. However, we realised it was absolutely imperative we won the first leg which was in the Midlands. We really needed something to take with us to London if we had to stand a chance. It was still goalless after the fifty-five minute mark and it was a wonder how the London team were even still in the contest. We absolutely bombarded them. It was a real backs-to-the-wall job from our visitors that evening. They pulled all their big guys back into their penalty area, including forwards Chivers and Gilzean, as we gave them a pasting. We had a stream of corner-kicks, free-kicks and throw-ins, but somehow they survived. Jennings probably had more touches of the ball than anyone else of the field up to that point. He was most certainly the most active performer on view as we pummelled away at their penalty box.

As so often happens in this game, they opened the scoring with the most simple of goals - a free-kick and a header. Just like that. All our good work was obliterated in a heartbeat. Big centre-half England slung in a deadball effort from just inside our half of the field. It was just a high diagonal ball launched into the mix that you would expect your defence to deal with as a matter of course. Sadly, football doesn't work like that. Phil Parkes elected to remain on his line while the guys in front of him must have expected our goalkeeper to come and claim the ball that seemed to be up in the air for an awful long time. Remarkably, no-one blocked off the run of Chivers, who, with his massive frame in an all-white strip, was hardly anonymous. However, he was allowed to race unobstructed into the danger zone and get his head to the cross from six yards. The ball simply floated over the prone figure of Parkes who was caught in no-man's land. Some of the Spurs players at least possessed the grace to look shocked that they had actually put the ball in our net.

It took us fifteen long minutes to get back on level terms. They looked as though they were content to play out the rest of the match and hold onto what they had. They slowed play right down and would take ages at throw-ins. You know the sort of thing. A player will go over and pick up the ball, clean it and shape to throw it. Then he'll place it for a team-mate to come along and go through the same rigmarole. Then he chucks it to another colleague and he feels the need to give the ball a rub, too. Of course, it's annoying and frustrating, but you cannot let it interfere with your concentration. You just have to hope the referee is taking all the time-wasting into account and adds on the minutes at the end. Some do and, alas, some don't.

However, a bit of quick-thinking between myself and Danny Hegan caught the London side totally unprepared at a free-kick. The Azerbaijani referee gave the award for a handball from Mullery most people would have missed. Kenny Hibbitt smashed in a shot that was deflected. Play went on for a moment or two before most of the players realised the match official had blown his whistle and pulled us back to the edge of the box. I raced after the ball, retrieved it and threw it swiftly to Danny. The ref had already indicated it was okay for it to be taken and my team-mate didn't hesitate. The Spurs players were still thinking about erecting a defensive wall when he slipped the ball to his left and I latched onto it, steadied myself and fired in a shot. The ball passed through the legs of Phil Beal who was too late in getting back to cover and I think the defender might have unsighted his keeper with my low effort striking Jennings' left heel on its way into the net.

Not the most spectacular goal I have ever scored, but they all count and it was extremely satisfying. With eighteen minutes still to play, our only thoughts were to go for a winner. We had Spurs right where we wanted them. They were rocking a little, we were in command and then we pressed the self-destruct button again. With three minutes left, a long ball was fired out to Chivers about fifteen yards inside our half on their left. He miscontrolled it, but one of our players inadvertently directed the ball straight back to him. To be fair, it was late in the game, limbs can begin to ache, tiredness sets in and these things can happen. Unfortunately, it was to have disastrous consequences. Chivers picked up the rebound, saw an opening and drove straight for it. Our defenders were out of position and as they tried to get back to nullify the threat, he suddenly let loose from about twenty-five yards. The ball took off like a heat-seeking missile and whistled low past our keeper low to his right. I have to admit it was a fairly special goal, although that was not my immediate thought, I have to confess.

We had failed to make home advantage count, but we were far from out of the silverware chase. Sometimes you have to accept a set of circumstances will go against you in a match. There was little point in feeling sorry for ourselves. Take that route and I guarantee you will end up a loser. If you become self-absorbed in believing the world has got it in for you, there is little point in going onto a football field. I had never been interested in being runner-up, even knocking the ball about with my pals in the streets as I grew up in the Gorbals. As far as I was concerned, we were ninety minutes away from winning the UEFA Cup. Okay, we were a goal adrift, but it was hardly an insurmountable margin. Maybe Dame Fortune would bestow a small smile upon us at White Hart Lane in a fortnight's time? That would have been welcome, but the bottom line was that it was down to us and our efforts that would dictate whether we would be winners or losers in London on May 17.

Had we learned from our expensive mistakes from the first leg? We got an answer inside half-an-hour. Spurs were awarded a free-kick about thirty-five yards out on their left. We had practically gifted them their opening goal from a setplay at Molineux, so we had been well warned of their capabilities from deadball situations. Martin Peters lined up to take it and we packed into the box to keep a wary eye on Chivers, Gilzean and England, all big guys who were dangerous in the air. However, we failed to adequately guard the front post. Peters was experienced enough to accept the invitation. He swung the ball into the unprotected area and his England international team-mate Mullery read his intentions perfectly. The ball dropped into the little pocket of space, Mullery's timing couldn't have been bettered and he arrived before our keeper to head in from six yards. Clearly, it was straight off the training ground. The presence of players such as the stature of Chivers and Co at the back post will attract attention, their pedigree goes before them. Spurs mixed it up and suddenly we were trailing 3-1 on aggregate with just an hour to turn things around.

A lot of things can happen in sixty minutes in football and you must adopt a positive attitude. It was all about how both teams reacted to the goal. Would Spurs, as they had done in the first game, retreat into defence to hold onto their two-goal advantage? Okay, they were playing at home in front of their own fans, but were they more interested on winning the trophy than putting on a show? No prizes for guessing which one they chose. We had little option but to open up and go for it. We couldn't leave the back door open, of course, but we would have to be a bit more aggressive and assertive going forward. We were back in the contest five minutes before the interval when David Wagstaffe scored with a fairly spectacular drive from about twenty-five yards. Waggy had a devastating left foot and he could conjure up all sorts of things when he was in the mood. On this occasion, he dragged the ball in from the right, the Spurs lads made the mistake of backing off and he accepted their invitation to have a crack at goal.

Pat Jennings was one of the greatest goalkeepers of his era and most opponents possibly thought it was a colossal waste of time trying to beat him with a long-range effort. Obviously, Wagstaffe was no great respecter of reputations. From nowhere he lashed the ball with his trusty left foot. The ball was a blur as it hammered off the inside of the right-hand post and ricocheted into the net like a bullet. Jennings didn't stand a chance. We were back in it. However, our name was not on the trophy that year.

We probed and prompted throughout the second-half, but they firmly closed the back door. Derek Dougan thought he had found the key when he turned in a John Richards flick from a Wagstaffe cross, but was adjudged to be offside. It was marginal, but you just have to get your head down and keep going. Jennings had a good save from one of my shots and Frank Munro joined the attack to force another good stop from the Irish giant. Frank got his head to my cross from the bye-line and it looked good from where I was standing. Alas, Jennings underlined his status yet again by getting one of his giant paws to the flashing effort to push it to safety.

The following day, the back page headline in the local newspaper, The Express and Star, stated: **WOLVES GET GLORY BUT IT'S SPURS' CUP**. That just about summed it up. Most neutrals agreed we had been the better team over the two legs, but we made mistakes and they counted heavily against us. I was bitterly disappointed, as you would expect. Sometimes you have to hold up your hands if you have been played off the pitch and beaten by a superior team. That was not the case with our UEFA Cup showdown with Bill Nicholson's side. And that is not sour grapes, please believe me. Still, it's history now, but you can never prevent yourself from thinking of what might have been.

Nor did we enjoy an overload of good fortune in the two domestic Cup competition in season 1971/72. Our League Cup campaign hardly got out of the blocks when we were stopped in our tracks at the second round stage by Manchester City in September. We managed to score three goals at Maine Road, but that counts for little when the opponents claim four. Even worse, we were ahead by two goals on two occasions and were leading 3-1 with only twelve minutes to go. And we still managed to throw it away. We were two goals to the good inside the opening twenty-five minutes through efforts from John McAlle and Danny Hegan. City were struggling, but they got one back just before the interval with a header from Wyn Davies, the rangy Welsh international who did all his best work in the air. However, Derek Parkin restored our two-goal advantage with a penalty-kick past Joe Corrigan nine minutes after the turnaround. That's the way it remained until the seventy-eighth minute when Davies knocked a ball down to Colin Bell who thumped it past Phil Parkes. Three minutes later City were awarded a dubious penalty-kick, but that didn't prevent Frannie Lee from burying a blaster into the back of our net. That old sinking feeling in the pit of your stomach was suddenly evident. In the eighty-fourth minute Bell hit the winner. Three goals in six minutes? Something wrong somewhere.

A similar tale in the FA Cup. We drew 1-1 with Leicester City at Molineux with me scoring the goal in the third round on January 15 1972. Peter Shilton, the opposition keeper, made a couple of good saves, but we didn't do enough to get over the line. The replay was at Filbert Street four days later and they won 2-0. We could have no complaints. They had brought in a new go-ahead manager in Jimmy Bloomfield and he was creating an interesting change of direction in the side's fortunes. They earned their place in the next round, but, after playing so comprehensively against us, they lost 2-0 to Second Division Leyton Orient on their own ground in the next round.

I was beginning to wonder if I would ever play at Wembley again.

Chapter Twenty-Seven

MIXED FORTUNES AT MOLINEUX

THIS would be my eighth season as a professional footballer, the career I chose as a young boy from the Gorbals. I had travelled a lot of miles, I had played with and against many great players and played under different managers with different ideas.

I was an intelligent player and loved responsibility. The only thing missing was trophies. I had won the League Cup at Chelsea when I was very young. Sadly I had lost in the FA Cup Final with Sheffield Wednesday in 1966, my first appearance and first goal at Wembley. Unluckily, I had been on the losing team in a UEFA Cup Final.

At the start of pre-season for 1972/73 campaign, could Wolves rival or better last year? I was optimistic. Our first two league games we lost away to Newcastle United 2-1 and Arsenal 5-2. We were also beaten by Bristol Rovers in the Watney Cup. It was so disappointing and I had my own thoughts on why things were going wrong. In my opinion, Mike Bailey always started slowly. I think the manager should have realised this and played Danny Hegan as Mike battled to find his form. It caused some resentment in the dressing room as competition for places in the team was a big part of our progress.

Mike and Danny were different players, Mike steadied things and Danny wanted to get forward. Both their styles had helped the team in different ways. Mike was more a team player and Danny more of an individual. The manager had a different attitude this season. He was a lot more cocky and less concerned. I don't know if the other players noticed, but I certainly did. The team started to play and in the next fifteen games we only lost one and drew five. We were still in the League Cup and our league form was picking up. Maybe the boss, Bill McGarry, fancied our chances of winning something at last.

The dressing room was united and we were ready. We didn't fear any team. I had fancied us to win a Cup because on our day we were capable of beating anyone and the team was a year older and more experienced. Most importantly, we were scoring goals. I think the fans knew we were a top team. I don't remember the boss getting overheated about anything, he was just letting games and events take care of themselves. And he wasn't rocking the boat over little things.

We were still involved in all the competitions with the FA Cup still to start. Sammy Chung, our coach, must have felt good not having to come between the players and the boss. I remember Sammy telling a group of players about his career. He said he broke his leg three times and The Doog asked him: 'Were you just unlucky or stupid?' Sammy and the group just laughed, there was no animosity. The Doog was always mischievous.

Talking about The Doog, he was in tremendous form ever since I arrived at Wolves. His fitness and mentality towards football made him stand out. Like I said before, the boss and The Doog didn't get on at all. We had five strikers at one point, Hughie Curran, Bobby Gould, John Richards and The Doog plus Steve Kindon, who was normally a winger, but the boss fancied him right up front. Hughie and Bobby were Wolves' top goalscorers in 1969 and 1970, but the boss knew The Doog's value to the team. He was first choice among the strikers. The Doog had been top goalscorer the previous season with twenty-four goals, but the best he ever managed when Ronnie Allen was in charge was fourteen. The Doog and the boss were good for each other. In my opinion, we were a very dangerous team with The Doog playing. He stretched defences and defenders panicked with crosses into the box. He was great fun in the dressing room and a great chairman for the PFA.

I MISS THE BIG MAN.

In our next fifteen games, we only lost one with four draws and ten wins. We were getting back in the groove. I think I spoke too soon as in our next eight games, we lost six and drew two. We were doing well in the League Cup and we had to face Blackpool in the quarter-finals. We drew 1-1 at Molineux and beat them 1-0 at Bloomfield Road. We had already beaten Orient 2-0 at Molineux, then my old club Sheffield Wednesday 3-1 at home and Bristol Rovers 4-0 to avenge the Watney Cup defeat at the beginning of the season.

Waiting for us in the semis were Spurs – again! We had beaten them earlier in the season in the league at Molineux 3-2. The next six league games, we lost one, drew one and won four. Our last two games we beat Everton at Goodison 1-0 and Chelsea 1-0 at Molineux, two good wins and no goals conceded. Next up it was Spurs in the first leg of the League Cup at Molineux. We lost 2-1and in the second leg at White Hart Lane, we kept going. It was 1-1 on the night and we tried so hard to get another goal to take it to a third game, but it wasn't to be. Martin Chivers scored the all-important goal. He must have loved playing against Wolves, we had no answer to him.

Our concentration was now on the league and the FA Cup. We lost our next league game at home to Southampton 1-0, but we won our next three games against Manchester United, Bristol City in the FA Cup and we beat Liverpool at home. I was involved in a bizarre own goal. Derek Dougan headed a high ball towards myself. It got stuck under my feet as I helped the ball goalwards. Emlyn Hughes lost control of the ball, too, and it went over the line to put us 1-0 up. Liverpool equalised through Kevin Keegan and John Richards scored a second as we won an important league game against the eventual title winners.

We went on a thirteen-game winning streak which came to an end when we lost to Manchester United at Old Trafford, but we still got through to the semi-final of the FA Cup. We beat Millwall and Coventry City in the fifth and sixth rounds of the FA Cup. Sadly, for myself, I pulled a hamstring against Coventry three weeks before the semi-final against Leeds United. Hamstring injuries normally take to between three weeks to six weeks to recover. I hoped I would be fit to help the team to the FA Cup Final, six years since I had played at Wembley for Sheffield Wednesday against Everton in 1966.

I had never had this type of injury before. I had played so much football all over the world and seldom missed any club games in my time at Wolves. The conditions versus Coventry in the quarter-finals were muddy. I sprinted and I felt my hamstring go, it made me pull up very sharply. I had treatment three times a day trying to be ready for the semi-final. I came close to being fit. The boss said he would wait until the morning of the game. Our physio Toby Andersen was tremendous and I got to know him well I this period as he tried to get me fit.

The boss stayed in the hotel as I tested my hamstring with the physio. It was touch and go. I was very close, I waited for a reaction after my test as it was such an important game. I knew I wasn't 100 per cent, but, with my experience, could I get away with it? Before the team meeting, I talked to the boss. He said: 'Tell me what you think.' I said I wasn't ready and that it was too much of a risk. I had to make the decision, I was so disappointed, but I knew it was right.

We started the game well and young Barry Powell who took my place had a great chance in the opening minutes of the game, but sadly missed. It was torture watching, I wanted us to win so badly. Our supporters were amazing and kept encouraging the team, but in the end to no avail. We lost 1-0 and Billy Bremner got Leeds' goal. Two semis, but no final. I think going out in the semis is the worst round to lose in. I went into the dressing room and it was just like a morgue. All the team were down it was best to keep quiet and let the result sink in.

On the coach journey back to Molineux, it was time to reflect on the game and the season so far. There were still six games to go until the season's end. I had treatment on the Sunday and I just couldn't believe I had missed a semi-final of the FA Cup because of a hamstring injury. I knew I could have made a difference. I was a player who rose to the big occasions throughout my career and I would inevitably put one over on my old teams.

The season had been very eventful, but sadly we missed out on two Cup Finals. Surely next season would bring us a trophy?

Chapter Twenty-Eight

BOMBSHELL WEEKEND - MANCHESTER UNITED MAKE THEIR MOVE AFTER SEVEN YEARS

THE beginning of the end of my Wolves career came on the bombshell weekend when Bill McGarry dropped me for the first time for the game against Everton at Goodison on February 9 1974.

There had been no indication of what was about to happen. After a pre-match meal, we had a team meeting in one of the hotel's function rooms. The manager read out the team. I was not in it! I was shocked and extremely hurt. I kept quiet, but my mind was racing. I couldn't believe I had just been dropped for the first time since my transfer from Sheffield Wednesday.

I had been a first-team regular for eight years at Wednesday and Wolves. I was in a daze, but kept my cool. It was a long weekend as I considered my future. It was a bolt from the blue and being left out I kept my own counsel as I worked out what I would do. I had missed games because of injury, but the boss would put me in as soon as I was fit again. This was something different. My pride was hurt and an explanation from the manager would have helped.

We lost 2-1 and I went to training as usual on Monday morning as I had done for nearly five wonderful years. I was happy at Wolves. I took everything into consideration. I had had to trust my decision-making to myself all my football career. My mind was made up, but I had to be patient. I went into the dressing room and enjoyed the banter before training. I never went into the manager's office. I decided I wouldn't waste my breath on the manager. I thought the ball was in his court, he made the decision to drop me. His call.

I never spoke to the manager again until he told me Vic Crowe, the Aston Villa manager, had permission to speak to me. The Villa boss was obviously keen for me to sign and, of course, it is always nice to feel wanted. Naturally, though, there are always rumours in this wonderful game of football and the grapevine was rife with speculation I might join up once more with my former Chelsea boss Tommy Docherty at Manchester United. I admit the prospect of turning out for the Red Devils had a massive appeal. I had no intention of joining Villa if there was a chance, even a remote one, of going to Manchester United. I actually went along to a game at Villa Park on the Tuesday night and talked to Vic Crowe who seemed a nice enough bloke with big ideas for his club.

I telephoned my Scottish newspaper contacts Jim Rodger, at the Daily Express, and Ken Gallacher, at the Daily Record. I knew they were friendly with Tommy Docherty and I wondered if they could shed any light on the situation. Time was running out and I had a big decision to make. I had every intention of getting it spot on. I was six months away from my twenty-eighth birthday and, to many, that is considered to be the beginning of a footballer's peak years.

So, back in March 1974, I was more than interested in discovering if there was anything to the tales of Tommy Docherty wanting to sign me for a second time. There was a Thursday transfer deadline at the time and I got the distinct impression Bill McGarry was eager for me to move across the Midlands to Villa. Why? That's easy. Villa were in the old Second Division and that would have prevented me from showing up the Wolves manager if I had started to turn it on which would have made him look bad and his judgement questionable. Out of the top flight, I would have been out of sight and out of mind. Well, that appeared to be the plan. Football doesn't always follow the script.

I went to training as usual at Wolves on the Wednesday morning and I sought out the manager. I asked him if there were any other clubs showing an interest in me. 'Just Villa,' I was told curtly. Bill McGarry would never have had a great career as a chat show host, that's for sure. So, I went through the routine with the lads and wondered where I would be twenty-four hours or so later. If my manager had his way I would be a signed, sealed and delivered Aston Villa player by the completion of the Thursday transfer deadline. I had other thoughts on the matter of my immediate future.

My newspaper pals came good. Later that day I received a call from Tommy Docherty. 'Don't do anything, Jim,' he ordered, 'I'm really interested. United are really interested. I'm going to talk to the board about the money. We want you here, me and all the directors. So, don't be in a rush to sign anything with anyone else, okay?'

'Look, boss, if you want me, I'll walk to Old Trafford,' I said. Okay, a wee bit melodramatic, but it conveyed the message. I was elated to know Tommy Docherty was on the case. The following day, I reported for training at Wolves. I sought out Bill McGarry to get an update. 'Anyone else showing an interest in me?' I asked and I could not disguise the small trace of a smile. The Wolves manager looked at me for a moment and then exploded. 'You effin' know, don't you?' he shouted.

'Know what?' I asked in wide-eyed innocence. 'Manchester effin' United!' he roared. I knew Tommy Docherty had made contact and the £60,000 move was in motion. As I was heading out of his office, he blurted: 'If you sign for United you will not get your £5,000 loyalty bonus.' I knew I was on the home straight. I had kept my counsel up until now, but could not resist saying my last words to him: 'Shove your £5,000 up you jacksy, I'm off to United.'

I went into the secretary Phil Shaw's office and he put me through to Tommy Docherty. I said: 'I am on my way.' He said: 'Good, Jim, see you at Old Trafford.'

After training, I was chatting to Frank Munro. 'So, you're off to Villa, then,' he said. It was more of a statement than a question. 'It will be in the evening papers, Frank,' I said. I didn't mention I was signing for Manchester United or anyone else. I shook hands with my team-mates and left the Molineux dressing room. I was sad as I loved my time at Wolves, but I was optimistic and couldn't wait to get to Old Trafford.

I realise there aren't too many players who are willing to drop thousands of pounds in cash to get a transfer, but that's exactly what I had done. Had I gone to Aston Villa I would have pocketed a £5,000 loyalty bonus from the club. The cash had been due after I had served five years at Molineux and I was sixteen weeks away from that milestone. They would have overlooked the four-month discrepancy if I had transferred to Villa. Alas, it was a different story if I decided on United.

I got into my car and drove to Manchester, it would take me about an hour. It was a great day for myself. To play for Manchester United was one of my football dreams. I was so thrilled and honoured and humbled to follow in the steps of so many wonderful Manchester United players, past and present. When I arrived at the Theatre of Dreams, I took a deep breath and went into the office to ask for the manager.

The boss came and took me into an office with Les Olive, the club's secretary, and I signed for Manchester United just before the 5pm deadline. There were no photographers. My new boss showed me around Old Trafford briefly and we drove to my hotel. It was at best a three star hotel, it was not what I expected. I called my parents to tell them I was okay and now a Manchester United player. I settled in my hotel and was looking forward to training and meeting my new team-mates.

Chapter Twenty-Nine

BILL McGARRY, A MAN OF FEW WORDS

I NEVER had a genuine problem with Bill McGarry, the manager who took me to Wolves from Sheffield Wednesday in August 1969. I doubt if the board members of the Molineux club would entirely agree with that sentiment. It would be fair to say the team boss was fairly unique, even among the world of slightly eccentric, dugout-dwelling characters.

Bill arrived in the Midlands in 1968 after a successful four-year spell at Ipswich Town. They loved him at the East Anglian club and their rather colourful chairman was a chap called John Cobbold, who made his millions through his vast empire of breweries. There was a tale at a stage when the team were going through a rough patch and a local reporter asked this laidback individual what would constitute a crisis at Portman Road. He didn't even hesitate for a moment as he replied: 'Oh, dear boy, that would be running out of wine in the boardroom.'

However, it would be fair to say the club supremo knew his football and he was willing to offer Bill McGarry a King's Ransom to remain at Ipswich. But the lure of a club with the prestige and history of Wolverhampton Wanderers proved too much of a challenge and attraction for the manager. Same for me, too.

On my first day at Molineux to finalise the details of the transfer, dotting the 'i's and crossing the 't's, I arrived in my dad's car and was welcomed by McGarry and club chairman John Ireland. I received a very warm welcome and I immediately felt at home. Once the formalities were out of the way and I was now a Wolves player, I spent time with the manager and the club chief. They showed me plans they had for restructuring their ground and all sorts of other improvements to take the club into an exciting new chapter. It was clear, though, the most important element of the club was the team itself. That sounds a little obvious, but there are clubs where the balance sheet is more important than the team sheet. That wasn't the case at my new club and I was eager and determined to play my part.

Later in my Wolves career, I heard the interesting tale of the boss in his first board meeting at the club. He took his seat at the large oak table in the company of the chairman and the directors. They discussed a few items on a prepared agenda and then they got to the team's performance in the last game. Without preamble, the manager pushed back his chair and, without a word, opened the door and left the room. He was persuaded to come back by chairman Mr Ireland and the meeting was reconvened. They skipped the team's previous display and next on the list was the line-up for the forthcoming game on Saturday. Once again, the boss pushed back the chair and went through the same routine as he exited the boardroom. I was reliably informed he never attended another board meeting.

It was evident there was only one person who mattered when it came to team business and that was the manager. Chairman John Ireland, who was a very approachable chap, and his directors could get on with their jobs, take their seat in the stand on matchday, support the team and leave the formations and line-ups to the boss. Obviously, any interference in team matters would not be tolerated. I'm not too sure the boss had to go to the extent of refusing to allow the board members to travel to away games on the team coach. But he did. They had to make their own arrangements and were forced to travel in their own cars.

Possibly, outsiders may have thought that was a little odd. It was just the way the manager did things. A lot of the players, I soon discovered, didn't actually like him. His attitude may have been difficult to fathom at times. For instance, he would be last on the bus to go training after Sammy Chung, his coach, had reassured him everyone else was in place and he would never acknowledge the players. There was no 'Good morning, lads' with the boss. He would take his seat at the front of the coach and order: 'On you go, driver'. The players came not to expect a 'Hello' every time the manager walked past them. He didn't waste time on the frivolities of good manners. I could see that it really annoyed some of the players, but, to be honest, I couldn't care less. I was there to do a professional job and I enjoyed training, so if the manager chose to blank me I didn't mind one bit.

I understood the situation with the players who had been at the club prior to the arrival of the boss. The previous manager had been Ronnie Allen and the players adored him. It seemed like a chalk-and-cheese situation and it was obvious Mr Allen and the boss had distinctly different personalities and methods.

I got the drift some of the players could get away with murder with Mr Allen as he appeared to be a fairly easy-going individual. On the other side of the spectrum, you had the boss who took no nonsense from anybody. You only had to ask the chairman and his directors to have that confirmed!

Another example of the boss distancing himself from his players was highlighted when Derek Dougan was sidelined for two months with a fractured cheekbone. I put my hands up here and now and admit I liked the man better known as The Doog. Obviously, he wasn't allowed to train with such an injury, but the boss refused to give him any time off. He wanted him at Molineux every day, but that was not a big deal for my mate. Being the infectious type of guy he is, he would have been at the ground every day, anyway. The Doog loved winding people up and even facial damage couldn't prevent him from getting involved in some merciless tongue-in-cheek antics. We would play six-a-sides and, although the rangy Northern Ireland international striker was absolutely superb in the air, by no stretch of the imagination could you say the same about his skills on the deck. With the ball at his feet, his first touch was not the best. Regularly, he would be the worst player on view and he would go back to the dressing room and pick on some poor unfortunate for being awful. He would shower, change and leave while whistling with not a care in the world. The poor wretch who had just had his cage rattled was left devastated.

But The Doog was fearless when it came to attacking the ball in the air in packed penalty areas which accounted for his fractured cheekbone which put him out of the game for eight weeks. Did he get any sympathy from the boss? Not a word. Or, as comedian Billy Connolly would say: 'Not a jot.' In fact, he didn't even get a pleasantry when they met at the ground and the tight confines of the stadium at the time meant it was impossible not to bump into someone. Coming in the main entrance at Molineux, the manager's office was on the left with the secretary's office on the right. There was a door that took you to a long corridor that led you down to the dressing rooms. Inevitably, you met just about everybody every single day. I don't think The Doog was that upset the boss blanked him on a daily basis. He would be working on the premise, the boss didn't say hello to him when he was fit, so he was hardly like to say hello to him when he was unfit.

There were a lot of players who would get an ear-bashing from the manager when he was unhappy, which, unfortunately, appeared to be most of the time he drew breath. They would take it and call him all sorts of names when he was safely out of sight. The Doog, on the other hand, would debate a few points with the manager and he didn't like it one little bit. He really didn't know how to handle my big mate. You have to say, The Doog wasn't bad at a wee verbal joust. He was self-taught and a lot of his knowledge came from the University of Life. I remember he was on the first football panel during the 1970 World Cup Finals in Mexico along with Pat Crerand, of Manchester United and Scotland fame, Manchester City's brash and outspoken manager Malcolm Allison and Arsenal full-back Bob McNab. The ITV show was chaired by Jimmy Hill.

The Doog was brilliant in that company with a lot of interesting comments flying around every night. He was also the chairman of the Professional Footballers' Association at Wolves which meant if a player had a grievance they could take it to him and, if he deemed it worthy of further attention, he would move it upstairs to Union boss Cliff Lloyd. That would be another reason for the boss's silent treatment, although, to be honest, he wouldn't have needed a reason.

The manager controlled what you ate, especially in the close season. That may seem extreme, but most of the clubs these days employ dieticians to look after this side of things, so possibly the boss was innovative for his era. The players, naturally, didn't understand this course of thinking. For instance, when we were in Germany for a game, my fellow-Scot Hughie Curran mimicked a rabbit chewing on a lettuce as we sat down for lunch. You can bet the boss noted his Bugs Bunny impersonation, he didn't miss much. We were not allowed potatoes or chips with lunch. Prawn cocktail was a very popular dish back then - still is, I suppose - but the players were not permitted this so-called culinary delight. For evening meals in hotels, we were given the selection of soup or pate, steak or chicken, fruit salad or ice cream. We weren't exactly spoiled for choice.

And, as you would expect, he also took total control of what the players could drink - or, more accurately, what you couldn't drink. In 1972, we achieved a marvellous 1-1 draw with Juventus in Turin in the first leg of the UEFA Cup quarter-final. Big John Charles, who was a god in the city after his years at the club, as I've stated elsewhere, was an invited guest of Wolves and the manager. After the match, in which I scored our goal, we were all well up for a small celebration when we returned to our hotel and Big John came back with us. Naturally, after such a fabulous result, the players were on a high and fancied a few beers. The boss, once again, put his foot down and told us firmly: 'You can have a glass or two of wine, but absolutely no beer.' As captain, my team-mates asked me to have a word with the boss. Waste of time. There was no way he would change his mind and the players were not happy. They were used to having a lager or two after matchdays at home, but, despite a commendable draw against one of Italy's top teams, they were given no leeway by the boss. No-one should have been surprised.

However, there was a light-hearted moment. As the wine continued to flow, the boss decided he was going to bed and got up to leave the premises. Big John intercepted him and practically growled: 'Sit down and drink like a man.' All the players loved the Welsh legend for telling the boss off. A compromise was reached, but I don't think the boss hung around for too long before making good his escape when Big John was otherwise engaged. But, of course, it was normally our gruff manager who had the last word. On another trip abroad, my mate Hughie Curran went over to the boss and, in all innocence, asked: 'Can we stretch our legs, boss?' McGarry didn't even smile as he answered: 'I know what you want to stretch, so just stay where you are.'

And, speaking of stretching, at the start of training each morning, the boss would order us to do a fast lap without being warmed up properly. It seemed back to front and in normal circumstances you would have some light jogging and then gather momentum as the session went along. The players hated this exercise, including me, and I was a good trainer. Dave Wagstaffe was the worst of the lot of us and moaned every single day when we were told to follow instructions. We did it through gritted teeth, but, strangely, the fast lap training seemed to work. Our complaints meant nothing to the boss and, fair play to him, he wouldn't be fooled by anyone.

The boss wasn't slow, either, to give anyone a blast in front of their team-mates. It could be belittling, but it didn't bother me. As far as I was aware, he had no favourites among his playing staff and we all got treated exactly the same. At least, he was saying it to your face and not behind your back and, as a Gorbals boy, that was important to me. I never spent any time in his - or any other of my managers - office. What was the point? I could take the criticism, especially if it was constructive and not just someone letting off steam. Either way, I accepted it and got on with the job.

One team-mate who didn't think along identical lines was my fellow-Scot Frank Munro, who had played for Dundee United and Aberdeen before he was signed at a fee of £55,000 by Ronnie Allen for Wolves in October 1968, a month before McGarry arrived. He didn't like it one bit when he was on the receiving end of a verbal mauling from the boss. Frank had been a midfielder in Scotland, but had moved into central defence because he was never going to be football's answer to Usain Bolt and, back then, the managers demanded their men in the middle of the park to be fairly mobile. Jim Baxter, who performed with a smile and a stroll, may have been an exception, but Jim Baxters were few and far between. Frank was a fine footballer who was capped nine times by Scotland, but lacked inherent defensive qualities. A rearguard operator such as Bobby Moore could smell danger in the penalty box and never seemed to stray too far from the danger zone where he wasn't asked to cover twenty yards to tackle an opponent. Maybe a rival could time his attacking run before Frank's defensive nous kicked in. So, there were the odd occasions where an opponent might get in front of Frank or behind him and the loss of a goal could be the outcome. When that happened, the boss never missed the opportunity to tear a strip off him. Frank hated it. But, for me, it was part and parcel of being a footballer.

The media were wary of the boss, too, and they must have thought he was softening a little when he invited them to a local hotel one Christmas time. A reporter friend told me the story that they arrived about an hour before the manager. Journalists appear to be a thirsty lot. Or so the story goes. Anyway, the press guys were racking up the bar bill before the boss arrived and everyone continued to have a good old time. Alcohol was coming thick and fast in all sorts of quantities and tastes and the food was going down well, too. They must have thought the manager of Wolves was a very generous mine host, especially as he wasn't indulging himself in the spirit of the season. Near the end of the day, the boss excused himself to pay a visit to what is euphemistically termed 'the little boys' room'. After about fifteen minutes or so, some of the press lads wondered if the manager was okay. After half-an-hour, they were somewhat perturbed. After an hour, they realised he had no intention of coming back to join the happy - and sozzled - throng and the reporters had to dig in to their wallets to pay the rather extravagant and hefty bill. Merry Christmas from Bill McGarry!

As you will have gathered by now, the boss would never have made it as a chat show host and Michael Parkinson and Terry Wogan's jobs were never under threat. However, despite his lack of joining in dressing room banter, he did give us a few laughs. Unintentionally, of course. One day he was criticising winger Steve Kindon and spluttered: 'Who do you think you are? Manley Statthews?' We held in our laughter until we got out of the room.

There was another occasion on our way to training and we were waiting for the boss, as usual. He duly arrived, jumped into the front seat and ordered the driver to get a move on. My team-mates and I exchanged quizzical glances. We all noticed there was something different about our manager - his hair was PINK. Goodness knows what had happened overnight, but his follicles had undergone a dramatic change in their colouring. No-one volunteered to ask about this inexplicable transformation in his barnet. We never did discover what was behind this clearly unintentional fashion statement from a rather staid character. Another one of football's mysteries.

However, I can only stress Bill McGarry knew his football. Well, he paid £70,000 for me, didn't he?

Chapter Thirty

UNITED'S CASANOVA AND A COACH CALLED CAV

MY career at Manchester United didn't even stretch to a full year. I have no doubt one of the main reasons for that was a character by the name of Tommy Cavanagh who did his level best to drive me out of the club. He was a horrible, sneaky individual who had befriended Tommy Docherty during their playing days at Preston North End.

Unfortunately, Tommy Docherty took him to Old Trafford in 1972 and he eventually worked his way into the manager's confidence to become his right-hand man at the expense of club legend Pat Crerand. This would-be bully went out of his way to be antagonistic to everyone. He couldn't help himself, he was just a loudmouth who punctuated every sentence with a blizzard of four-letter words. Listen, I'm hardly a prude and footballers can curse like drunken sailors when they feel the urge.

However, in general conversation we don't pepper sentences with the f-word. That displays a lack of class and also the deficiency in the command of the English language. Needless to say, Cav, as he was called among a few other unprintable monikers, fitted neatly into those categories. He was a Scouser who clung to Tommy Docherty's coat-tails to get noticed in football. He certainly did not possess the qualities to make it under his own steam. I had a quick look at his record at Preston. How many first-team appearances? None. That would emphasise his inability to actually play the game.

His incompetence in the art of engaging his brain before saying anything interesting might be explained in his first foray into club management. When his nondescript days as masquerading as a professional footballer were over, he got a job as team boss at Cheltenham in 1961. It would be fair to say he was not a resounding success as an astute, deep-thinking coach. In fact, he was sacked after four games by a board who could not tolerate his bad language! That might get him a place in the Guinness Book of World Records because he certainly wouldn't achieve that feat with actual ability or football knowledge.

You may be getting the idea I did not quite see eye-to-eye with this individual. You would be dead right. I am not a confrontational character, but I will not be intimidated and that was where Cav went wrong with me. In truth, I had no respect for the guy or his foulmouth. The air was never anything other than blue at the Carrington training complex when this guy was around. That was no big deal. You would just try to switch off the steady stream of diatribe by a pathetic individual trying too hard to be noticed. I do recall Cav being told to try to curb his language by Matt Busby and some members of the board. He did his best, but he seemed incapable of keeping curse words out of his bletherings. There may have been a very slight possibility he may have said something actually worth listening to once, but no-one would have noticed with his words, as usual, buried under the mandatory rubble of nonsensical prattling. He was a monotonously annoying specimen.

He went out of his way to make life difficult for me at United. I didn't take his vindictiveness personally. To be fair, he adopted the scattergun approach to browbeating and just about everyone was on the receiving end. However, he was a tiresome individual who was forever running to Tommy Docherty with tales about players. What a way to go about your life. Sad, really.

I'll give you an example. United had hastily arranged a friendly game in Ireland. I had arrived in March and this was around November. The club, of course, was enormous in that part of the universe. There is a great affection and also a huge support for United in the Emerald Isle. The club also nurtured so many young hopefuls who made the trip across the Irish Sea to make a name for himself at Old Trafford. The midweek match had been speedily put together and the players were told we would be staying only one night and flying home the following morning. I can't recall the circumstances for the match, but it could have been another fund-raiser for a club needing an urgent financial fix. United played quite a few of those sort of games. The encounter itself was of no great consequence. At that stage of the season, you are reasonably matchfit, so the main thing is to make sure you don't pick up an injury.

The game passed by and the United players were given permission by the boss to go for a couple of drinks before returning to the hotel. There was no mention of a curfew, but we were well warned not to overdo it. That wasn't a problem for me because, unlike a fair percentage of my countrymen, I was not a drinker. My team-mates used to laugh at me when we went into a bar. My tipple was a half-pint of lager. 'Come on, Jim, push the boat out, have a pint,' they would say. 'No thanks,' I would reply politely. 'I'll stick to a half-pint.'

On this particular evening, I was out with my team-mates in a bar and a few of the local girls mixed in our company. I got talking to one of the girls and one thing led to another. I was single, so I enjoyed myself as you might expect from a fit and healthy young sportsman. I didn't see it as a big problem to ask the girl back to the team's hotel. As far as I had been aware, there had been no strict regulations covering this area. Of course, I got the drift the club may not have been overly-enthused if there had been a full-blown orgy taking place in the foyer with all their players involved, but there was just me and my accommodating colleen who, thankfully, was likeminded. She was a female out for some fun with no strings attached. Neither of us had any thoughts of catching the first flight out of Dublin for Las Vegas to get hitched or anything like that.

I thought it may be clever not to advertise the fact I had had a sleeping companion when my team-mates and the management got ready for breakfast the following morning before heading for the airport. The girl left around 5am and there was no fuss. Maybe she didn't see me as husband material! I went back to my room to catch up with some sleep. I was sharing with Tony Young at the time and I'm glad to say he was dead to the world. Anyway, my head was on the pillow for a couple of hours before I was rudely awakened by an incessant clattering on the door. I thought the place must be on fire. It seemed quite urgent given the continuous heavy thuds that rained down on the woodwork.

'Let me in!' came the bellow from the excitable voice on the other end of the door. It was the unmistakeable tones of our dear friend Cav. 'Let me in!' he screeched again. Not for the first time, I wondered what was bothering Tommy Docherty's assistant. I opened the door and he sped past me. It was almost comical. Clearly, word had reached his ears that I had been 'entertaining', not sure if that's the right word, but it will have to do for now. The night porter had seen me arrive with my associate for the evening, so I surmised he had seen fit to pass on the information to someone in authority. Goodness knows why.

Cav was searching for my overnight companion. Tony Young was wiping sleep from his eyes, completely baffled about what was unfolding. Cav ran into the bathroom and looked behind the shower curtain. He wasn't going to give up his quest for 'Find The Lady' without a good snoop. He dived to the floor and looked under my bed. Nothing there. I wondered if Benny Hill was going to show up at some point.

Cav looked inside the wardrobes. Nope, nothing there. He was running out of places to explore. He actually opened a bedside cabinet in the hope I had been spending some time with the smallest person on the planet. He stopped short of looking in the cupboard drawers. He was raging. His face was turning a strange shade of crimson. His white hair was standing on end. I could see he was searching his limited vocabulary for something to say. I awaited the usual barrage of four-letter oaths. Cav looked me straight in the eye, took a deep breath, stabbed a forefinger at me, struggled to formulate a sentence and shouted: 'You're a...you're a...you're a fuckin' playboy!'

I had never been called a playboy before. I didn't know whether I should take it as a compliment. I don't suppose my stifled laughter did anything for the United assistant's blood pressure. 'You're in trouble,' he screamed as he left the room. 'I'm in charge. The Doc's taken an early flight home.' He repeated 'I'm in charge' as if to reassure himself. He just about took the door off the hinges as he slammed it behind him while muttering: 'The bus leaves at 10am sharp.'

Okay, hands up, maybe what I did was wrong. It wasn't against strict regulations, as far I was aware. If United had insisted on such a policy back then we might never have heard of a bloke called George Best. I thought that might be the end of it. Cav had given his four-letter words their ten-minute airing and we could all get on with life. Alas, not with Cav around. He thrived on turning everything into a full-blown crisis. On the coach travelling to the airport, I thought I detected that all was not quite right. It was just a gut feeling, but my gut could be uncannily accurate at times.

We reached our destination and, as usual, we were all hanging around waiting for our flight to be called. Cav headed in my direction, his face still a picture. Evidently, he was not one to forgive and forget. Quite the opposite, as I found to my cost. He began needling me. 'What's your problem?' I asked. Cav was aware a couple of my team-mates were listening and he backed off. The players were having a laugh and saying things like: 'Cav's the boss...you're in trouble.'

Of course, Cav was meant to hear their comments and he took the bait. He about-turned and made straight for me. I had found a way to shut out the burble he would come away with and he was banging on about this, that and the next thing. He could have been discussing the price of fish for all I knew or cared. I got a wee bit fed up with his face in mine, so I said: 'You are getting on my wick now. Go and pester someone else.' He looked at me and I'm convinced I saw steam coming out of his ears. 'Just you wait,' he fumed and stormed off. My tranquillity lasted about two minutes. The little nuisance wasn't finished with me. He came back to continue his irksome droning. He was trying to pull his bully boy stunts on me with my team-mates watching. I had had enough. 'Why don't we go outside and sort this out right now?' I offered. He dismissed my suggestion and, under his breath, threatened: 'Just wait till we get back.'

We got back to Manchester and Cav informed us Tommy Docherty wanted to see all the players at Old Trafford. Obviously, Cav had given the manager chapter and verse of what had gone on in Ireland. He probably threw in a few gratuitous expletives, as well. I would say the boss would have had a fair idea about my nocturnal liaison. Presumably, the night porter would have gone to the manager with his snippet of information before he would go to anyone else. Cav would have been called in and he would have relished the opportunity of trying to belittle one of the players.

Tommy Docherty was waiting for us as we filed into the home dressing room. It was like being back at school. The boss looked at us with a grim expression. My gut feeling had proved to be correct once again. 'I was wakened up in the middle of the night by the night porter,' he said. 'I was informed one of my players had a girl in his room. I can tell you I am not happy about this situation.' It looked as though the manager wanted to make an example of his errant player. To this day, I can't see that I did too much wrong. I repeat I was a single guy with no ties and I met a girl in Ireland and we had a one-night stand. I don't know what Cav whispered in the boss's ear. He could have added all sorts of extras. Either way, he did a good job on me.

The boss rambled on for a while before I took the opportunity to step forward and say: 'I am the player you are talking about. Why don't you let the others leave and you can say what you like to me?' It was a reasonable solution and there was little point in bringing the other players into a situation that only concerned me. There was no need for them to be delayed going home, it had already been a long day. The boss agreed and my team-mates filtered out leaving just me, the manager and Cav. I think the boss had been caught on the wrong foot by my admission of being the so-called guilty party. I was fairly certain he knew I was the Casanova culprit. The hotel worker may have identified me. Why was the room I shared with Tony Young the only one that was subjected to the sleuthing skills of the frustrated Sherlock?

In the peace and quiet of the dressing room, the three occupants stared into space. For once, Cav kept his mouth shut. 'Can I go now?' I asked after an interminable couple of minutes. Tommy Docherty nodded and replied: 'Okay, I'll deal with this in the morning.' The following day, I expected to be summoned to the boss's office to discover what fate awaited me for the heinous crime of spending some time with a female a couple of nights earlier. I was surprised to find I would be going straight into a light training session with my team-mates. Nothing was said during the stint and I returned to get showered and changed. I did not think for a moment the boss was going to let it slide. Not with Cav muttering in his ear, that's for sure.

As I prepared to leave, some of the players were looking at the team sheet. I walked over to have a look at that weekend's line-up. There was no sign of the name Jim McCalliog. I was out. And I was furious. I went straight to see the manager. I knocked on his door and he growled for me to come in. I wasn't in the mood for pleasantries, so I cut to the chase: 'You're the boss and I accept what you have done, but you don't have to humiliate me.' Tommy Docherty sat on his chair behind the desk and said nothing. I couldn't stop myself from adding: 'At least, I owned up and, as for Cav, keep him away from me. I have no respect for him.' There wasn't much the boss could add and I left the room. I didn't feel the need to apologise for my actions in Ireland. However, I had no idea how all this would one day rebound on me.

The last time I looked, I wasn't suffering from paranoia. My distrust of Cav was absolute after that episode in Ireland. I know this may seem childish, but I loved making him look stupid in training. Obviously, he had never been gifted too many silky soccer skills, but he joined in when we were going through a routine in six-a-side games. Needless to say, no-one ever wanted Tommy Cavanagh in their line-up.

It was two-touches only, so it was control, pass and move. Cav was never far from my side in these exercises and you could see he was desperate to get the ball off me. On occasion, I would deliberately mis-control the ball and that was the signal for Cav to charge in. As soon as he did that, I slid the ball through his legs. You probably know it is a nutmeg. It happened time and time again. He never cottoned on to what I was doing. It was like a matador and the bull. I felt like shouting 'Ole!' every time he was left looking foolish.

During these training exercises, it was easy to see why he never played a first-team game for Preston.

Chapter Thirty-One

LOVING MY TIME AT MANCHESTER UNITED – FANS AMAZING

I WILL never forget my tenth First Division game for Manchester United. How could I? The Old Trafford club were relegated from the top flight for the first time since 1938.

I was well aware of what I was getting into when I left Wolves for Old Trafford on March 1 1974. I realised I was joining a team low on confidence with players terrified to make mistakes. It's a lethal combination that normally leads to disaster. Tommy Docherty wanted to put me in his midfield to utilise my experience and, hopefully, my ability. I had always been happy on the ball. I could take a few touches as I tried to size things up.

I was confident I had the qualities to sit in the middle of the park and attempt to lead by example. I wanted to show my new team-mates we didn't have to do everything at one hundred miles per hour. We had to take control, get rid of the fear factor, put some passes together, play to the manager's instructions and take it from there. People often talk about players treating the ball like a hot potato. When I arrived at United they were treating it like a live grenade. No-one wanted to dwell on the ball, there weren't too many ready to take responsibility. It was all too clear everyone dreaded making a fatal error.

Of course, there was enormous pressure on everyone at the club. The spectre of losing our place in the First Division was intolerable to just about everyone at Old Trafford - and by that I include the tea ladies, as well. The team were losing far too many games, but there was that feeling that United were too good to go down. Relegation didn't happen to the likes of Manchester United, that was for other teams who usually made up the numbers.

However, the harsh reality was beginning to bite by the time I turned up. The strain was showing and, as they say, the league table does not lie. It proved conclusively the great Manchester United, the team of all stars who won the

European Cup only six years beforehand, were in serious decline. If you had told anyone after United's thrilling 4-1 extra-time win over Benfica, Eusebio et al, at Wembley in 1968 they would be plummeting out of the top league they would have recommended you see a doctor. As George Best, Bobby Charlton, Nobby Stiles, Alex Stepney, Brian Kidd and even manager Matt Busby, before his knighthood, cavorted on England's national pitch that night it would have been utterly absurd to even insinuate the club would be in terminal decline only a few years later.

I was happy to hook up again with Tommy Docherty. He didn't have to work too hard to get me to sign those transfer forms. He didn't sugar coat anything, either. I don't believe he thought for a moment the team would disappear through the trapdoor. Yes, he accepted things could be a helluva lot better, but he was confident the players would get their act together and pull clear. He didn't bother with an enticing sales pitch, but I had always wanted to play for the one-and-only United and, of course, my hero Denis Law had been the idol of the Stretford End for so many years. Unfortunately, I never got the opportunity to play alongside my all-time favourite footballer in that famous red shirt.

The Lawman had left the previous summer. Denis still insists he was 'double-crossed' by Tommy Docherty, but I don't know the ins and outs of that particular scenario and it wouldn't be fair to take sides. What I would say is that Denis and the boss were two exceptionally determined, headstrong and proud Scots. It would be an impossibility to see either of them walking away from an argument. And, of course, Denis was to play an unwilling and unexpected part in the demise of United, in front of the very fans who had entitled him 'The King' from day one of his arrival from Torino. Manchester United and Denis Law were meant for each other, an association made in heaven.

After sitting down with the boss to talk about how he saw my role at the club I was left in absolutely no doubt what was required. I made my debut against Birmingham City at St Andrews on March 16. On the day I signed, Tommy Docherty, being the ebullient character he was, didn't actually want to talk about relegation. He could point to players such as my good friend Willie Morgan, fellow-Scots Lou Macari, Jim Holton and Martin Buchan, English internationals David Sadler and Brian Greenhoff, Northern Ireland's Sammy McIlroy and the Republic of Ireland's Gerry Daly to demonstrate why there was such optimism. Unfortunately, that positive outlook was not being transferred into the required results. I looked around that dressing room and wondered why were these guys not at the other end of the division fighting for the title.

So, naturally, I was looking forward to making my first appearance against Birmingham City and I was one of seven Scots playing for us that afternoon with Alex Forsyth and Stewart Houston, both Scotland internationals, playing at full-back in front of veteran Alex Stepney, who, bizarrely, was also the team's penalty-kick taker. Holton and Buchan were in central defence with Mick Martin, George Graham, Brian Greenhoff and myself playing in the middle of the park with Macari and a young Englishman Paul Bielby up front.

It was noisy with almost 38,000 in the ground with the game as crucial for the Midlands outfit as it was for us with both clubs far too close to the relegation zone for comfort. It wasn't a classic, games played enveloped with stress rarely are showpieces, and it looked as though it was heading for a goalless draw until their big centre-half Joe Gallagher knocked one past Stepney in the 73rd minute. The goal gave us a jolt and we tried to respond immediately, but, as you might anticipate, our opponents retreated deep into defence to hold onto what they had earned. The remaining seventeen minutes seemed to zoom by and we were left with nothing for our efforts. It was United's eleventh loss by one goal at that stage. Those single goal losses were to prove so crucial at the end of the campaign.

A week later, it was an identical story against Spurs at our place. We were stunned when Ralph Coates scored and the points went back to White Hart Lane. That was the only game in which I played alongside Brian Kidd. It was his last outing before he was transferred to Arsenal the following August. I had played against Kidd and I had watched him in action and had always been impressed with his talent, but he didn't show that as a team-mate. He moped around complaining endlessly about all sorts of things. He always seemed to be injured and one day I just cracked up. 'Why don't you stop moaning and get out there and do something about it?' I said. 'There's no point grumping about this, that and the next thing. If you are that concerned you should show it.' I suppose tension was getting to me, as well.

Seven days after the disappointment against one London team, we had joy against another from the capital. It was a happy homecoming for the boss and I as we beat Chelsea 3-1 at Stamford Bridge with strikes from Morgan, Daly and McIlroy. We saw that as being an extremely important two points, as it was back then, and we hoped it may be the catalyst for sprint up the table. We hit three goals in the next game against Burnley at Old Trafford with Forsyth, Holton and McIlroy on target, but, unfortunately, we conceded three at the same time so we had to be content with a point. Would it be good enough? That was the question.

We had seven games left to play to ensure First Division football for Manchester United in the new season. Three were at home against Newcastle United, Everton and Manchester City. Four were away against Norwich City, Southampton, Everton and, on the last day of the campaign, Stoke City. Our next match was at Carrow Road where the home side were in dire straits. We just could not afford to concede anything to fellow-strugglers and goals from Greenhoff and Macari got the job done with a 2-0 victory. We were fairly happy with ourselves on our way home from East Anglia and we were convinced our professionalism would pull us through.

West Ham, Birmingham City and Southampton were also in the dogfight to stay in the elite division. The boss continued to stress we were far too good to be relegated and his confidence - whether it was real or manufactured for our benefit – managed to get through to a player. I scored my first goal for the club against Newcastle United in front of almost 45,000 on April 13 at Old Trafford and fortunately it was the only strike of a tense encounter. Two days later, it got even better as I claimed a double in a 3-0 success over Everton with almost 48,500 watching. Stewart Houston hit the other goal. I was on the mark again when we drew 1-1 against Lawrie McMenemy's side at The Dell. As it transpired, a point apiece was no use to either side that day. I would have happier times at Southampton.

Four goals in three games was fairly satisfying for a midfielder. A centre-forward would be happy with that strike rate. In fact, I had just scored double the total the great George Best had contributed that season. Maybe that tells you why United had got into such trouble. The pressure, though, was unremitting. We had three games to shape our destiny.

And then the unthinkable happened.

Chapter Thirty-Two

MANCHESTER UNITED DOWN – REALITY BITES

THE Manchester United players travelled to Goodison Park on Tuesday, April 23 1974 with only one thought in mind: We had to win at all costs. We had been on the football tightrope without a safety net in sight for some considerable time. Now a blindfold had been applied. One slip would put our First Division lives in jeopardy.

Tommy Docherty attempted to be upbeat as he primed us before kick-off. He was still the same positive character, but I just might have detected a little desperation punctuating his mannerisms. You couldn't really blame him. The eyes of the world were on Manchester United. And for all the wrong reasons.

There were only three games to be played and this was one we could not afford to lose, it was as stark and simple as that. The boss was not gambling on this occasion. He sent out eleven internationals that evening on Merseyside where a crowd of 46,000 waited with bated breath for the action to start. I was in my usual berth in the middle of the park and my fellow-Scots Martin Buchan, Alex Forsyth, Stewart Houston, Jim Holton, Willie Morgan and Lou Macari were also in the line-up. England's Alex Stepney was in goal and his compatriot Brian Greenhoff was also stripped and ready to go. The Republic of Ireland's Gerry Daly and Northern Ireland's Sammy McIlroy were also paired in midfield.

Battle lines were drawn before kick-off when the Everton manager, Billy Bingham, told the local press: 'We wouldn't like to see Manchester United go down, but they can expect no favours from us. It is far more important for them than it is for us and it will be a titanic battle, but we are out to improve our points total. We aim to get as many as we possibly can.'

So, we knew what to expect from the opposition. In any case, we did not want anyone doing us any favours. We were determined to remain in the top flight by our own efforts and we didn't expect anyone to do us a turn. It was a fairly even first-half, with a lot of effort and endeavour from both sets of players. It was goalless as we trooped off the pitch when the tannoy system at Goodison crackled to life. I'll never forget the bulletin. We were informed of the half-time scoreline concerning one of our main rivals in the fight against relegation. **BIRMINGHAM CITY 2 QUEENS PARK RANGERS 0**, bellowed the announcer.

It was not the news we wanted to hear. The boss went ballistic in the dressing room. I had never seen him so angry at half-time, even when we had been losing. That break was normally very productive when our manager giving us a gee up and pointing out little things that could help our game. He was just settling down when the announcer blared out the scoreline once more. He almost hit the roof. The boss was doing his best to motivate his players and bad news was bouncing around the stadium. It certainly wasn't designed to help our morale and it didn't matter afterwards when we were told this is normal practice at the ground for half-time scores to be read out for the home fans.

Once the boss collected his thoughts, he emphasised the requirement for us to keep our concentration. We had to push what we had heard out of our thoughts. 'It's what we do that matters,' he said. 'Keep moving the ball around, look for that opening and when it comes, make sure you take it. We'll get that chance and that will turn the game.'

Five minutes into the second period, we were a goal down. Our defence didn't deal with a free-kick, the ball broke to their centre-half Mick Lyons and he fired the ball beyond the helpless Stepney. That simple goal dealt a fatal blow to us. Watching the net ripple behind our keeper was like getting punched in the stomach. But we didn't have time to feel sorry for ourselves. We had forty minutes to do something about the scoreline, but it wasn't our night. No matter what we tried, there was an Everton limb materialising at the last moment to deflect a shot or a pass. Efforts on goal were flying high or wide or being mopped up by opposing keeper, David Lawson. And then the final whistle went and we had failed by a solitary goal. Yet again.

As we came off the pitch we had to hope QPR had staged a dramatic, if unlikely, revival against Birmingham at St Andrews. Was it impossible for the Loftus Road outfit to come back and possibly take a point or, even better, two off the Midlands club? No such luck. We were informed the home side had won 4-0. We all felt sick. We did our calculations. It was clear we needed to beat Manchester City at Old Trafford on the forthcoming Saturday and Stoke City in our final game two nights later. At the same time, we needed Birmingham City to somehow drop points in their home match against Norwich City who had already been relegated. Even the world's greatest optimist would have agreed it looked ominous for us in our quest for survival. It looked as though we were trying to swim to safety with a boulder attached to each ankle.

To be fair, the St Andrews club had responded a lot better than United as the spectre of relegation hovered. They lost only one of their final nine games, winning four and drawing four. Their form, with Trevor Francis, Kenny Burns and Howard Kendall playing very well at the time, helped heap the pressure on United. It was up to us to do something about it and the best place was out on the pitch. But, once again, we had stumbled. We may have been on the floor, but the referee hadn't quite counted to ten and signalled the fight was over. However, the game against our city neighbours and my idol Denis Law was beginning to look like the condemned men being taken out to face the firing squad.

The boss fielded the same team that had lost to Everton. He told us to forget all the permutations that were flying around. We were in twenty-first position - one from rock-bottom - on thirty-two points, three adrift of Birmingham City who were sitting above the drop zone in nineteenth. We had a game in hand over the St Andrews club and needed at least a draw against the Maine Road side and pray for a Birmingham City loss against doomed Norwich City. We had to hope as we took the field that eventful afternoon.

A lot was being made of Denis Law, at the age of thirty-four, almost certainly playing his last game at Old Trafford in opposition to the supporters who had feted him since his arrival in 1962. No wonder they christened him 'The King'. A total of 236 goals in eleven years and one third of the wonderful United trio of Charlton, Best and Law, three players who would have been welcomed by any club in the world. Tommy Docherty ordered us to ignore all the nostalgia that was swirling around the ninetieth derby between two famous old foes. I hadn't been signed in time for the first derby which had ended goalless. It had been a feisty confrontation. Just before the interval, Lou Macari and their defender Mike Doyle had squared up to each other and referee Clive Thomas was quick to banish the pair. Both Lou and Mike protested their innocence and refused to leave the field.

The match official, universally known as Clive 'The Book' Thomas for his enthusiasm in producing his pencil and little black notebook with the speed of an old Wild West gunslinger, reacted in his usual dictatorial fashion. With over 50,000 fans watching on, he led the teams off the pitch. This authoritarian figure marched the players towards the dressing rooms and no-one had a clue what was going on. About ten minutes later, the teams reappeared, without messrs Macari and Doyle. Battle then recommenced.

David Smith was the nominated official for the second occasion and if Thomas reckoned he had it difficult at Maine Road in the previous meeting, then it was nothing to what Smith was about to experience at Old Trafford on the windy, dry afternoon of April 27 with a crowd of 56,996 in attendance. I do recall it was not an encounter for the football purist as both sets of players went at it in helter skelter fashion. The best chance of the first-half came early and it fell to me.

Willie Morgan flighted over a right-wing corner-kick into the congested penalty area. Big Joe Corrigan, the City keeper, left his line in an attempt to cut out the cross, but that was always easier said than done with Jim Holton around. Our central defender's strength was his aerial power and he attacked the ball. It was half-cleared by Corrigan at full stretch and the ball fell to Sammy McIlroy who cleverly returned it first time to me, standing unmarked around the penalty spot. I flighted in a looping header that had the goalie scrambling, but just when the ball looked like dropping into the net, their left-back Willie Donachie appeared on the line to head it to safety.

A goal at that point would have been more than welcome. It remained goalless going into the second period, but once more United were denied by a goal-line clearance when Colin Barrett hooked away an effort from Gerry Daly that had eluded Corrigan. Do you ever get the feeling Dame Fortune is snarling at you? We continued to press, but we had a let-off when Dennis Tueart let fly from outside the box and his effort sizzled over Alex Stepney's grasping fingers before thudding against the crossbar. Maybe it was going to be our day after all?

With eight minutes to go we conceded the only goal of the game that condemned us to football outwith the First Division for the first time in thirty-six years. It had to be Denis, hadn't it? A writer of far-fetched fiction would have been laughed out of town if he had come up with that scenario. Denis Law? King of the Stretford End? It's true, though, isn't it? Fact is often stranger than fiction.

The clock was ticking down and we did not know what was happening in the Midlands with Birmingham City and relegated Norwich City. Ignorance is bliss - on this occasion, anyway. The game ebbed and flowed without any great strategy or pattern. And then disaster struck. Frannie Lee drifted across our box and mishit a shot at goal. Alex Stepney had already started to move to his right to take care of the danger when Denis Law materialised about six yards from goal to back-heel the ball in the opposite direction. It was an instinctive reaction from the Lawman, displaying those lightning reflexes that had been witnessed so many times at this venue. Normally, Old Trafford would cheer to the rafters at such ingenuity from their favourite, but on this occasion there was a stunned silence. Stepney, with his weight going to the right, could only stand flat-footed as the ball rolled over the line.

I have never seen a goalscorer look so crestfallen in all my life. I doubt if I ever will. Denis did not celebrate at all as his team-mates congratulated him. He stood rigid to the spot for a moment before cantering back up the pitch for the re-centre. Before the game could restart, though, there was a pitch invasion by unruly fans whose aim must have been to get the game postponed with the possibility of it being played again. It was a waste of time. In the midst of the supporters racing around aimlessly, Denis, clearly, had no appetite to play on. He looked ashen-faced. Tony Book, the City manager, took the opportunity during the enforced hold-up to take off Denis and put on his substitute, a youngster by the name of Phil Henson.

Denis looked devastated as he walked down that tunnel, a journey he had taken so many times with thousands of fans cheering his name. He made his way past concerned police officials, stewards and others milling around in the congested area. He disappeared out of sight and the match restarted. It was brought to a halt again with a mini invasion and kicked off for a third time. Matt Busby, such a revered figure at the club, had made an appeal to the intruding supporters. 'For the good name of Manchester United, please leave the pitch,' he implored. Alas, it was to no avail. The fans were not in the mood for reason. The match did get going again and there were actually forty-five minutes on the clock when there was yet another field invasion. There was at least five minutes stoppage time to be played, but on this occasion, with the chief of police in attendance and his officers forming a dark blue line, referee Smith blew his whistle for the final time that day. There was no way the English football bosses would order another game.

I didn't hang around. I was the first United player to get through the throng and make my way to the dressing room. I pushed open the door and I couldn't believe my eyes. Sitting in the corner was Denis Law, still wearing his City strip. His head was in his hands and he looked disconsolate. He looked up at me and was in an emotional state. He didn't say anything, he didn't have to. He had just scored a goal and his beloved United had lost their First Division status. It was all too much to comprehend. He was utterly distraught.

The boss came in with the rest of the players and I wondered what would happen next. Here, in the United dressing room, was the player who had been given a free transfer by the boss the previous year and who had just knocked in the winning goal in such a monumentally important game in the history of the club. Our manager could be a fiery character and he had still to go out and face the TV interviewers shortly afterwards and admit to being 'ashamed and embarrassed' at what had just occurred. How would he react to Denis sitting in the losers' dressing room?

The manager came over and put out his hand. Denis looked at him and took it. The two men shook without a word being spoken. Denis was a City player, they paid his wages and he did what he was asked to do when he wore the light blue colours of the club. The boss would have admired his professionalism. And you better believe he would have done the exact same thing if he had been in The Lawman's boots.

In 2010, Denis was asked how long he had remained miserable after that goal. He replied: 'I was inconsolable. I didn't want it to happen. How long did the feeling last? How long ago was the game? Thirty odd years. There is your answer.'

Let's put the record straight, Denis Law did NOT score the goal that put United down. On the same day we lost to the Maine Road club, Birmingham City beat Norwich City 2-1 in the Midlands. They had been leading at half-time on that day, too. They completed the campaign on thirty-seven points, the same total as West Ham who had also struggled. Southampton joined United in the second tier, finishing on thirty-six points.

So, it's simple arithmetic that tells you United wouldn't have survived even if the game against City had finished goalless. A draw would have put us on thirty-three points and the best we could have achieved was thirty-five with a win over Stoke City in our match. As it happened, we lost 1-0 in that match to complete a miserable season.

Denis Law was not to blame for the demise of Manchester United. I think the culpability for that failure lay a little nearer home.

Chapter Thirty-Three

'WILL THE REAL TOMMY DOCHERTY PLEASE STAND UP?'

TOMMY DOCHERTY was a chameleon. Sometimes I felt like asking: 'Will the real Tommy Docherty please stand up?' He actually thought it was okay to look you straight in the eye and tell you a bare-faced lie. He wasn't even trying to be 'economical with the truth,' as some may say. He believed it was perfectly acceptable behaviour for a football manager to tell whoppers, he saw it as mandatory in his position.

By the way, this is not to denigrate the boss. Okay, it's not much of a compliment to be labelled a liar, but I honestly believe he didn't think he was doing anything wrong if he told an untruth. 'All managers are the same,' he told me. 'We have to say what is best at the time to get things done.' It's a strange philosophy and I have to say it is not one I ever adopted. My parents brought me up with the belief of 'the truth hurts, but the lies will kill you'.

So, as the great Manchester United prepared for life in the Second Division in season 1974/75 after conquering Europe in 1968, I wondered what lay in store. I had agreed a three-year contract when I had arrived from Wolves in March and I had hoped to see it through. Performing in the second tier was not ideal for a 28-year-old professional who still harboured hopes of rekindling my Scotland international career, but I was well prepared to give it my best shot and do my utmost to get the team back where they belonged after a one-year 'interlude'.

However, I didn't require the wisdom of Solomon to realise I would never be allowed to overstay my welcome at Old Trafford. I also had a fair idea Tommy Docherty's ear would have been well and truly bent out of shape by the scheming, deceitful Tommy Cavanagh. I made up my mind to push all the speculation and uncertainty into the background as I concentrated on the job at hand.

But I could not help but look at the situation concerning George Graham at the club. He played twenty-four games in the fateful relegation campaign, but must have done something to annoy the boss because he never figured in the first team squad during my first few months at the club. He was even stripped of the captaincy which was handed to my friend Willie Morgan. George, of course, knew the boss from their days at Chelsea and, in fact, the man nicknamed 'Stroller' had been the manager's first signing for United in December 1972 when he arrived in a £120,000 deal from Arsenal. The boss had also capped him during his stay as Scotland's international gaffer.

You may have thought there was some rapport going on between the manager and the player. Alas, you would be wrong. It was clear to everyone that George, an elegant, thoughtful midfielder who could pass the ball, was brilliant in the air and could score a goal or two, was bombed out. Why was George frozen out? Although I had known him during our time together at Stamford Bridge, I never asked him about his situation. It was none of my business, but possibly he could have done a job in the first team when we were really struggling. It just seemed such a waste of obvious talent. I don't think an explanation was ever given for his sudden fall from grace at United. George played one game in the second tier before being offloaded to Portsmouth in November 1974. Maybe Cav had got to work with some of his over-zealous character assassination. We'll probably never know.

Brian Kidd was involved in a similar situation. He was a top striker and these guys are gold dust in football, irrespective if you are up at the top fighting for trophies or at the bottom striving for safety. I played alongside him just once in my First Division games for the club. To be fair to the boss, Kiddo did carry a few injuries. Like Graham, he must have wondered what was going on, though, when he was fit and good to go. He had won a European Cup medal as a teenager, but he was far from being a diva. His feet were firmly planted on earth and he wanted to play his part for the club, but he didn't get the opportunity. Kiddo was out the door when he was sold to Arsenal for £110,000. He finished his first season at the London club as their top scorer with nineteen goals from forty appearances. How United could have done with a few of those goals the previous year. For the record, Kiddo and I were the only United players to score two goals in one game throughout my time there.

To me, George Graham and Brian Kidd were two big players who were treated shabbily. They could have been held up as examples for the younger players at the club. They had both been winners, Graham notably did the double during his days at the Highbury club. Instead, the players were basically shunned and it just underlined how ruthless our manager could be when he decided he thought you had served your purpose. I thought the boss called it wrong in both cases. It's interesting to note that their experiences with the boss didn't put off either of the individuals from taking up management or coaching and both were great successes at this level.

The boss ruled with an iron fist. It was his way or the highway. I recall an evening when I was with Stuart Pearson, better known as 'Pancho', in a nightclub called 'Slack Alice', part-owned by George Best. It was in midweek and we were both injured. Nothing too serious, as I recall, but enough to make sure we were not fit enough for ninety minutes of rigorous football at the weekend. As I have said, I was never a drinker. I never touched alcohol until I was twenty-three and I was content to have a few half-pints of lager to see me through a convivial evening. Pancho and I decided to have a night out in the city and we were minding our own business when Pat Crerand, a favourite player of mine during his days at Celtic, came over to us. Pat was Tommy Docherty's assistant manager at the time and he thought it might be a good idea if we made ourselves scarce.

'There's a white Mercedes drawing up outside, lads,' he said. He didn't have to elaborate, we got the drift. The boss drove a white Mercedes and it was obvious he would be arriving for a couple of drinks. It was clear from Pat that he would not be overly delighted to see two of his players in the vicinity. I can only stress we were not doing anything untoward, we were simply minding our own business in Bestie's place and whiling away some time, simply two team-mates having a night out. But that may have triggered something in the manager and Pat, a Gorbals boy like myself, was tipping us the wink it may be better if we were elsewhere. We both got out of there pronto like two naughty schoolboys before the headmaster caught us copying each other's homework. We got down the stairs just as Tommy Docherty was getting out of his car.

Speaking of Pat, I wish I had been given more time to work with him at Old Trafford and get to know the bloke. As a kid growing up in Glasgow, Pat Crerand was a player I would walk from Caledonia Road in the Gorbals to Celtic Park in the east end of the city to watch in action. He was such a cultured player and United bought him for over £50,000 in 1963. That was a helluva lot of money at the time. He quit playing in 1971 after becoming a legend at the club and playing his part in United winning the European Cup in 1968. He became a coach at United and then moved up to assistant boss when Tommy Docherty came in. However, there were warning signs soon afterwards when the boss added Tommy Cavanagh and Frank Blunstone to his coaching team. Their arrival pushed Pat to the side and it was no surprise when he left in 1976 to spend a year at

Northampton Town. I don't think for a heartbeat that was how a proud Scot saw his career panning out.

With the boss around, strange things could happen. Even before we kicked a ball outside the top flight, the players were rewarded with a week's break in Mallorca. One of the days we went to United chairman Louis Edwards' massive villa in Formentor. What can I say? Sir Matt Busby treated the players to a few serenades. He was a real gentleman who had a calmness about his persona. God knows what he thought about his beloved United being relegated. Spending some time with Sir Matt was precious to us all and you could see quite clearly why he commanded so much respect among the players. You could listen to his tales all day. Not sure about his singing, though!

I had always wanted to ask him about what happened in 1967 when I knew he was interested in buying me for United. I was aware of some genuine intent after my winning goal against England at Wembley. And then it all went quiet. I also realised Sir Matt did not get along with Allan Brown, who was the Sheffield Wednesday manager at the time. Naturally, I was intrigued to the reason the move never materialised. I had hoped Sir Matt might reveal all, but I never did discuss the situation with him. He was no longer the Manchester United manager and out of great respect for the man I let it go. However, I can still only wonder what might have happened in my career if I had joined the Old Trafford club seven years earlier than I did.

The reality, though, was that I was now a Second Division player. And I had to rectify that situation as swiftly as possible.

Chapter Thirty-Four

STIRRING TIMES AT OLD TRAFFORD

MY last win and my final goal for Manchester United both arrived on the same afternoon on January 11 1975. Ironically, I scored two that day in a 2-0 success over Sheffield Wednesday, the club where I had enjoyed the bulk of four happy years after leaving Tommy Docherty first time around when I quit Chelsea in October 1965. After the game, the boss introduced me to the Scotland manager, Willie Ormond. He was drunk. Obviously, my two goals hadn't registered with him. Somehow I believe the hospitality at the club hadn't aided my chances of an international recall.

Things were going well for the club in the Second Division, winning ten and drawing four of our first seventeen games, losing three to Norwich City, Bristol City and Hull City, all away from home. The fans certainly rallied to the cause, one look at our attendance figures at Old Trafford emphasised that point. United averaged crowds of 47,781 which, remarkably, was around 2,000 higher than any team in the top flight. In fact, it was 13,000 more than all but three of the clubs in the league above us.

Derby County were the First Division champions with an average gate at the Baseball Ground of 26,719. Their highest crowd was 38,000 on the last day of the season against Carlisle on April 26 1975. United's best attendance was 60,585 for a 3-2 victory over Sunderland on November 30. I have always insisted supporters are the lifeblood of football and the way the United fans rallied round when the team most needed them was both extraordinary and exemplary.

I recall a league game against Notts County at our place on October 12 when all the players were on a high after dismissing Manchester City 1-0 from the League Cup the previous midweek. Gerry Daly had taken over the penalty-kick duties and he was on target from the spot twelve minutes from the end of a pulsating confrontation. So, the United half of the city was still buzzing by the time Saturday rolled around and we had 46,565 fans in the ground. And they had every intention of letting us know they were there. Tommy Docherty couldn't pass up the opportunity of putting those vocal chords to a good use.

The boss held the players back in the dressing room right until the last minute and then released us. We raced onto the pitch and the place erupted. The County players actually looked a wee bit scared. With that din going on, it would have been impossible for opposition players not to feel a little apprehensive. Sammy McIlory gave us the advantage in the seventeenth minute and the supporters must have hoped for a procession. Sadly, that was the only strike of the afternoon. County shut up shop, they were clearly unwilling to risk being on the receiving end of a humiliating scoreline. We had to settle for the win and the two points.

Our lone marksman that day, Sammy Mac, was an impressive performer. He had broken into the first team as an eighteen-year-old at the same time as Law, Charlton and Best were playing. Right away, you could see the Northern Irishman had a marvellous future in the game. He possessed great ball control and had the confidence to enjoy nutmegging the opposition players, something I quite enjoyed myself. Sammy Mac flourished in that division and just got stronger and better with the more appearances he piled up in the top side. His big pal was Brian Greenhoff, a very positive and dedicated young lad. He could operate in midfield and central defence and, like Sammy Mac, you were not taking a huge risk to predict a wonderful future lay ahead of him.

To my mate Willie Morgan fell the honour of scoring United's first goal in the Second Division when he rifled in a pass from Greenhoff just before the half-hour mark. It came on the Saturday afternoon of August 17 against Leyton Orient at Brisbane Road where about 10,000 of our supporters had crammed into the tight little arena with the crowd recorded as 17,772. There were newspaper reports of some United fans sleeping overnight outside the ground to make sure they could gain admittance the following day. And to think some sceptics doubted if those followers would remain loyal to the club. Just to make their trip south was worth their while, Stewart Houston added a second midway through the second-half for a 2-0 win. There were a few cynics who would have been delighted to see us fall flat on our faces at the first hurdle, but we were delighted not to oblige.

However, as we all know, it is dangerous to take anything for granted in this game and we had to be content with two draws in the following league matches against Nottingham Forest, 2-2 at Old Trafford, where good chums Greenhoff and Sammy Mac shared the goals, and 1-1 against West Brom at The Hawthorns where Stuart 'Pancho' Pearson got his first goal for the club since his £200,000 arrival from Hull City in May. In between those encounters, we eased to a 5-1 triumph over Charlton in the League Cup opener at our place. We were three goals ahead inside fifteen minutes, so there was no sign of a shock result. Lou Macari fired in a double that evening. Wee Lou possessed a lot of great qualities. He was two-footed and it was difficult to guess which one was the stronger. I still don't know!

He put them to good use, as well. He could strike a fine goal and the boss was obviously a huge admirer of the former Celtic player. He took him with the Scotland international squad to a tournament known as the Independence Cup which was held in Brazil in the summer of 1972. Lou scored two goals in the opening game against Yugoslavia which ended 2-2. The Scots were leading with three minutes to go when Martin Buchan unfortunately deflected an effort into his own net. Lou played in the next game, a goalless draw with Czechoslovakia. That game was played in Porto Alegre on July 2 and over half of the team's outfield players that evening would be reunited with Tommy Docherty at Old Trafford five months later after he quit the international post; Buchan, Alex Forsyth, Willie Morgan, George Graham, Denis Law and, of course, Wee Lou.

I liked Lou. He enjoyed a good laugh and he was a willing team-mate, supremely fit, could run all day, had a good footballing brain and, despite not scaling the heights, remarkably proficient in the air.

Thankfully, after our two draws, we picked up the pace again and collected three back-to-back wins over Millwall (1-0), Bristol Rovers (2-0) and Bolton (3-0). A double whammy awaited us as we travelled to Carrow Road to take on Norwich City on the Saturday afternoon of September 28. We lost our unbeaten tag and we failed to score a goal for the first time. Ted MacDougall, a Scotland international who had been brought to United by Frank O'Farrell for something like £250,000 from Bournemouth, hadn't impressed Tommy Docherty and was rather quickly shown the Old Trafford exit door. It was a shade ironic that the snubbed Scot should get the opening goal from the penalty spot that day. Just for good measure, he got the second in his team's 2-0 victory.

The boss was asked about MacDougall's display and, never one to shirk a controversial reply, answered: 'I still think he can't play.' Norwich City boss John Bond, an individual who enjoyed a headline or two, immediately fired back: 'I am willing to bet right here and now that Ted will score twice as many goals this season than Macari.' I don't know if Tommy Docherty took the wager, but for the record, MacDougall netted seventeen goals, including six penalty-kicks for the Carrow Road outfit, while Wee Lou clocked up twelve without the assistance of a spot-kick.

I believed United now faced the acid test. Up until that defeat, we had been receiving glowing media coverage. Very swiftly into the new season, according to the national scribes, it had become a case of when Tommy Docherty and his entertaining team were back in the First Division and not 'if'. From a personal point of view, I was more than interested to see how we reacted and what we were made of after we had taken a knock. 'Pancho' Pearson provided the answer with a double salvo in a 2-1 win over Fulham at Craven Cottage. I had struck up a friendship with a very likeable personality and it was great to see him getting back on the scoresheet after four consecutive blanks. That sequence may not be seen as a crisis, but Pancho only felt really happy after he had put the ball in the opposition's net.

Next up was our League Cup third round tie against Manchester City at Old Trafford on October 9 in front of an attendance of 55,159. For a lot of the home support the memory of City's last visit six months earlier was still raw. They say revenge is a dish best served cold, so it was worth the wait to get that result. It was another fairly nervy derby confrontation and I recall the goalkeepers, our Alex Stepney and their Keith MacRae, a tall Scotsman bought from Motherwell a couple of years earlier, were more than playing their part in keeping the scoreline blank. Something had to give and it went in our favour when we were awarded a late penalty-kick. Garry Daly left MacRae without a chance. I couldn't have done better myself!

We enjoyed the kudos of not only beating our city neighbours but also overcoming high-quality top-flight opposition. We were aware of people saying 'United were a First Division team playing in the Second Division', but that cut no ice with the boss or anyone else at the club. There was a helluva long way to travel before we could accept that accolade. We duly beat Notts County in the next outing through Sammy Mac's early strike to continue on the crucial points-gathering crusade. Frustratingly, we were held to a goalless draw with Portsmouth at Fratton Park three days later.

Up to this stage, I thought I had been playing well, but I was more than acutely aware I had yet to score a goal. I prided myself on being a midfielder who could bag a few during the season, but it wasn't happening for me and I had to rectify that as swiftly as possible. We travelled to Blackpool on a brisk Saturday afternoon on October 19 to play at their famous old Bloomfield Road which to this day still only holds a capacity 17,338. United must have taken about 10,000 fans to the seaside resort that day and the place was packed. It made for a great atmosphere and it turned out to be a wonderful day. Alex Forsyth got the opener halfway through the first-half and Lou Macari doubled our advantage following a pass from myself on the hour mark. I was desperate to get involved and, thankfully, I got off the mark in the seventy-second minute with the final goal in our 3-0 win.

The Press acclaimed our display. I recall a headline in 'The Sun' proclaiming: **'McCALLIOG OUTSHINES THE LIGHTS'**. Their reporter, a chap by the name of Ian Gibb, obviously a very astute observer, wrote: 'United, led in midfield by a glorious performance from Jim McCalliog, were irresistible.' Beaten Blackpool manager Harry Potts very sportingly added: 'United are the best team we have met this season.' And, just to underline a good day was had by all, World Cup referee Jack Taylor chimed in with: 'That was one of the most pleasant afternoons I have ever spent refereeing.' Praise from a match official? Thanks, Jack, we did our best.

Everyone likes a pat on the back if you think you deserve it and Ronald Crowther, writing in the Daily Mail, stated: 'It was in the midfield zone that Jim McCalliog, with a scintillating service of slide-rule passes, showed that United's four-year quest for another Pat Crerand has ended at last in success. McCalliog's goal when he floated the ball over the head of keeper George Wood was as skilful a contribution as his cross that led to the one which Lou Macari richly deserved.' The headline in the Sunday Mirror read: **'MAC MAGIC'**. The sub-deck told us: 'Jim steers The Reds to a four-point lead'. The scribe wrote: 'Not only did Jim McCalliog call the tune, he sang it, too, with a brilliant 72nd-minute goal.' These Fleet Street hacks certainly knew their football, that's all I can say. To that little round of applause you can add an appreciative Tommy Docherty. He was quoted in the newspapers as saying: 'I don't like singling out exceptions, but McCalliog was just that in this game - exceptional.'

I was walking on air, but football has the horrible habit of dumping you when you least expect it. After my Blackpool success, I went nine games without a goal and when I brought the drought to a welcome end with my double against Sheffield Wednesday, I had only four more outings in that famous red shirt of Manchester United. Everything looked so good when we brought October to a conclusion with a 1-0 home success over Southampton where Pancho Pearson got the only goal near the end. We opened November with a 4-0 romp over Oxford United, once again played at Old Trafford. Pancho was on fire and walloped in a first-half hat-trick. Lou Macari added the other goal.

However, the juggernaut was derailed at Ashton Gate the following week when we lost 1-0 to Bristol City. They were a good workmanlike side and they scored around the half-hour mark. No-one was panicking in the United dressing room at the break, but, try as we might, we just could not get a goal that day. We could probably have played until midnight and not scored. You get games like that. Once again, though, the trick was to get up off the canvas and land a few knock-out punches of our own.

Our character was put to the test in the midweek League Cup confrontation against Burnley at Old Trafford. The lads from Turf Moor were one of those sides that could make life difficult for anyone when they decided to turn up. They decided to grace us with their presence that evening. We were a goal adrift in the twentieth minute when Peter Noble scored, but Lou Macari responded within ten minutes. Before we had the opportunity to settle, we were a goal down again when their big striker Ray Hankin beat Alex Stepney. It remained that way until half-time. The Doc remained calm as he got across a few points. He made an inspired substitution when he put on Willie Morgan for Brian Greenhoff. The youngster hadn't done much wrong, but the manager changed the shape a little to make us more direct. He got his reward four minutes after the turnaround when my pal Willie equalised with one of his first touches of the ball. Willie always had a good sense of timing. Wee Lou popped up with the winner with only three minutes remaining. His timing wasn't bad, either!

Cup wins were all well and good, but, naturally, our main objective was promotion and it was back to points-gathering when we played Aston Villa on November 16 and once again we had to make life difficult for ourselves before gaining a hard-fought victory. The Midlands club took an early lead and we weren't helped when Pancho Pearson limped off early and the boss had to shake up the formation a little after using his only substitute, Brian Greenhoff, which was hardly a like-for-like replacement. It was turning out to be a very frustrating day against the team I had knocked back to come to United. Once more, we refused to roll over and two goals from Gerry Daly, one from the penalty spot, in the last twenty minutes gave us a 2-1 win. It had been too close for comfort. As I am sure the 55,615 onlookers would have agreed.

A week later we were at Boothferry Park to face Hull City and we lost 2-0. No-one saw that one coming. Their manager Terry Neill, who had been Tommy Docherty's boss at the club in 1971, had quit after ten games following fierce criticism with the team in disarray. They had already lost by four, five and six goals by the time we turned up. We were still without the injured Pancho, but, in truth, we should have had enough firepower to have the job done by half-time. Instead, goals from Malcolm Lord and Ken Wagstaffe sent us home pointless and fairly dispirited.

We opened December with a visit to my old haunt of Hillsborough to face relegation-threatened Sheffield Wednesday who had won only four games and had a mere fourteen points from twenty matches. On this occasion we found our shooting boots and hammered in four goals. Lou Macari claimed a double and Pancho Pearson celebrated his return with a typical effort. The only problem that day was that the home side responded by thumping four past Alex Stepney. We opened the scoring through a Stewart Houston free-kick, but they actually led 3-1 at the interval. We brought it back to 3-3 with Macari and Pancho on target before a lively lad by the name of Dave Sunley headed their fourth past Stepney. With five minutes remaining, Wee Lou smashed a low drive past Peter Springett, brother of my old mate Ron, and we had earned a point.

It was a dreadful day in Sheffield and the news got worse when we were informed that our giant and uncompromising centre-half Jim Holton, who had been taken off in the fifteenth minute, had suffered a broken leg. Sadly, he never played again that season and snapped the same leg when he was attempting to come back in a reserve game. His United career came to an end that December 7 afternoon in Yorkshire. In the summer, he had been playing for Scotland in the World Cup Finals in West Germany against Brazil, Zaire and Yugoslavia and was the nation's established No.5. The big chap eventually moved to Sunderland and Coventry City and had stints in the States with Miami Toros and Detroit Express. He chucked the game in 1981 and went into retirement at the age of twenty-nine.

We were back on League Cup duty eleven days later and, thankfully, there was no drama against Middlesbrough when we beat them 3-0 at our place with goals from Pancho Pearson, Sammy Mac and Wee Lou. I sat out an FA Cup meeting with Third Division Walsall at Old Trafford on January 4 1975 which ended goalless. I got the nod for the replay at Fellows Park in midweek. Some critics had made the reasonable point that the last thing United needed was cluttering up their fixture list with domestic Cup-ties when the main aim had to be getting out of the Second Division. Those same observers didn't have to worry about us having a run to Wembley as we lost 3-2 in extra-time in the second game.

On their tight playing surface, our opponents were right up for it and took the lead before Gerry Daly equalised with a penalty-kick just before half-time. That's the way it stood after the regulation ninety minutes and we were forced into another thirty minutes on a pitch that had cut fairly badly. Alan Buckley put the home side ahead again only for Sammy Mac to level once more in the 114th minute. It looked as though the tie would go to a second replay until Walsall were awarded a spot-kick in the fading moments and Buckley gleefully rammed the winner behind Alex Stepney.

We knew we had let down our supporters with the FA Cup exit, so we had to concentrate fully on the task at hand when we played Sheffield Wednesday in my landmark outing at Old Trafford on January 11 1975. Gerry Daly, of course, had been taking the penalty-kicks all season, but the Irish midfielder was on the substitutes' bench on this occasion when we were awarded one in the twenty-second minute. I was happy to accept responsibility and slide it beyond keeper Peter Fox. My final goal for United was a bit more memorable. It arrived five minutes after the turnaround and I was set up by Wee Lou. His ball forward was precision and I caught it with my right foot just inside the eighteen-yard box to flash another effort wide of Fox.

When the smoke of battle cleared that afternoon, United were sitting top of the division with thirty-nine points from twenty-six games, six ahead of nearest challengers Sunderland who had lost 4-2 against Portsmouth at Fratton Park. I was happy enough with my two goals and the team stretching their advantage at the top. I had no way of knowing I would never celebrate another United victory and I would be heading through the Old Trafford exit four games later. The boss was stirring things up at the club and had taken the captaincy off Willie Morgan and handed it to Martin Buchan. There had been some friction between my mate and the manager around that time, so no-one asked for an explanation.

Four days after my double against the Hillsborough side, it was back to League Cup duty where we were due to meet Norwich City in the first leg of the semi-final at Old Trafford. A truly astounding crowd of 58,010 turned up to see if they could roar their favourites towards a glamour showpiece occasion at Wembley. Achingly, we were two minutes away from a 2-1 victory when the Carrow Road levelled through Ted MacDougall. Could you believe it? For the second time that season the player who had been shown the door by Tommy Docherty had come back to haunt him.

It was a real struggle on a rain-lashed evening against the visitors who had set up their team to hit on the break. They did that very well and took the lead through Tony Powell. Lou Macari wiped that out six minutes after the interval and my wee Scottish pal was on target again in the seventy-first minute and that looked like being the winner. However, MacDougall still had something to prove against our manager and he snapped on to a passback from Brian Greenhoff that held up in the treacherous conditions, swept round the outrushing Alex Stepney and rolled the ball into the net. I will never forget the hush that descended on Old Trafford at that precise moment.

We didn't get too much time to reflect on what-might-have-been when we were launched straight back into league action three days later against our nearest rivals Sunderland at Roker Park. There was almost 46,000 noisy fans in the ground that chilly day on Wearside. The football was fairly raw, too. Pancho Pearson was missing again through injury and Tommy Baldwin made one of his rare appearances for United. Despite the raucous crowd, the encounter failed to ignite and ended goalless. Painfully, we fired blanks in the next match, the second leg of the League Cup semi-final at Carrow Road. There wasn't much in it and it was settled by a strike from Colin Suggett in the fifty-fourth minute, a scrambled effort which was in keeping with most of the play. A report in one newspaper stated: 'The tackling began at the knee caps and worked progressively higher'.

I was as disappointed as any of my team-mates as the coach took us home from East Anglia that evening. We had passed up the opportunity of reaching Wembley and that was still a special place for me. Now the domestic knockout competitions were out of the way, we could keep our focus sharply on the Second Division title and returning to the top flight with a bit of flair and flourish. Those were my thoughts as we drove out of the Carrow Road car park, but things, as we know, can change very rapidly in football. On the first day of February we prepared to play Bristol City at Old Trafford. Over 47,000 hardly souls braved the elements to greet us as we took the field. It was a phenomenal response considering their obvious disappointment of seeing their team lose a Cup semi-final only a few days beforehand.

Bristol City had turned us over at their place in November and they surprised us again with another 1-0 victory. Tommy Docherty also had a surprise for me. I was told my Manchester United career was at an end.

Chapter Thirty-Five

GALLANT BATTLE AGAINST THE DROP

ON moving to Manchester United, I knew Pat Crerand was assistant manager to Tommy Docherty. I was delighted as Pat was one of my football heroes. I loved to go to Parkhead specifically to watch him play, his passing of the ball was special. I was looking forward to playing six-a-sides with him as I knew the boss would also join in as he did at Chelsea.

As we battled relegation, Pat was calm and upbeat. It must have been hard for him to see United struggle. I played against Pat a lot of times in my career in England. I would have loved to have played in the same team as him. It nearly happened in 1967 when United were reportedly interested in myself. At the end of the season, Pat came with the team to Majorca. He was great company and obviously United wanted to come back up straight away from the Second Division. Also with the players were chairman Louis Edwards and Sir Matt Busby.

Sir Matt was a wonderful man and it was great to spend time with such a special, well-respected football great. You could see why the players wanted to win the European Cup so badly for Sir Matt, making United the first English club to win the trophy. I was glued to the television for that match at Wembley. When United beat Benfica it was very emotional, but well-deserved. I never got the chance to talk to Pat Crerand about the game and what he thought, especially with Celtic, his old club, winning the European Cup the year previously.

After I signed, the boss introduced me to the players. Most of them I had played against a couple of months previously when I was at Wolves. We drew 0-0 at Old Trafford and I didn't feel overawed with any of the players, but I knew I could help. Their confidence was very low and we were in serious trouble. We looked certs to go down. We couldn't buy goals and nothing was going our way (no pressure, Jim). After training, the team sheet was up the board. I was in against Birmingham City away from home in a six-pointer as our opponents were also in relegation trouble. It was the second time I had made my debut against Birmingham City. The previous occasion was when I made my league debut at eighteen years of age for Chelsea. We won 6-1 and I scored two. More of the same would do nicely.

I was now twenty-six and this was my fourth professional club. We lost 1-0 to Birmingham and I got injured after about fifteen minutes in a goalmouth scramble. I got a crack on my shoulder blade. It really hurt. It was a long match and I was in pain. Not the best of starts, but I was determined to be fit for the next game as there were not a lot of games to go. I was in for treatment on the Sunday morning and I thought I might need an x-ray on my shoulder, but Laurie Brown, our physio, said: 'You'll carry on with your treatment for a couple of days and see how you are.'

Our next game was on Saturday, March 23, against Spurs at Old Trafford and I had to be fit and play through the pain. The atmosphere in the dressing room was mixed. The boss and the coaching staff were upbeat. The players were low in confidence. We needed goals. The team had scored twenty-five goals in thirty-three games. The figures speak for themselves. I thought we did well against Spurs, but we lost 1-0. We were running out of home games. We had four more and five away. It is okay looking at the fixtures now, but at the time we needed wins and goals. Talking with the players, they felt down on their luck. As Alex Forsyth said in the newspapers after the game: 'I think we're doomed.' Perhaps because I had just arrived, I was optimistic. Our next match against Chelsea at Stamford Bridge was looming. We travelled on the Friday and stayed at the Russell Hotel in Russell Square. I had stayed there before with Sheffield Wednesday. I roomed with Willie Morgan, one of my best friends in football. It was great to catch up with him. Willie, like myself, didn't want to go down to the Second Division. We won the match and Willie got the first goal and Gerry Daly and Sammy McIlory scored the other two in a 3-1 win.

It was a great victory, 3-1 away to Chelsea was a good result in most people's book. The players were upbeat and the boss was in good form. The journey home to Manchester was great. Our next match would be against Burnley at Old Trafford. As we arrived in Manchester the boss said: 'Have a good night, but remember we have an important game coming up against Burnley.'

I went to Slack Alice's Nightclub with a few of the players. It was part-owned by George Best. I was hoping he would be in. After a few drinks, George came over and had a few drinks with us and introduced me to lots of people. It was a great atmosphere and I enjoyed myself. It took my mind off our dangerous position in the First Division for a few hours. Speaking of Bestie, reminds me of the time he invited me to play in a charity match with all the proceeds going to Lytham Amateur Football. After the game, there was a sportsman's dinner which would finish with a Q&A with George. Bestie was in good form and one of his early questions concerned one of his ex-girlfriends, Marjorie Wallace, a former Miss World. He was asked for a reply to a remark she had made about only giving him three out of ten for his performance in bed. George, quick as a flash, said: 'It's f****n' three more than I gave her.'

Training on Monday was very enjoyable and we were all looking to getting a positive result against Burnley on Wednesday. The crowds had been down on other seasons, so we had to give our supporters encouragement to get them back to Old Trafford for the run-in.

Our defence had been good throughout the season and kept the goals against quite respectable, but we had lost a lot of games 1-0. After Saturday's three against Chelsea, we were determined to make the goal for column more respectable. Brian Kidd had made his final appearance for Manchester United against Spurs. I think Kiddo would have liked to have gone out in style. In the eleven games I played, Kiddo played in only one, He had made 203 appearances for United and scored 52 goals. In his last season before moving to Arsenal, I don't know what was going on. Brian Kidd was a great player and goalscorer and we needed goals.

Before the match against Burnley, the team was changed from the Chelsea game. We had Jim Holton back, no Lou Macari again and one striker, Sammy McIlroy. It was an exciting match, but the result was disappointing, three goals each. McIlroy, Forsyth and Holton were our scorers. Sammy Mac had scored two goals in two games and was up front on his own. He was a marvellous young player. Our crowd got behind us as we looked for a fourth goal. We had a six-pointer coming up against Norwich City at Carrow Road on Saturday. We were below Norwich in the league and we had to win. Lou Macari was back. We were playing with a lot of confidence and pushing the ball around and I was on top of my game. I was dictating matches from midfield, but I wanted some goals. We beat Norwich with Macari and Greenhoff the goalscorers. We had a settled squad that the boss was keeping together. I couldn't help think about the players he had discounted.

Our next league game was against Newcastle at home and we came onto the pitch to a bigger crowd, nearly 45,000. The boss made sure Newcastle were already on the pitch before he would let us leave the dressing room. He wanted to let Newcastle hear our crowd as we went to the centre circle and waved to them. My thoughts were that if it gives an edge then why not? But some of the players were embarrassed because of our league position. We beat Newcastle 1-0. I scored from a diving header (I was Supermac, not the other No.9 at Newcastle). After the game, our dressing room was buzzing. We had won three games and drawn one out of our last four games. We were on a roll, but we had a tough schedule in April, we had eight games, four at home and four away.

After the game the boss said: 'Well done, we have given ourselves great hope. We have a huge game against Everton at Old Trafford on Monday, so let's rest, we will do a light training session and be ready.' It was great coming in for training on Sunday, such a different atmosphere from when I first arrived five games ago and it was going to get better for myself. I had been thinking a lot about our league position and where I was playing. I decided I could go forward and look to score more and pick up loose balls further forward.

It would be interesting to see what the crowd would be and when we came out the tunnel the noise was deafening. There were 48,500 fans at the game. Our supporters were amazing. David Meek, the Manchester Evening News reporter, a great guy and an honest reporter who had seen all the success at Manchester United down the years, said: 'Play it cool, Manchester United…or you will fritter away the chance of First Division survival. Seven points from the last four games have breathed new life in the Reds. But it will count for nothing if they again succumb to the pressure and tensions of fighting for survival.'

We started the game on fire, we pushed Everton back as we stormed the Stretford End. Cheered on by our fans, it was exciting as we went for the Toffees. We were awarded a free-kick just outside the 18-yard box. I placed the ball, stepped back and I curled the ball with my right foot into the goalkeeper's left-hand side high up into the top corner. We talked in training about putting one of our players on the end of the wall and pulling the wall in so I could get the ball down the outside of the wall. I decided against it as I thought the referee might give a foul against us.

What a way to open your goal account in front of the Stretford End. I was overjoyed as I went towards the fans. So many great United players had scored in the same net before me. I felt elated. Stewart Houston scored our second goal from a Willie Morgan cross. I scored our third goal after Sammy Mac hit a post. I was so excited I lifted a ball boy as we celebrated at the scoreboard end of Old Trafford. I had another goal disallowed. I don't know what for.

It was a great day for everybody, especially myself in the dressing room. The atmosphere was great. We had now taken nine points out of ten in five games. The boss was delighted and said: 'Have a couple of days off, but we have a six-pointer at Southampton on Saturday.' As a team we went out afterwards together, a new team was evolving. The papers the next day were very good to the team and myself. David Meek said, under the headline **UNITED'S VERDICT:** United's bold bid for goals paid dividends against Everton at Old Trafford today. Jim McCalliog, now proving a bargain buy at £60,000, scored two of them in an authoritative display.' Peter Fitton, in the Sun, said: 'United back with Magic Mac. Doc's new boy does the trick.' Peter Moss, in the Daily Mail, said 'Incredible United can do it' and he quoted myself saying: 'Now we can sleep soundly in our beds. Southampton and the others can do the worrying.' John Roberts, in the Daily Express, said: 'Mac has magic touch.' Bob Russell, in the Daily Mirror, added: 'The great escape act.'

When we reported back for training, we were now looking forward to the upcoming games and again we had a six-pointer with Southampton. Training was enjoyable, Wednesday and Thursday, but Friday was more serious. I fancied we would get a result, we wouldn't get beat. We were travelling down south on the Friday. The boss told me Brian Moore, the ITV commentator and presenter, wanted me to go to London the night before the game to do an interview. I wasn't keen as I wanted to relax with the boys before an important game. The boss said: 'We will ask for cash, they will not agree.'

I said: 'Can I leave it with you?' He said okay. A little while later, the boss told me they were agreeing to pay cash. I said I didn't want to do, I wanted to relax. God knows what the boss told him.

Southampton were in freefall. They had a young, inexperienced manager in Lawrie McMenemy who had taken over from Ted Bates when the Saints were fourth in the league. They had some great players and were a better side at home. It would be an interesting game, we were on the up and they were on the slide. There was a big crowd and the tension was apparent as both sides started tentatively and then the deadlock was broken. Sammy McIlroy went through and Eric Martin, the Saints goalkeeper, pulled him down for a penalty-kick.

On the coach travelling to The Dell, I was sitting beside Willie Morgan and he said if we get a penalty he would take it. So, I was extremely surprised when I could feel Willie pushing me forward from the back: 'Go on, Jim, you take it,' he was saying to me. I couldn't believe what was happening as I took the ball and placed it on the penalty spot. I did my familiar penalty run, I would stop just as I was about to hit the ball and put it in the keeper's right hand side, low down. I scored to put us one up.

Both teams fought bravely. Mick Channon equalised for the Saints. The way I looked at it we had taken a point from them because they were dangerous at home. On the journey back to Manchester, we had time to relax as we had three games to go, two away and the derby match against City at Old Trafford.

Our next game was against Everton at Goodison on the Tuesday night. We were in for training on the Sunday for the most important eight days of our careers. Could we pull it off? I didn't want to go into the Second Division just yet. We had been unchanged for the last four games. So we were ready, we had turned over Everton easily at Old Trafford 3-0, but they would be a different team at Goodison Park. I liked playing Everton, they were always a good footballing side, but had nothing to play for. Teams always wanted to beat Manchester United, so we took nothing for granted. It was 0-0 at half-time. Mick Lyons got the only goal of the game and the pressure mounted.

Travelling back from Liverpool, the players were all feeling low. How did I feel? The reality was that the Second Division was now a distinct possibility. Relegation had been far removed from my thoughts when I arrived at Old Trafford, I genuinely believed we would be too good to go down. Now, though, it was staring us in the face.

The following day at training, Tommy Docherty was still remarkably upbeat and no-one even dared talk about relegation in his presence. I've covered the derby fairly extensively in a previous chapter, but I can still recall the build-up to the occasion. If we won our next two games, we knew we could stay up, so we had it all to play for. As we went out to the centre of the pitch to wave to our fans, we were determined to rattle City. Willie Morgan and Denis Law were captains and the crowd gave them an enormous cheer. It was wonderful to hear the United fans' support for Denis. He was an extraordinary footballer, especially for Manchester United.

After an emotional day, I got showered and went to the players' lounge. We were due to play Stoke City at Victoria Ground on Monday night, but we didn't know what would happen in the aftermath of the derby. There would have to be an urgent meeting with the football bosses. I sat with my team-mates and I think we were all in shock. Everything was a mess. I was thinking would we lose two points? Could the club appeal? We were in training on the Sunday and would things be clearer then?

For the final match against Stoke, the boss made one change, bringing in Mick

Martin for Gerry Daly. On the journey to Stoke, the boys got on with being professional, but it had been an unbelievable time in my career and that of my team-mates, but we had to complete the league programme.

On a personal note, I thought losing the FA Cup Final with Sheffield Wednesday was my most disappointing day of my footballing career, but now I have had time to think more and it doesn't compare to being relegated with Manchester United. We were all numb over the weekend and after the Stoke game, which we lost 1-0,. It all came flooding back. I had to have time to myself to let what had just happened sink in. That we had just been relegated with probably the best football club in the world. It was so embarrassing.

I had dreamt of playing for Manchester United and being a Busby Babe when I was young. My initial thoughts of our relegation was to ask for a transfer. I did want to go into the Second Division. Period. Full stop. I could hide behind the fact that United were bottom of the First Division when I joined the club, but that would be unprofessional. I had been a senior professional at the club and it hurt getting relegated. The boss had said in the dressing room that we would come straight back up. But maybe that was his way of handling relegation. It was so frustrating, five 1-0 losses in our last eleven games. On top of that, how did the fixtures, four games from April 20 to April 29, come about?

Every game was a pressure situation. How would you agree to this fixture scheduling? When you play matches it is important players are recovered and ready for the next game, four games in nine days is poor value for supporters of football. At United, we only used thirteen players in our last eleven games, myself, along with Stepney, Houston, Greenhoff, Buchan and McIlroy, played in all the games. We also had the uncertainty the boss could get sacked at any time. It wasn't fair on Manchester United and our supporters that we had to finish our fixtures because of the World Cup Finals' schedule in 1974. I don't think I was ever so low in my football career. I was keeping it to myself as I worked out my next move. I knew at least one team in the First Division was very interested in my situation.

The boss had a meeting with all the players and told us we were going to Spain for a week's break. I couldn't believe it at first. I didn't think it would go down well with the supporters. Also Stuart Pearson was lined up for Manchester City, but the boss had sneaked in and signed Pancho from Hull City for £200,000 and he came to Spain with the team. Pancho was scored to sign goals in the Second Division and whether he was the answer only time would tell. These moves cleared up my fears about the boss being sacked. Surely the board would not sanction a signing and a first-team break in Spain if they were going to sack the boss?

On our break in Spain, I had time to think away from all the heartbreak of relegation. I got on well with Pancho and we became good friends. He was a great lad. I had never seen him play, but the boss had managed him at Hull City so he knew about him. If he could score goals he would be a bargain. Three of the team were on World Cup duty with Scotland – Jim Holton, Martin Buchan and Willie Morgan. I thought myself and Lou Macari might have got in the squad. I finished the season well, but I didn't get the call. When we got back from Spain, my mind was clear and I felt the boss had bonded the team ready for the new season and we had signed a goalscorer.

In my second year, when we returned for pre-season training, we had two new staff. Tommy Cavanagh became Tommy Docherty's assistant manager and Frank Blunstone was in charge of the youth team. Tommy Cavanagh was at Hull City with the boss and would work with the first team alongside him. Frank would work with the youths. I knew Frank as he was a player at Chelsea when I was a young player. Frank had a lot of respect from the young Chelsea side and revelled in being the elder statesman at The Bridge.

With these changes to the staff. It meant that Pat Crerand would decide to move to manage Northampton Town in the Fourth Division. What an absolute waste of football talent and a man so passionate about football who played at the top level who could have passed his knowledge down to young players. What would I learn from Tommy Cavanagh? Not a lot compared to Pat Crerand. Pat did not last long at Northampton. With due to respect to Northampton, it must have been so hard for Pat, having played at the top for so long with Celtic and United.

Cavanagh was keen and enthusiastic and had a great rapport with the manager which is why the boss wanted him as his assistant. He quickly got his feet under the table and worked the players, but was a crap six-a-sides player.

At the start of the season there was a new rule. All clubs had to write out a team sheet signed by the manager which had to be taken to the referee's room one hour before kick-off. Team sheets would be exchanged and taken back to the manager in the dressing room. The boss would take the team sheet from Cav and in front of the players scrunch the team sheet up and throw it in the bin, saying: 'We will play our game.' When the boss and Cav were not looking, we would get the team sheet out of the bin to see what the opposition's team was. Once the season started at Orient, we had a comfortable win, but I hurt my

Achilles and missed the next three games. It was hard for me to watch. But the team were doing well as I was recovering. The atmosphere in the dressing room was getting better.

Chapter Thirty-Six

LEAVING OLD TRAFFORD

I HAVE no idea why Tommy Docherty wanted me out of the door at Manchester United. He never thought to explain the matter to me. You may have thought I deserved some sort of clarification as to how I was now expendable and no longer part of his first-team plans. As a manager, Tommy Docherty never thought he had to justify himself to anyone and, basically, that was the start - and end - of the matter.

I had read some of his comments in the newspapers in the aftermath of the 1-0 loss to Oxford United. He was clearly unhappy with what he had witnessed and hadn't been slow to go into print with his thoughts and criticisms. I was rather surprised to note the boss thought we should have seen the game out in the last ten minutes and been content with a point in a goalless draw. Try telling that to over 47,000 fans roaring you on for a winning goal. We were hit by a classic sucker-punch when Donnie Gillies scored, but I don't recall the manager giving us any instructions from the touchline to ease off and settle for a draw.

I am well aware football can drop some bombshells on unsuspecting individuals, but you never think it will happen to you. Now I am a little older and, hopefully, a little wiser, I acknowledge no-one in this game is bomb-proof. And that fact would hit Tommy Docherty, too, in his United career. It was the Monday morning after the weekend loss and I was at the ground as I prepared for training. One of the coaches informed me: 'The boss would like a word in his office'. I hadn't a clue what to expect, but I admit I was not particularly apprehensive. I made my way to the manager's office and wondered what this was all about.

I took a seat and the boss blurted out: 'Lawrie McMenemy has made an offer and has been given permission to talk to you.' I was speechless. The boss delivered the news in such a matter-of-fact way he could have been discussing the weather. I looked at him blankly as I tried very quickly to make sense out of his few words. I knew he was a personal friend of the Southampton manager. As my mind whirred away, it was obvious the boss had said his piece and had no inclination to add anything to his five-second delivery. I was numb for a moment and then I heard myself saying: 'Thanks' and then getting up to go through the door. The manager said nothing. It was a fairly ruthless way to tell someone their Manchester United career was over.

I left his office and I realised it would be for the last time. As I walked along the corridor, I couldn't help but think Tommy Cavanagh had been up to his old tricks. What nonsense had he filled the boss with this time? There were a lot of politics played at the club and, on this occasion, I was most certainly on the receiving end. Maybe I should have had it out with the boss there and then. Possibly I should have demanded a reason. There were a lot of things I could have told him. But experience had taught me to sleep on major decisions. It might have ended in a rammy and that wouldn't have done either of us any good. So, I bit my tongue and said nothing apart from that one word: 'Thanks'.

Inside, though, I felt destroyed, utterly devastated. I didn't have time to take it all in. It hit me like a wrecking ball that this would be my last time inside Old Trafford, at least as a Manchester United player. It didn't seem that long ago the boss had been telling me he would move heaven and earth to get me to the club. Now I was being discarded. I had outlived my usefulness as far as the manager was concerned. Even looking back all these decades, I can still sense the emptiness I felt in that moment. Somehow, I actually felt ashamed, I had failed him in some sort of way. If the manager had wanted to hurt me, he certainly achieved his ambition.

Very quickly, I realised I had to sort out things in my own mind. Southampton? How did they get linked with me? Had the boss dropped a word in the ear of Lawrie McMenemy? Had a price already been negotiated? Agents were not in plentiful supply back then, so it was down to me to sort out this situation. And quickly. It wasn't of my making, but it had been dumped on me. Clearly, I wouldn't be hanging around anywhere I was not wanted. I had never been part of the cliques that can crop up around a manager. I was never anyone's yes man. That's never been my style right to this very day. I have got no intention of following the crowd. I'll make my own decisions and I'll stick by them. If nothing else, Tommy Docherty would have known that about me.

I also had to wonder if my old sparring partner Cav had played a part in my shift from United. It was evident things had never been the same between us following the head-to-head incident in Ireland. I still find that fairly impossible to comprehend. Talk about making a mountain out of a mole-hill. Cav clearly saw it as an ideal opportunity to flex his muscles and didn't pass up the chance. From that moment, I had tolerated the pest and kept my head down. I was a professional footballer and I always acted like one. I think anyone who knows me will verify that statement. But Cav could be poison and maybe enough of it seeped through to the boss for him to make a career-changing decision for me.

I stopped at the boot room to collect my gear. As bad as I felt, I still possessed the common sense to pick up my boots. I didn't have time to feel sorry for myself. My career, as far as United was concerned, was in pieces. The big professional football world had enhanced my life so much that maybe this was payback. I had dodged a lot of bullets since my first day as a teenager at Leeds United. Looking in from the outside, people will believe being a footballer is a glamorous profession. And, yes, I was extremely fortunate to make money by doing something I loved, but, believe me, it is not all a bed of roses. There are some rocks along that road and players can suffer as well as anyone in their chosen profession. Very few folk go into football and come out the other end unscathed one way or another.

Anyway, while I mulled all sorts of things around in my head, arrangements were made for me to see Lawrie McMenemy at the club's ground, The Dell, the following day. There was absolutely no point in hanging around. As a single man, I was answerable to no-one but myself. I had to remain positive. I was determined I still had a lot to offer in the game. I wasn't even thirty years old and if Tommy Docherty thought I was past my best then I had all the impetus required to emphasise what I had to offer elsewhere. All sorts of thoughts bombarded my mind as I drove to Southampton.

I had played at The Dell for former clubs Sheffield Wednesday and Wolves, as well as United, of course, and by a quirk of fate I had scored for all my ex-teams on that ground. Whereas Old Trafford was vast and imposing and capable of easily holding crowds of 50,000-plus, Southampton's arena was a homely little place with a capacity of 15,200. In truth, there was no comparison and I drummed that into my head as I made the trip. I had to give any negativity a body-swerve. I had to remain open-minded, but, instinctively, I knew I would give the club my best shot if talks went well with the manager.

I arrived at the ground and there was no red carpet treatment awaiting myself. I went into the stadium, announced myself and told someone I had an appointment with Lawrie McMenemy. I was shown to his office and immediately

I was struck by his affability. He was six-foot plus and could fill a room. I was informed Southampton had offered £60,000 for me and it had been accepted by United. Now it was down to him and I to discuss personal terms and see where it takes us. We had a good, progressive chat. We both got our thoughts over and I was feeling good about the possibility of a move. Helpfully, Lawrie gave me a guided tour of The Dell. I remained upbeat throughout and he made all the right noises.

The players had gone home after a morning training session, so we virtually had the place to ourselves. We discussed a few more details before I agreed to come back the following morning when I could meet the players who were likely to become my new team-mates at my sixth senior football club. It was a case of farewell United and hello Southampton.

Chapter Thirty-Seven

TOMMY DOCHERTY AND A PRICELESS QUALITY

I DIDN'T always see eye to eye with Tommy Docherty - I think that will be fairly evident by now - but that does not mean I could not appreciate his qualities as a manager. We had our fall-outs and we had differing opinions on occasions. However, I thought he had an awesome presence, a real player's type of team boss who was an incredible motivator who could get every ounce of energy out of an individual to make him the very best he could be as soon as he stepped onto that football field.

I still insist Tommy Docherty should have won two English First Division championships - one with Chelsea and another with Manchester United.

He appreciated talent and encouraged his players to put on a show. Winning was the be-all-and-end-all, of course, but if we could achieve it with a flourish, a splash of colour and a mixture of excitement and entertainment, then you would be guaranteed a massive smile from the manager in the dressing room afterwards. He was an infectious character and his players responded to that encouragement. He saw it as part of his job description to lift the players and push them all the way to advance their ability.

In my time with him at Chelsea and Manchester United, I cannot recall him ever missing a training session. Hail, rain or shine, Tommy was in the thick of it. He would undertake the office work that was required of a football manager back then, take care of the media tasks and, more often than not, head out that evening to watch a game. If there was a new kid on the block, he wanted to see him for himself to make up his own mind. He could travel the length and breadth of the country and the following morning he would be out on the training pitch with the players, cajoling, inspiring, teasing and stimulating individuals as he prepared for the next fixture.

Unlike a lot of other loudmouth managers who took advantage of their position, he kept criticism to himself. The player would get to know the boss' thoughts, but they were shared between the two of them, no-one else needed to know. Of course, he could get his message across with a crafty leg-pull and a joke, but that was his style.

Tommy Docherty did not get involved in a lot of tactical jargon, he left the mumbo-jumbo to others. However, he worked his players hard in training, he demanded they could last the entire game at full pelt, slackers were not tolerated, but, as I have said, they were galvanised and invigorated to perform with style. That was always important to Tommy Docherty. Look at what he did at Chelsea, for a start. When I joined in 1964, their nickname was 'The Pensioners', not exactly a moniker to strike fear into opponents. He set about changing that image. As he would continue to do so later in life with clubs such as Wolves in 1986, the man possessed seemingly boundless enthusiasm.

He was thirty-two years old when he was asked to move up from playing for Chelsea to become player/coach. Inside a year, Docherty was manager when the legendary Ted Drake left the post and, although he could not save them from relegation from the top flight, he made sure they came straight back. He sold a lot of the older players and brought in youth in the shape of Terry Venables, Bobby Tambling and Peter Bonetti. He gave the entire place a real shake-up. He even changed the colour of the shorts to blue to match the shirt. He really did have an eye for detail, even the smallest things.

Suddenly, 'The Pensioners' had been transformed into 'Docherty's Diamonds'. London was a vibrant, lively place to be in the sixties and Docherty intended to take full advantage of the situation. He was eager that his Chelsea team should play their part in the entire spectacle of so-called 'Swinging London'. The eyes of the world appeared to be on England's capital city and Docherty sensed football could take a share of the spotlight. He had hungry and ambitious young players and a go-ahead chairman in Brian Mears. In the first campaign back in the big-time, the club finished fifth in the league which was no mean feat. And, just as importantly to the manager, critics and neutrals were saluting what Chelsea were bringing to football grounds everywhere they performed.

Docherty could spot a player, but he also knew how to put the jigsaw together away from the pitch. He appointed Dave Sexton as his coach and, coincidentally, he also managed Chelsea and Manchester United. Eight of his young players in 1964 went on to become full internationals for Scotland and England. As a stroke of genius, he signed a more experienced campaigner in Tommy Harmer who was thirty-four years old when he arrived from Watford after making his name at

Spurs where he had nine years after kicking off a fine career at White Hart Lane in 1951. Tommy, an old-fashioned inside-forward who made the ball do all the work, was used sparingly on the pitch, playing only nine games, but his appearances on the training field and in the dressing room got through to his younger team-mates. He scored one goal for the club, but what an important one it proved to be - the winner against Sunderland at Roker Park in the second last match of the promotion campaign. A thoroughly likeable gentleman, Tommy Harmer was the team's youth team coach until 1967.

Terry Venables was still in his early twenties when he was told he was the new captain of Chelsea and, of course, my old colleague thrived on responsibility as he later proved during his managerial career as the England international manager as well as boss at Spurs and Barcelona. Docherty did not exactly give his chairman nightmares for demands for transfer cash, either. He spent £30,000 on wing-back Marvin Hinton, from Charlton Athletic, £8,000 on my future Scotland international team-mate Eddie McCreadie, the left-back from East Stirling, and an extremely modest fee for another Scots cap in midfielder George Graham from Aston Villa. An absolute steal at £5,000. At least Dick Turpin had the good grace to wear a mask in such transactions. A Dochertyism!

I've already said elsewhere that I blame Tommy Docherty for Chelsea failing to win the title in 1965. Much as I admire and respect the guy, I will never be able to get my head around what happened when eight players broke the curfew at Blackpool. To send these players home on the eve of a game we really should have won which led to a disastrous fall-out at Stamford Bridge. The punishment did not fit the crime, that's for sure. When Tommy Docherty left in 1967. Dave Sexton, who had spent a year at Arsenal as first-team coach, returned and won the FA Cup in 1970 and the European Cup-Winners' Cup the following year. It would be fair to say Docherty had laid solid foundations for that double success.

At Manchester United, Tommy Docherty was again offered the ideal platform from which to display all he worshipped in football. He had spent sixteen months with Porto, but couldn't knock Benfica or Sporting Lisbon off their joint perch at the top of Portuguese football. Slightly frustrated, he returned to Britain and accepted the No.2 post to Terry Neill at Hull City, but it was obvious Docherty was his own man and he was on his way shortly afterwards to become full-time boss at Scotland. About fifteen months later, after revamping the international system with his nation, he was lured to Old Trafford.

I often wonder why it took United so long to get around to making Docherty their manager. They were made for each other. Matt Busby, he wasn't a 'Sir' at the time, quit the post in February 1969 after being in charge for twenty-four incredible years. That's several lifetimes in football at that level. He brought in Wilf McGuinness, who had been a former United player and trainer. Without any disrespect, the job was too big for an inexperienced coach to cope with. McGuinness was sacked in December 1970 and Busby returned to the dug-out once again. I thought they had made a mistake missing out on Tommy Docherty first time around and I could hardly believe it when Frank O'Farrell, the Leicester City boss, got the nod to try to succeed Busby in June 1971. Eighteen months later, O'Farrell was handed his P45 and, after two hiccups, United got it right by naming Tommy Docherty as manager.

It was a job my old manager tackled with a relish. He had inherited players who had been brought in by two previous bosses over a relatively short period of time, plus, of course, he had the Old Trafford legends such as Denis Law, Bobby Charlton and George Best. A lot of work lay ahead and Docherty dipped into his Scotland international squad to bring in players such as Lou Macari, Jim Holton, Stewart Houston and Alex Forsyth. George Graham teamed up with his old Chelsea and Scotland boss once more and I'm delighted to add I, too, was brought in. We also had my mate Willie Morgan and Martin Buchan around the place, so it was no wonder one newspaper dubbed us 'Mac-chester United'.

Tommy Docherty obviously welcomed a challenge and in his first few months at the club, he managed to haul United away from the relegation trapdoor. The following season, though, United could not get out of the mire. I signed from Wolves with ten games to go, but the team was in a flat spin and we just could not arrest the nosedive that took the club into the Second Division for the start of season 1974/75. I remember Tommy Docherty's demeanour at the time. He vowed to the United fans he would get them straight back up in one year. He was under extreme pressure, but he was as good as his word.

I recall one of the first things he did was go out and find a proven goalscorer who knew what life in the second tier was all about. He brought in Stuart Pearson in a £200,000 deal from Hull City. Not too many people had heard the name before Tommy Docherty signed him, but he did exactly what he was bought for - he scored goals. He even went on to win fifteen England international caps and I think we could agree he was money well spent. Docherty set about installing all the virtues held in high esteem by Manchester United followers and they stormed back to the top division with a certain amount of style. The fans returned in droves to Old Trafford.

A year later, they were challenging for the crown and narrowly missed out.

They had to settle for third behind Liverpool and surprise packets Queens Park Rangers, managed by Dave Sexton, and that was nothing short of phenomenal. I still believe United should have been crowned English champions on that occasion. I talk about their FA Cup Final experience against Southampton elsewhere, but they did get their hands on the silverware when they beat old foes Liverpool 2-1 in 1977. As far as the supporters were concerned, Tommy Docherty had United back on track. I have to say I was overjoyed for my old manager. I was with Chicago Sting when they overcame the Anfield side at Wembley and I gave them an extra cheer. When Southampton had beaten them the previous year, Docherty had been gracious in defeat. I admired that.

Tommy Docherty, of course, was not given the time required to win that coveted First Division championship with Manchester United. He lost his job at Old Trafford for a non-football related matter. It's been well documented, he left his wife Agnes, to whom he had been married since 1950, for Mary Brown, wife of United physiotherapist Laurie. Headlines were plastered all over the newspapers and it was one of the lead items on the television news. Subsequently, Tommy and Mary married in 1977 and remained together until my old boss sadly passed away on Hogmanay 2020 at the age of 92. Two weeks after United's FA Cup triumph, Tommy Docherty had been fired.

One evening I was sitting in the audience when Tommy Docherty talked about his sacking. Simply, he stated he 'had fallen in love with Mary' and pointed out they had been at each other's side ever since. Wherever Tommy's football travels took him, Mary was with him every step of the way. Since United, he has been manager of Derby County, Queens Park Rangers, Sydney Olympic, Preston, South Melbourne, Sydney Olympic (for a second time), Wolves and Altrincham before retiring from football management at the end of the 1987/88 season at the age of sixty.

Players who have come in contact with this colourful character will have their own stories to tell, but, as far as I am concerned, he was never a diva and always retained the ability to laugh at himself. That's a priceless quality.

Chapter Thirty-Eight

MICK AND OSSIE WANT ME AT SOUTHAMPTON, LAWRIE TELLS ME

I THINK it would be safe to say my debut for Southampton was a fairly low-key affair. A crowd of 12,397 turned out at Boundary Park on Saturday, February 15 1975 to watch a 1-1 draw with Oldham where I set up our goal for Paul Gilchrist. An attendance of almost FOUR times that had witnessed my last game for Manchester United at Old Trafford, the 1-0 loss to Bristol City.

I had realised that any move away from United would be a step down. I wasn't kidding myself or anyone else and I had to acknowledge and accept that fact. At the same time I realised I still had a lot of football to play and Southampton were now paying my wages. I owed it to them to give them everything I had. In fact, I owed it to myself to show I was too good to be rejected by anyone. So, I went into my new career with a resolve that has followed me throughout my life. I was there to be a winner.

I played alongside Mick Channon that day for the first time and, of course, I had heard so many good things about the England international forward. He and Peter Osgood, my former Chelsea team-mate, were the big stars at the team at the time, but Ossie was missing from the line-up on this occasion. We had to be content with a point, but I had been reasonably satisfied with my own performance and I could see there was talent in the team in the likes of Bobby Stokes, Nick Holmes, Mel Blyth and goalscorer Paul Gilchrist. Fellow-Glaswegian Hugh Fisher was in the engine room of the side and he was a good, solid professional who gave every ounce of endeavour.

There was another performer that day who also hailed from the city of my birth, a winger by the name of Gerry O'Brien. Former manager Ted Bates had travelled north to watch the tricky, little attacker in action for Clydebank in a Division Two game against East Fife. He liked what he saw and a £22,500 deal was struck that evening. That was a helluva lot of money for the Kilbowie Park outfit and I believe it was a record fee for a club in that division at the time. There was a fourth Scot in that line-up, goalkeeper Eric Martin who hailed from Perth. He was a bit of a personality at the club after signing from Dunfermline in 1967. He wasn't there too long after I arrived as he headed for the States, a route I would be taking myself.

Okay, I would have preferred a victory on my baptism, but I did see some positive signs. A week later, I was looking forward to teaming up with Mick Channon and Peter Osgood. We were due to play Bolton at The Dell and I was reasonably confident. I had had another week working with my new team-mates and getting to know them a little better. It's all part of a bedding-in process, familiarising yourself with new colleagues, a new system in a different line-up and with a new set of fans to impress. I had always enjoyed a good rapport with the supporters of the clubs on my travels and I was determined to show Saints' followers I could provide for their favourites. A healthy crowd of 18,339 were there to roar us on against the Wanderers, but it didn't go to script. We lost 1-0 and, in truth, we hadn't played well.

It was far too early to say, but I could already see Mick, Ossie and I would have to work on our understanding. Their talent was not in question, both of them oozed class, but there are occasions when you have to get your sleeves rolled up and get down and dirty. I wondered if Mick and Ossie fancied that side of football. A week later, we headed for Blackpool where I had enjoyed some welcome headlines in the not-too-distant-past after a performance for United. That memory was obliterated this time out as we were thumped 3-0. Ossie was one of the lucky ones, he sat this one out with an injury. The record books showed that thrashing was the team's eleventh league defeat of the season from thirty-one games. There were ten draws included in that sequence. Ten wins was a poor return from a team that had been playing top-flight football the previous season.

It was a fortnight before we played again and once more we were on our travels to the Midlands to face Aston Villa. If I had followed Bill McGarry's 'advice' just over a year earlier, I might have been lining up in the claret and blue of the home side instead of the red and white stripes of Southampton. Funny old game football, as someone once said. Actually, I wasn't feeling too disposed towards humour at the end of a fairly one-sided ninety minutes when we were on the receiving end of another 3-0 hammering. Ossie, Mick and myself had been given the runaround by a team that looked a lot more determined. Three games, three loses, seven goals conceded and none scored. Not too impressive is it?

I had to draw on some positive thought and tell myself the only way was up. I've never been one for letting my head go down, so I just buckled in for a bumpy ride to see if we could get back on track as swiftly as possible before the season fell apart. Some teams fall into the bad habit of losing. Confidence is shredded, players are terrified to try anything, it's safety-first all the time. No-one wants to dwell on the ball, no-one wants to be the one who makes a mistake that could lead to another lost goal and another defeat. No-one wants to accept responsibility, but we all know what will happen if we don't get our collective act together - we would all be playing in the third tier of English football next season.

That's not where I wanted to ply my trade and I just didn't see Mick or Ossie looking forward to games at Port Vale, Colchester, Aldershot or Hereford, with no disrespect to those teams - when I'm sure they saw themselves at Old Trafford, Anfield, Highbury or White Hart Lane. That where I saw myself, anyway. I had no intention of fading into the wilderness. Without any conceit, I thought I still had something to contribute at the top end of the game.

We got a quick chance to turn things around when we played Oxford United at our place only three evenings after the trouncing at Villa. Thankfully, we arrested the descent with a 2-1 win. Paul Gilchrist and Mick Channon were on the mark and it was such a relief afterwards to sit in a dressing room with your team-mates when a bit of the anxiety had been eliminated. For the time being, at any case. We weren't kidding ourselves, we had a lot of hard work ahead.

Around this time, Lawrie McMenemy looked fairly relaxed. I wondered what he knew that his players didn't. He was still relatively new to management and had a certain charm and warmth. He was forty-six years of age and he was no tactical genius. I do not say that as a slight to the boss who obviously knew enough about the game to shell out £60,000 for me! Lawrie's claim to fame was winning the Fourth Division championship with Grimsby after taking over as a boss for the first time in 1971. Two years later he was on his way to Southampton as assistant to Ted Bates and he took over as manager in November 1973. In a strange twist, Ted Bates then became his No.2 and was on the bench when the Saints won the FA Cup. Then he stepped up to the board where he served as a director for twenty years before taking on the role of club president.

So, Big Lawrie breezed around and I didn't know the character well enough to work out if it was an act or the real deal. Was he working on the principle that if he looked a nervous wreck it might filter down to the players? Or if he exuded confidence and a devil-may-care attitude that, too, might tell the players they had nothing to worry about, everything was under control? I would find out in time.

In the space of nine days, the team faced four games as March came to an end. It was a fairly hectic schedule and we won two and lost two. We began with a 3-2 victory over Notts county at home and then went down 3-2 against Fulham at Craven Cottage, were on the receiving of a 1-0 scoreline at The Dell against Bristol City and then picked up two precious points with a 1-0 victory over my old club Sheffield Wednesday at Hillsborough where Peter Osgood got the only goal of the encounter.

On April 5, Tommy Docherty and my former Manchester United team-mates were the opposition at The Dell. It was a vital game for both clubs. We were mid-table and didn't want to sink closer to the relegation dogfight. The Old Trafford side, on the other hand, knew a win would see them make a quickfire promotion to the First Division with four games to play. How did I feel about that situation? Envious? That's second nature, isn't it?

I had been allowed to leave and I will never know why, but you have to accept these things. Bitter? No, definitely not. I had made too many friends in my short spell at the club, so I was happy for them. In the main, they were a good bunch of guys and I knew they had been working their socks off to get straight back up. The fans, too, backed the team right from that opening Second Division game against Orient and you have to think they, too, deserved to see their favourites take their rightful place among the elite.

However, if I could delay their celebrations by another minute, you better believe that would be my intention. It seemed Peter Osgood was of a similar mind. He had been linked with a reunion with The Doc at United when it was evident he was on his way out at Chelsea. Dave Sexton had taken over as manager at Stamford Bridge and the word was that he had grown tired of Ossie's lifestyle. I knew Dave and I was aware he was a strict disciplinarian. He didn't rant and rave. Instead, he was very softly spoken, but there could be a hint of menace hidden in the tones.

The Chelsea fans were not happy about the news their great hero was no longer a fixture in the team and they threatened to picket home games. Sexton was not fazed and eventually Ossie was moved onto Southampton in March 1974 for £275,000, a club record for the Saints. Undoubtedly, he would have preferred to have been strutting his stuff at the Stretford End than at The Dell and that may have explained his rather explosive start to this confrontation. Maybe he thought Tommy Docherty had let him down somehow; join the club, my friend!

Anyway, Ossie, who would never have been famous for his hard graft or solid tackling, went out like a man possessed. It wasn't long before he was booked for a lunge at my old mate Willie Morgan. There was another fairly reckless challenge on Lou Macari and that incurred the considerable wrath of the United manager. Old friendships were forgotten when Tommy Docherty seethed afterwards: 'He could have broken Macari's leg.' It was a fairly rugged head-to-head and if United were going to get the points they would have to earn them. One goal settled it and it came from United with Wee Lou the scorer.

We should have been ahead at that stage. The Saints were awarded a penalty-kick nine minutes after the interval. Mick Channon stepped up to take it and sent Alex Stepney the wrong way. Alas, the effort lacked accuracy and smacked off the outside of the post and rebounded to safety. Wee Lou demonstrated how to finish in style when he raced onto a pass from Sammy McIlroy and fired a shot away from Ian Turner, the keeper who had replaced Eric Martin the previous month. Tommy Docherty, still fuming, talked to the Press afterwards and, referring to the match-winning goal, said: 'Ossie crawled into a hole. You should have seen his head drop. Who wants players like that? Anybody who tried to do what he did to Macari is a cheat.'

Strong words and all the more extraordinary when you consider what these two individuals meant to each other at Chelsea in another decade. I got the distinct impression Ossie wouldn't be getting an invitation to join United in the top flight any time soon. Wee Lou was quite funny after the game where the celebrations were distinctly low key. It was clear United wanted to return as champions and they would have to wait for the title. Asked about his crucial strike, my little sparring partner replied: 'I was so angry that after that tackle it was a case of me getting sent off or scoring a goal. I was desperate to score.'

Our season limped to a tranquil conclusion with two wins, two losses and a draw in our final five games. It had been a fairly nondescript season. We finished thirteenth in the table, twenty points adrift of United after forty-two games with fifteen wins, sixteen losses and eleven draws. That brought in forty-one points. The Saints scored fifty-three goals and conceded fifty-four. You don't win prizes when you lose more games than you win or concede more goals than you score. United went up as champions with Aston Villa runners-up and Norwich City in third place. Alas, my old club Sheffield Wednesday completed the campaign rock-bottom with only five wins all season.

Did I feel just a little upset that Villa, the team I had rejected for United, had gone up alongside the Old Trafford club? No. You don't knock back the opportunity to play for Manchester United.

Somehow I knew I still had some unfinished business with that club. And Tommy Docherty.

Chapter Thirty-Nine

I AM ON MY WAY TO WEMBLEY – AFTER TEN YEARS ABSENCE

YOU would have thought there was nothing left Tommy Docherty could do to surprise me. My old manager had signed me twice and sold me twice. The departure at Manchester United and how it was handled still left a bad taste with me. I wasn't so much transferred as discarded when he decided I was expendable. I think you could describe it as a low point in my career.

However, on the first day of May in 1976, I was congratulated by that same manager in the most unusual of settings. Tommy Docherty, wearing the expression of someone who wished he was elsewhere at that precise moment, walked almost the length of a football field in my direction. He extended his right hand and I accepted his acknowledgement. We shook hands in an embrace that was hardly noticed by anyone else in the vicinity. 'Well done, Jim,' he said. 'Well played.' And with that extraordinary gesture, he turned on his heels and headed towards the Manchester United dressing room.

There were 99,115 supporters at Wembley that memorable afternoon, half of them dancing in delight, half of them staring in disbelief. Southampton, who were perceived to be merely making up the numbers, had just beaten Tommy Docherty's Old Trafford side and we had the FA Cup to prove it. Second Division teams are not expected to beat their opponents from the league above them and not too many shrewd observers gave the nod to Southampton against a United team who had done exceptionally well upon their return to the top flight. Asked about the Saints' chances of triumphing at England's national football mecca, most folk reckoned we had two chances: Slim and none.

It was difficult to argue with that forecast. United had had a storming campaign in the First Division and could have actually won the championship. They were four points adrift of title winners Liverpool and three behind surprise packets Queens Park Rangers. It had been a mighty effort from a club just coming up from the Second Division in their gallant attempt to go all the way and be crowned champions of the country. Of course, it had been done before. Ipswich Town had pulled off the incredible feat in the early sixties when they ran away with the Second Division in 1960/61 and then startled everyone by doing likewise in the First Division the following year. They were managed by Alf Ramsey.

Two weeks before Wembley, Southampton had been turned over 1-0 by Plymouth Argyle, our thirteenth loss in the Second Division that season. We followed that up with a 2-0 defeat from Bristol Rovers. That is no way to prepare for an FA Cup Final. We did steady the ship somewhat as we had odd goal wins over Oxford United and Hull City to bring the league campaign to a disappointing conclusion, limping in sixth with only twenty-one victories in forty-two matches, fourteen losses and seven draws. It wasn't particularly impressive and I didn't believe for a moment that our form kept Tommy Docherty awake at night.

As a matter of fact, my old boss had already written us off long before the Wembley encounter. I recall Tommy Docherty didn't make too many friends on the south coast when he declared the winners of the trophy would come from United's semi-final against Derby County. We were scheduled to meet Third Division Crystal Palace - and Malcolm Allison and his lucky fedora - on the same day, April 3, at Stamford Bridge, my old stomping ground where a certain Mr T Docherty esq has been my boss. Tommy Docherty insisted: 'This is the first time the Cup Final will be played at Hillsborough. The other semi-final is a bit of a joke, really.' Joke? It was more of an insult and, as you may have gathered by now, my fellow-Glaswegian did sometimes make the most outrageous statements. I've always found it a reasonable idea to engage my brain before I open my mouth.

Basically, my old boss had told the nation the outcome in our last-four meeting didn't matter a jot, the eventual winners of the competition would be the team that emerged victorious in Yorkshire. It is more than a little annoying to be dismissed in such a nonchalant, flippant fashion. The Saints had worked hard to reach the semi-final of the national competition. We had to go to Aston Villa in a replay at the start of our run and I was in the right place at the right time to score twice in a 2-1 victory in the Midlands. Two goals from Mick Channon helped us to overcome Blackpool 3-1 and we needed a second game to get past West Brom at the next hurdle. Bobby Stokes, who had also netted against the Seasiders in the previous round, got our goal in a 1-1 stalemate at the Hawthorns and we clicked in the replay with Mick hitting a hat-trick and Paul Gilchrist getting the other in a 4-0 romp.

Then it was onto the fifth round on March 6 and a trip to unfashionable Valley Parade to take on Fourth Division Bradford City, a team with the ability to make life difficult for anyone, especially on their own tight, threadbare pitch. To be honest, we all thought we would be playing First Division Norwich City at this stage, but Bradford, after two postponements, had other ideas and beat their more-fancied opponents 2-1 at Carrow Road. That win underlined their threat. Their manager was a Scot by the name of Bobby Kennedy, who had played as a non-nonsense full-back for Kilmarnock and Manchester City. Like Lawrie McMenemy, he had had a spell in charge at Grimsby Town before moving to Yorkshire.

We had a good idea of what to expect at their place. We knew they would get in about us. Who could blame them? They were ninety minutes away from a place in the FA Cup semi-final and they had the massive advantage of playing the tie on their own claustrophobic ground. I could almost hear Kennedy ordering his troops: 'Get into them'. As I recall, it was not a day for the football purist and the ball was probably black and blue after a bruising confrontation in which I managed to get myself booked. Thankfully, I did something else of note and that was score the only goal of a keenly-contested match. My big moment arrived just before the interval when I accepted a Peter Osgood free-kick and volleyed into the net.

I admit there was a little ad-libbing between Ossie and myself. We tried all sorts of set-play permutations during training routines. When we received the free-kick, I knew immediately what I wanted my big mate to do. I stood beside him just to his right. We were a couple of yards outside the area, almost smack in front of goal. 'What do you fancy, Jim?' asked Ossie. 'Just flick it up and I'll hit it.' The referee blew for the kick to be taken, Ossie did as he was asked and lofted the ball in front of me. I smacked it full on the volley with my right foot and the effort flew straight into the net with the keeper hardly moving a muscle. I hit it as sweet as a nut. I didn't even look. As soon as I made contact, I knew it was in and I ran away and performed a Highland jig or something like that in celebration. I hadn't a clue what I was doing, I was lost in the moment. But it was worth it.

Next up was our non-event, according to Tommy Docherty, against Malcolm Allison's Palace. I have to admit I got more than a little wound up before the game. I had been talking to my old Chelsea team-mate Terry Venables, who was a coach at the Selhurst Park club, and he told me he was absolutely convinced Palace would beat us. Even back then, he was the master of mind games. Clearly, he was working on me. He knew the right buttons to push and he didn't miss. It really got me going because Terry could be a fairly persuasive character. Chatting to him, I wondered if it was even worth our while turning up at Stamford Bridge. He did a good number on me, but when I got to thinking about it I had a laugh to myself for almost being taken in by him. I looked at our players and I went through their probable line-up. They had one player, outside-left Peter Taylor, who might get a game for us. No disrespect to the others, but that's the way I called it. I knew we had the better side.

There was an amusing incident on our way to the ground. By a strange coincidence, our coach drew up at a set of lights right beside the bus carrying the Palace players. The usual pleasantries were exchanged between two sets of combatants who would soon be locked in battle on the field to see who would get the opportunity to contest the main prize, the FA Cup. Lawrie McMenemy told our driver to step on it, we had to get in front of our rivals. The man at the wheel, obviously a frustrated Formula 1 devotee, took our manager's order to heart and took off as soon as the lights changed to green. We nudged in front of our opponents' transport and remained in pole position all the way to the Stamford Bridge car park. All we needed was Norman Wisdom to turn up to complete the comedy moment.

Both sets of players went out about 1.45pm to have a walk around the playing surface just to check out conditions. Normally, it is quiet at that time, but it was fairly noisy on this occasion with a few thousand fans turning up early to get a good vantage point for an all-important semi-final for both clubs. Malcolm Allison was a larger-than-life character and in a strange way he actually took the pressure off Southampton with all his appearances on TV and the newspapers as he rattled out predictions with machine-gun speed.

It was around this time, Big Mal, one of football's most colourful characters, invited soft porn actress Fiona Richmond to join him and his players for a training session. As you could guess, the topless model ended up in the bath with the manager and his bug-eyed footballers. A News of the World photographer just happened to be on hand to take the snaps and they duly appeared plastered all over the Sunday tabloid. My old puritanical pal at United, Tommy Cavanagh, would probably have required an overdose of smelling salts if he had witnessed any such frolics at Old Trafford.

While the players were out going through their usual pe-match routine, the

Palace manager, fedora firmly in place, was wandering around with his right hand in the air with two fingers visible, indicating his predicted scoreline. Okay, he was a genuined showman and he brought a bit of razzmatazz to the game, but he was beginning to get on my wick. My team-mates were thinking along similar lines. Lawrie McMenemy talked to the players before the game. It was all basic stuff, but he agreed the main threat from our opponents would come from Peter Taylor. He may have been a Third Division player, but he had still been deemed good enough to make his England international debut the previous week when he came on as a substitute against Wales at Wrexham and scored a goal. The player he replaced? None other than our own Mick Channon!

Thankfully, Peter Rodrigues, a good friend and one of the most dependable full-backs in the game, kept the Palace dangerman in his pocket throughout the ninety minutes. Without Peter Taylor performing, our opponents were minus their main weapon. It gave us the opportunity to build our game and we took control, slowly and surely. The first-half passed without too much incident apart from the fact I managed to incur the wrath of referee Pat Partridge who booked me for a challenge on Phil Holder. There wasn't much in it, but I never saw the point of arguing with a match official once he has taken action. He was hardly likely to change his mind, was he?

Big Lawrie didn't go into any specific details on how to win the game during his half-time talk. Basically, he reassured us if we kept playing the way we were, then the goals would come. A crowd of 52,810 watched as the tussle developed and we were on top without the required goals to emphasise our superiority. We went seventy-four minutes without scoring and then we claimed two in five. The breakthrough strike from Paul Gilchrist came after he played a clever one-two with Ossie and decided to try his luck from twenty-five yards. It eluded their goalie. Paul Hammond, down at his right-hand post and as my team-mate later recalled: 'I just decided to have a shot. I think their keeper was probably unsighted and I remember seeing their net move, hearing the crowd and then realising it had gone in'.

Our second and clinching goal came shortly afterwards following a clattering challenge on Mick on the edge of the box and we were awarded a penalty-kick. Mick was our usual taker, but he had missed his last one and didn't fancy this one. David Peach had been given the responsibility - I would have happily taken it if I had been asked - and the defender smacked the ball right down the middle with Hammond electing to go left. Asked about how he felt just before he took the kick, Peach didn't indulge in fancy soccer jargon and answered: 'My old arse was twitching'. I doubt if you'll find that phrase in too many coaching manuals.

I hadn't realised that our player Mel Blyth had put on a small wager with Malcom Allison. Apparently, Mel was in the vicinity when Big Mal was on the pitch giving it the 2-0 signal - well, he did get the scoreline right, but chose the wrong team - and our player told the Palace gaffer there was no way his team were going to win. They struck a bet there and then. Mel said: 'I bet him his fedora against £50'. In the aftermath of the celebrations, our dressing room door opened and a fedora hat fluttered into our midst and then the door closed again. Big Mal had kept his side of the bargain.

It was a great day at Stamford Bridge and it continued on our way home. Ossie persuaded Lawrie to get the bus driver to pull in at a pub for a drink. The players scrambled out of the coach and the place was bouncing with Saints fans. It was absolutely brilliant. We stayed for about an hour and the bevvy was flowing. We eventually got home to Southampton and it all started again. I think there may have been a few sore heads among my team-mates the following day.

Mick Channon struck a slightly more serious note, though. While we were giving it yahoo, he said somewhat sombrely: 'Now we have to win the bloody thing.'

Chapter Forty

SAINTS AND WINNERS

ON the day of the FA Cup Final, the headline in the national newspaper didn't need too much explaining. It read: **I'M GUNNING FOR THE DOC**. Under the big, bold words was a photograph of Tommy Docherty and myself in happier times before I left at Manchester United.

I had done an exclusive interview with a tabloid journal and this was their take on what I had to say. All the money that came in for publicity work in the media, TV, radio or newspapers, went into a pool for the Southampton squad and backroom staff and would be divvied up after the game. Back then, the FA Cup Final was **THE** big one. It was the glamour fixture on the soccer calendar. This was the match that was beamed worldwide and the audience figures were astronomical. There was genuine glamour about the Wembley occasion and, of course, royalty attended the sporting extravaganza.

The countdown to the Wembley grand finale is exciting - and exhausting. Quite apart from people looking for tickets, everyone wants to get the inside info on what is going on, what are your thoughts, who do you fear in the opposition, who will be your team's key men, what's your best starting eleven, how will you prepare, any superstitions and so on. In the midst of all this furore you have to prepare for one of the most monumental games of your career. I had played in a Wembley Final, of course, with Sheffield Wednesday ten years earlier and had seen the trophy snatched from us by Everton after leading 2-0. So, I knew the heartache of the occasion. Now I wanted to experience the other side.

I really looked forward to the encounter and I accepted the challenge of facing old team-mates such as Stuart Pearson, Lou Macari, Sammy McIlory and Martin Buchan. I watched a lot of the countdown to Wembley on TV and I picked up a few football periodicals, as well. I read the ***SHOOT!*** magazine and noted they had contacted players from the two divisions, ten from the First and ten from the

Second to get their predictions on the outcome. I wasn't too surprised to see United were overwhelmingly tipped to succeed, eighteen to two. One of the players who fancied us was my old Leeds United pal Peter Lorimer who insisted: 'Peter Osgood, Mick Channon and Jim McCalliog have the necessary experience for the big occasions. I've a sneaking feeling Southampton are going to pull off the shock of the season.' Peter Houseman, of Oxford United, also gave us the nod, saying prophetically: 'Southampton by the odd goal'. Those Peters knew their football. Everyone else blew us out of the water. We'd show them!

The Press, of course, explore every angle of the match. Ken Montgomery was the chief sport reporter for the Sunday Mirror and he got in touch with me to see if I would be interested in chatting to him for a piece for the newspaper. He wanted an exclusive and his paper were willing to pay for it. The money went straight into the fund. Ken was one of the biggest names in Fleet Street and was a Scot who never lost his accent. Some of his own colleagues even said he should provide sub-titles when he was talking.

We met for the interview and it was clear Ken was going to major on my history with Tommy Docherty. That was fair enough. He was there to write up that angle and words such as 'grudge', 'feud' and 'revenge' littered the article. Of course, once it is actually put in print and is spread across two pages with banner headlines it can take on all sorts of sinister connotations. My old boss was probably saying something similar about myself in another journal. It all helped set the scene for the encounter the world wanted to see.

On the day of the game, the BBC, who owned the television rights at the time, had cameras everywhere. They were at the hotel showing images of the players eating breakfast, stretching our legs and having a walk around the area before returning and getting into our club suits, shirts and ties. I have to say the suits were not to most of our tastes. They were beige and had been supplied by a local boutique called Squires. We also had dark brown shirts and massive cream ties. I felt as though I was going for an audition with the Doobie Brothers for a Top of the Pops appearances instead of preparing for the FA Cup Final. BBC's Grandstand programme was always given access to the team coach and covered the journey towards the stadium live. Intrusive? Not really. For a lot of players this would be a one-off experience and the saturation coverage was all part and parcel of the big day.

A day or so before the match, Lawrie McMenemy had been chatting to me after training. He wanted any pointers about United that may help him put things together. If anyone at Southampton had a clue how Tommy Docherty set his side out it was me. I told Lawrie the defence came out very fast in an effort to catch opposing players offside. It was a simple enough tactic, but it was so effective. They didn't operate with a sweeper because they didn't need one. Martin Buchan was exceptionally quick. One of Mick Channon's greatest assets was his speed off the mark, especially over thirty yards. He could leave defenders in his slipstream when he got into his stride, but I reckoned Martin could match him stride for stride. Anything Mick got that day he would have to earn.

Naturally, a backline all rushing out at once must be in total synchronisation. There is little point of three guys following instructions and one bloke falling asleep. They had to get it right in unison or one swift pass and someone playing on the shoulder of the last defender could wreck their plans. It was something I had thought about. We had to get players coming out with their defenders or else a fast return would catch someone in an offside position. It would have to be a disciplined performance from everyone when we were pressing forward or moves would continually break down, which, of course, was United's strategy.

It was clear, too, there was a lot of speed and skill on the flanks with Steve Coppell and Gordon Hill two very exciting newcomers who were earning rave reviews. So, we would have to cope with their menace and in Peter Rodrigues and David Peach we believed we had the full-backs to cope. We were also aware they would come out the blocks at a fair toot, so the first twenty minutes or so would be absolutely crucial. But we didn't want to spend too much time highlighting the strengths of our opponents, we could look at ourselves and see we had good players. Ossie and Mick could always provide something a bit off the cuff if the boys at the back and in midfield were doing their jobs properly. In my mind, I knew we would get two or three opportunities. The trick was to take at least one of them, especially if that was going to be the deciding strike. Games like this are often won on fine margins. I found that out at the same venue ten years earlier.

We settled well and my big pal Jim Steele was having the game of his life in central defence. One of the London newspapers had said he and Mel Blyth were weaknesses in the side and would be ruthlessly exploited by United. Big Jim didn't need any more motivation than that. Our keeper Ian Turner had a ten-minute or so spell when he was blocking shots with every part of his body including his head. There were little moments of anxiety when he thwarted attempts by Steve Coppell, Stuart Pearson, Sammy McIlroy and Gordon Hill. That might make it look like we were under siege, but it didn't feel like that at the time.

Just after the half-hour mark, we should have opened the scoring. It was the type of opening I knew we could fashion against a backline eager to rush out. I was about midway in our own half when I screamed for Peter Rodrigues - or Pedro as he was known to his team-mates - for the ball. He passed it in front of me, I took a touch, looked up and rifled a forty-yard pass towards Mick. I had spotted Martin Buchan had drifted off him and an accurate pass would catch him turning. I struck the pass in a manner it would hit the turf and either sit up or spin back a little. Mick wouldn't have to hare after it.

The ball dropped exactly where I intended and I hoped Mick would do the rest. Unfortunately, the fans' favourite rushed his shot and it smacked off keeper Alex Stepney's legs and bounced away to safety. Some people have said Mick should have attempted a lob, but he didn't have to try anything too fancy. The ball was there to be hit and, on this occasion, his finishing and accuracy let him down. It should have been a goal, I will never be convinced otherwise.

It was scoreless at the interval and Big Lawrie said all the things expected of him. I think we had taken confidence from the way we had performed, it certainly didn't look like two teams from different divisions in competition. United, of course, were a dangerous team and I knew that The Doc in the dressing room next door would be exhorting a little more effort from his players, he would be demanding more on the wings from Coppell and Hill and he would have been insisting to my old buddy Stuart 'Pancho' Pearson to let Jim Steele know he was in a game.

There was another bout of sparring going into the second-half and, increasingly, I reckoned one goal was going to settle the issue. It was that sort of game. We were nullifying them and they were doing exactly the same to us. Neither keeper, the Saints' Ian Turner and United's Stepney, were being brought into action too much. Having said that, we rode our luck on the hour mark when we failed to clear a corner-kick and Sammy McIlroy sneaked in at the far post. He strained his neck muscles to get his head to the ball and he managed to divert an effort towards goal. Turner was at the near post while Rodrigues was guarding the other upright. The ball looped over his head, struck the junction of bar and post and, thankfully, was scrambled to safety.

We had to capitalise on that good luck. Dame Fortune had smiled on us and we had to make the most of it. With just seven minutes to play, I seized that opportunity. Mick knocked a pass to me and I could see Bobby Stokes in a great position on the left and already in motion. I anticipated United coming out in a line and I just lifted a pass first time to my team-mate. Bobby's timing was perfection. He was never offside and he didn't waste any time when the ball dropped at his left foot. Bobby hit his shot very quickly and that didn't give Stepney a chance to set himself. The keeper may even have thought our player might have carried the ball forward for a clearer view.

Bobby, though, knew precisely what he was doing when he placed the shot. The keeper may have looked a little slow in diving for the ball as it went across him, but to be fair to my former colleague he really did not get a chance to move his feet. The swiftness of the shot had taken him unawares. It was a sweet sight as the ball nestled in the back of the Manchester United net.

The game seemed to zoom past after that. Normally, you might think seven minutes can stretch into seven hours when you are defending a single-goal advantage in a Cup Final, but it honestly did not feel like that. Not to me, anyway. Maybe I had an adrenalin rush or something like that. Either way, I felt good when referee Clive Thomas put that whistle to his lips and blew for full-time. Southampton had won the FA Cup for the first time in their history and it was an absolute pleasure to be part of that for a wonderful club with a marvellous set of fans. Chairman George Reader told me afterwards he had been terrified that I might stick two fingers up at a certain invidual on the United bench right in front of the Royal Box, but that was never going to happen.

The players danced and hugged and I wanted to savour the atmosphere. The pain of losing with Sheffield Wednesday a decade earlier wasn't wiped away, but this was a fairly acceptable compensation. It was then I noticed Tommy Docherty striding in my direction. He didn't have to acknowledge my presence, I wouldn't have thought any less of my old boss if he had walked straight to the United dressing room with the rest of his team. He must have been utterly disappointed, probably devastated, but he did well to keep his emotions in check. That's when he offered his hand and I took it without hesitation. 'Well done, Jim,' he said. 'Well played.'

I looked at him and answered: 'Thanks.' It was a few days afterwards when I was kicking things around in my mind that I realised that was the exact same word I had used when Tommy Docherty had told me I wasn't wanted at Manchester United.

Chapter Forty-One

THE THREE AMIGOS

MICK CHANNON jumped to his feet in front of his team-mates in the dressing room and exclaimed loudly: 'That's the biggest load of shite I've ever heard.'

You may be surprised to learn that the man on the receiving end of the less-than-complimentary remark was Lawrie McMenemy, the Southampton manager. Our boss had been chatting about how he thought we should approach a forthcoming fixture. He was midway through his speech when he was fairly rudely interrupted by the experienced England international player, one of his key performers in his side.

As soon as Mick had made his feelings known in a fairly emphatic manner, the place went quiet. I wondered how Big Lawrie would react. Let's face it, I had worked with a couple of team managers who may have forcibly responded in such a manner that my playing partner may have been having his lunch later that day through a straw. The least he could have expected would be the loosening of a molar or two. Everyone looked in the direction of Lawrie. He was a big lad and could have gone up like Vesuvius. Instead, he merely said: 'Oh, of course, Mick, you know everything. Now sit down and listen and, if you don't mind, I'll carry on talking.'

Lawrie must have been blessed with the temperament of a Saint, no pun intended. Others may have taken Mick warmly by the throat and given him a good throttling. I'm all for freedom of speech and it's only fair a player should have his say, but you can't do it in that fashion. I don't know about Lawrie, but I was embarrassed. For a start, it shows a complete disregard for the manager. He is the guy who is supposed to be in charge, whether you agree with his tactics or anything else he says, for that matter. There are ways and means of getting your point across and I don't think it is right and proper to do it in a manner that belittles another individual. A manager must have the respect of his players. If not, he is doomed.

I had been told Mick could be a disruptive influence in the dressing room before I joined. Look, there cannot be one rule for a particular individual and another one for everyone else. The clue is in the word team. I can recall a story I heard about Celtic's legendary gaffer Jock Stein and Jimmy Johnstone, who was the side's star player at the height of the club's fame in the sixties, the era in which they became the first British club to conquer Europe when they beat Inter Milan 2-1 in Lisbon on May 25 1967. That was a phenomenal achievement and broke the barrier for other UK teams to follow, notably Manchester United the following year when they overcame Benfica 4-1 in extra-time at Wembley.

However, there was a flashpoint incident during a game at Celtic Park when Big Jock thought he would freshen up the side and take off Johnstone, known to everyone as 'Jinky', a mesmerising wee winger who was one of the best in the world in his hey day. As the manager prepared to put on a substitute, Wee Jinky, who clearly did not agree with his boss' decision, threw his jersey in Big Jock's direction as he headed up the tunnel. Not the smartest thing the little guy ever did, especially with thousands of spectators looking on. Big Jock, who walked with a limp which was a legacy of the ankle injury that ended his playing days, took off as quickly as he could in pursuit of his player.

Tommy Gemmell, my Scotland international team-mate, told the story of Wee Jinky locking himself in the dressing room as Big Jock arrived and pounded on the door. The folly of his actions had dawned on the fans' favourite. The furious manager demanded that his player open the door and Jinky pleaded: 'I'll come out if you promise not to hit me!' The way Tommy told it, the manager actually burst out laughing and made his way back to the dug-out. Jinky only came out when he was certain the coast was clear. He told Tommy he was prepared to run right out of the stadium that afternoon and flee for his safety in the streets of Glasgow if he hadn't been able to find sanctuary in the dressing room. That conjures up an interesting picture, doesn't it?

So, Mick was a lucky chap he was giving his backchat that day to Lawrie and not Big Jock who, as everyone knew, was a no-nonsense former miner who dug for coal for a living before he made the grade as a rugged centre-half. I don't know if Mick was ever punished with a fine for his indiscretion, but he was certainly never dropped. Lawrie gave us the impression he would have put Mick in the team with a broken leg. Maybe a slight exaggeration. but you get the drift.

Peter Osgood was a bit of a favourite, too, with the manager. Probably not surprising because Lawrie had parted with a club record fee of £275,000 for him in March 1974 when the player was twenty-seven years of age and, realistically, represented no sell-on value. It may even have been seen as a bit of a gamble with Os clearly on his way out of Chelsea after reported friction between him and manager Dave Sexton. There was only going to be one winner in that confrontation and it was inevitable Os would leave his beloved Stamford Bridge.

I had a lot of time for Os. He was a supremely-gifted individual whose skill on the ball was fairly breathtaking and he had displayed his attributes all those years earlier when I first met him in London. His lifestyle was regularly mentioned when people queried why such a talented performer won only four caps for his country. There could be a few reasons for that. One being that it was fairly obvious Sir Alf Ramsey, the international manager for most of Os' prime-time career, was not too keen on flair players. He preferred performers who faithfully stuck to his rigid 4-4-2 system and he would have found it difficult to find a place for a player with the maverick attitude of my team-mate. Same goes for other free spirits who were around at the time such as Os' ex-Chelsea colleague Alan Hudson, Manchester City's Rodney Marsh, Sheffield United's Tony Currie and Queens Park Rangers' Stan Bowles.

If Os enjoyed a wild way of life away from the football pitch, I was certainly never invited to join in. We did spend time with each other off the field and, as I say, I liked his company. He had a dry sense of humour. Os used to travel by rail from London to Southampton every day for training and he would often be joined by Mel Blyth. Our central defender was said to be a bit of a skinflint. All I would say is that there was every chance he still had his first wage packet intact. Os used to buy a newspaper for the journey and Mel asked to borrow it when he had finished. This went on for a few months with the routine being played out in a carriage every weekday. Os clocked that Mel never had any intention of buying reading material for himself to help while away the journey. So, Os would read the paper from cover to cover and then restart until they reached their destination. Then he would hand it to Mel and say: 'Oh, have you been waiting for this? Well, you can pay for it for once.'

I was involved with Os and Jim Steele as part of what became known as 'The Hayling Three' that cast doubt in some minds if we would be selected for the FA Cup Final against Manchester United. There was a bit of a local furore about the fact three of Southampton's team over-celebrated the semi-final victory over Crystal Palace. After our 2-0 triumph at Stamford Bridge, we were due to play Portsmouth at Fratton Park three days later. Our local rivals were toiling at the foot of the table and another loss would see them playing their football in Division Three the following season.

Naturally, the players enjoyed ourselves on the Sunday - our day off - and it was business as usual on Monday when we turned up for training. Lawrie told the players to make their own way to Hayling Island, where the team was staying before the short trip the next day. We were told there was an 11pm curfew and he expected us all to be in place and good to go for the following day. As he imparted this information upon his squad, the sound of something like a cow mooing softly could be heard among the players, obviously just outwith the manager's hearing. The fairly awful mimicking of a farmland animal normally signalled a visit to a pub called The Cowherds. For the uninitiated, it was a pub situated at the other end of Northlands Road from The Dell.

Os, Jim and I were among quite a few Southampton players who frequented the establishment some evenings. To be fair, we were still on a high after winning through to Wembley. We had not been serious contenders for promotion for long enough and had been knocked out of the League Cup in the opening round, beaten 1-0 at home by Bristol Rovers in September. Now we were preparing to bring the campaign to a conclusion by playing in the silverware showdown in the most prestigious Cup competition of the lot. Could anyone really blame us for letting our hair down a little? As the evening wore on, a few of our team-mates drifted off in the direction of the team HQ.

Suddenly, before we knew it, it was getting close to curfew time and we ordered a taxi to take us to Hayling Island. Let me state here for the record, none of us, Os, Jim or myself were drunk. Sure, we had sunk a few, but we were perfectly okay without ever having the remote chance of passing a breathalyser test. The cab duly showed up at the pub and we piled into it. Jim was first out as he headed for the hotel entrance. The taxi driver was paid and Os and I prepared to follow Jim. I think we missed the curfew by about ten minutes, nothing too drastic. Or so you might have thought.

There was no sight of Lawrie, but he had left one of his coaches, a chap by the name of George Horsfall, on sentry duty. He must have been doing a head count of the players arriving. We made our way towards the steps and we saw Jim talking to George. Our team-mate walked back in our direction. 'Lawrie has left a message that we can just go home,' he said. Jim wasn't smiling, nor was George. We looked at each other. 'No room at the inn,' said someone. There was little point in debating the matter. Lawrie might have made certain he was there to deliver the news in person if he thought it was that important. We weren't welcome. We ordered a taxi and went elsewhere.

Of course, once the press get a hold of these things they can grow arms and legs. I've always got on well with the media and you understand what sells newspapers. It will shift a few more copies if you can conjure a story that goes along the lines of **'WEMBLEY AXE FOR THREE CURFEW CULPRITS?'** or something of that ilk. Your circulation will not be enhanced with **'THREE GET RAP ACROSS KNUCKLES'** emblazoned on the back page. These tales also get the fans talking and, as we all know, everyone has an opinion. It can get out of hand as something is blown way out of proportion.

Hands up, we were late, but we are not even talking about half-an-hour. We were fined and we took our punishment. Let's move on, we hoped. Football, alas, doesn't work like that. There's always got to be that little bit extra and, on this occasion, it was the three of us being dropped for the match at Portsmouth. It was a non-event, as far as Southampton were concerned, but it was crucial for our neighbours. Would Lawrie have left us out if it had been a meaningful game for us? What if it had been a match where a win was a must as far as promotion was concerned? You can make up your own mind, but one guy who was not one bit perturbed as far as Wembley was concerned was Os. 'We'll be playing against United,' he said with a firmness. Afterwards, he was quoted: 'I wasn't worried about my place. We had stepped out of line and we were correctly punished, but I knew we would get in.' And, of course, he had been proved quite correct.

The three 'curfew-breakers', as we had been labelled, were left on the sidelines at Fratton Park and Steve Williams, who went on to have a great career at Southampton and was capped six times by England, made his first appearance for the Saints in my place. A crowd of over 24,000 - almost three times their average gate - crammed into the ground in a last-ditch effort to inspire their favourites in their survival battle. Bizarrely, they booed every touch taken by Pat Earles, the youngster who had taken over from Os. It was explained afterwards that the home support mistakenly thought Pat was, in fact, Peter Osgood and they had decided to jeer his every touch. Os had no idea why he was so disliked by the Pompey support, but poor Pat got it in the neck for ninety minutes. The mood of the home support would hardly have been enhanced when Mick Channon got the only goal of the game with a last-minute shot that went in off the post.

Although Mick appeared get away with a few things, Lawrie wasn't slow to fire out fines for other players. I recall a time when the manager told the players to make their own way back to The Dell after we had been training at the Sports

Centre. Normally, we would get a coach back, but every now and again for no discernable reason, he would order us to do our own thing. On this particular day, I began jogging towards our ground which was something like two miles away and I said to Os and Jim Steele: 'See you back at The Dell'. The extra shift never bothered me because I actually enjoyed training. As I headed in the direction of my destination, I was aware there was no sign of two-thirds of 'The Three Amigos'.

I thought nothing of it until I got back to the ground, went to the dressing room to have a shower and get changed only to be greeted by my two sniggering team-mates. They were a couple of jokers and I could see they were desperate for me to ask them how on earth they got here before me. I decided to bodyswerve them. I cleaned up and I could see they were still hoping I would crack to discover their secret. Silence was golden because I could see they were bursting to tell me how I had been beaten into third place. Shortly afterwards, my two chums, who would been fortunate if they even got close to my slipstream in a foot race, were summoned to see the boss.

Slightly shame-faced, they returned to inform me they had been fined £40 each. Someone had told Lawrie the players, in their muddy tracksuits and filthy boots, had got a bus back to the ground. Jim tried to argue the case with the manager that he had instructed them 'to make their own way back', but hadn't specified they should not utilise public transport. Good try, Jim, but no cigar. The fines had to be paid.

By the way, a week after our banishment at Fratton Park, the 'curfew-breakers' were all back in the first team for a game against Charlton which we won 3-2 with a strike from myself and a double from Mick. Nineteen days later, the 'The Three Amigos' were celebrating big-style at Wembley.

Chapter Forty-Two

BIG LAWRIE AND THE WRECKING BALL

JUST eight months after enjoying FA Cup success with Southampton, I was called in by Lawrie McMenemy for 'a discussion'. Shortly after our meeting, I knew I would be leaving The Dell. It seemed such a short period from making history at the club with our unforgettable triumph over Manchester United to realising my time was up at the Hampshire outfit.

Coincidentally, it was a United legend who played a massive role in shifting me from the Saints, a chap by the name of Billy Foulkes. He had been the centre-half when the Old Trafford side won the European Cup by overcoming Benfica, Eusebio and all, at Wembley in 1968. His travels in football had taken him to America and he was now the head coach at Chicago Sting.

Lawrie didn't waste time as he cut to the chase. 'Billy Foulkes has been on and has asked for permission to speak to you,' he said. 'Are you interested?'

My immediate reaction was: 'Yes.' It wasn't a complete surprise. The boss had signed Alan Ball in December 1976 from Arsenal for £60,000 just as he was winding down his career at the London club. He was thirty-one years of age, but Lawrie clearly believed there was mileage left in those legs that helped England win the World Cup a decade earlier. I liked Bally, but I realised my first-team appearances could be marginalised with his introduction. For a start, Bally required players around him who could do his running, a youngster such as Steve Williams. That would leave me out of the equation.

I had had a word with Lawrie about the situation. I had celebrated my thirtieth birthday three months earlier in September and I had no intention of playing as back-up to anyone. Eight months earlier, I had been good enough to set up the FA Cup winner for Bobby Stokes and I wasn't quite ready to be stuck in football's twilight zone. There were no tantrums, I hasten to add. When I spoke to Lawrie about the position I was quite calm. So, when I got the call a month after Wee

Bally's arrival, I was not left rocking on my heels as I had been at United by Tommy Docherty.

One aspect that helped me make up my mind fairly swiftly was the fact I knew Billy Foulkes, who had been the reserve team coach during my eleven months at United. It was arranged that Billy would phone me at home that evening and he duly did. We had a good, old natter and I was impressed when he told me of his plans for Chicago Sting. He informed me my best pal Willie Morgan would be joining and Billy Jennings, who won an FA Cup medal with West Ham in 1975, was also heading over on a three-month loan to see how things progressed. Bill pressed all the right buttons in that phone call. I asked for time to think things over, but I was fairly certain I was ready to join the Great American Adventure that had attracted some of the world's greats such as Pele, Johan Cruyff, Franz Beckenbauer and, of course, George Best.

I played my last game for Southampton in a drab 2-0 home loss to Millwall on January 15 1977. Alan Ball and I were in midfield, but I was replaced by Bobby Stokes after the interval and as I came off the pitch that miserable afternoon in front of a crowd of just over 20,000 I had a feeling my Saints career was coming to a halt. I was one of seven FA Cup winners to leave the club that year and another, Paul Gilchrist, had already moved in September the previous year when he joined Portsmouth.

People have often asked if Lawrie McMenemy broke up his Wembley conquerors far too quickly. Broke up? I think Lawrie took a wrecking ball to that line-up. He reasoned he needed to change things because we were not winning enough games. Lawrie had enjoyed the taste of success and he wanted more in the shape of a promotion back to the top division. He didn't have to work too hard to convince his squad of players, I can tell you that. To a man, we were all eager to play in the First Division and that was our main target, too. We kicked off the season in the annual Charity Shield encounter with the champions, Liverpool, and, on a swelteringly hot August 14 afternoon in London in front of 76,500 fans, we played well enough, but conceded five minutes after the interval when Kevin Keegan nodded the ball down for John Toshack to volley in the only goal of a tight encounter.

Despite the narrow defeat to the best team in the country, we went into the league campaign full of confidence. It didn't quite go according to plan. We couldn't manage a single win in the opening seven league fixtures, losing four and drawing three. Worse still, we were humiliated at The Valley when we were turned over 6-2 by Charlton. We were 4-1 down at half-time and just weren't at the races. That line-up included six FA Cup winners, including myself, while new signing Ted MacDougall, who had arrived in a £50,000 deal from Norwich City, scored one of our consolation goals. It was a double whammy for us because we had been knocked out of the League Cup at the same venue on July 9 when we went down 2-1 in a replay following a 1-1 stalemate.

It was back to the drawing board for Big Lawrie. Possibly there was a bit of a knee-jerk reaction to how the results were falling. You cannot argue with the sequence of scorelines that saw the team on the backfoot in the promotion race so early into the campaign - and would ultimately see them spend another season in the second tier - but it can also be said that our collection of individuals had not all become bad players in an equally short space of time. Football is a results-driven business and everyone has to stand up and be counted - and that includes the manager. His answer to a team struggling for form was to have a fairly drastic clear-out. Just take a quick look at the exodus.

After my departure, FA Cup matchwinner Bobby Stokes and my fellow-Scots Hugh Fisher and Jim Steele were next out the door in March. Wee Bobby was expendable after the arrival of MacDougall and was another who made the short trip to Portsmouth. Hugh switched to Southport as player/manager while my old sparring partner Jim, one third of 'The Hayling Three', joined Rangers after a loan spell. Sadly, skipper Peter Rodrigues, at the age of thirty-three, was forced to quit the game when he could not overcome a persistent knee injury. Mel Blyth had a spell on loan with Crystal Palace before switching to Millwall.

Inevitably, Mick Channon and Peter Osgood left before the year was out. Mick moved to Manchester City for £300,000 in July, but was back two years later after scoring only 12 goals in his first season and 11 in his second. In November, Os had a three-game stint on loan at Norwich City before heading to The States for a season with Philadelphia Fury. He rejoined his first love Chelsea in December 1978 and retired a year later. Goalkeeper Ian Turner had loan stints at Newport and Lincoln City before joining Walsall in January 1978, David Peach moved to Swindon Town in February 1980 and last man standing was local lad Nick Holmes who completed his entire fifteen-year senior career at the club in February 1987 at the age of thirty-three.

European football had been a bit of a diversion for Southampton when we took our place in the Cup-Winners Cup. It was only the third time in the club's history they had played in European competition, following a stint in the now-defunct Inter-Cities Fairs Cup where they reached the third round in 1969/70 and their appearance in the UEFA Cup a year later which was cut short at the first hurdle when they lost 3-2 on aggregate to Athletic Bilbao. So, it was a treat for the Saints supporters to prepare for the glamour of Europe and I was delighted for them. When I arrived, they were quite quiet and reserved. However, our win at Wembley over United helped them find their voice and that carried on in the Charity Shield against Liverpool.

A double from Mick Channon and a single from Peter Osgood helped the team to a 4-0 win over Marseille in the first leg at The Dell in front of over 17,000 followers who thoroughly enjoyed the occasion. We lost 2-1 in France and were drawn against County Antrim club Carrick Rangers in the second round. We played the first game away from home and it was a bit of a stroll as we won 5-2 and I chipped in with a goal. Mick claimed another two with Os and Bobby Stokes adding to the scoreline. We took care of business at our place with a 4-1 victory to go through on a fairly convincing 9-3 aggregate. By the time Southampton met Anderlcht in the quarter-final of the tournament I was no longer at the club. I was disappointed when I saw they had lost 2-0 to Anderlecht in the first leg in Brussels and, despite winning 2-1 at home, went out 3-2 to a very good Belgian club who went all the way to the Final before going down 2-0 to SV Hamburg.

I enjoyed my time at the Hampshire club and I went to see Lawrie before I finally said my goodbyes to my team-mates. I wished them all the very best for the future and I really meant it. It had been quite an experience. I will never forget the scenes when we paraded the FA Cup in front of the fans. What a marvellous memory. It was great to see those supporters lining the streets to applaud us for our efforts. Naturally, the Cup triumph was as much for them as it was for us. We have had a few reunions since that afternoon at Wembley in 1976 and it is so sad that neither goalscorer Bobby Stokes nor my big mate Peter Osgood is still here to join in. Their part in that momentous day for Southampton will never be forgotten.

As you will no doubt have gathered by now, Os was a bit of a favourite, a genuine charismatic character. The two main men at Southampton in my time were Os and Mick Channon. Lawrie McMenemy gave them both their place as experienced pros and listened to them when they spoke - maybe on occasions when he should have told at least one them to belt up and listen. If the players wanted to get a message to the manager, we went through Mick and Os. Basically, that was a silly situation and Lawrie should have been there for everyone. I think that helps harmony in the dressing room and prevents a them-and-us situation.

Both of the players had exceptional strengths, but it may surprise you when I say they were part of the Southampton problem while we struggled for consistency in the league. I am convinced the FA Cup win, as welcome and wonderful as it was, papered over a few cracks. Maybe some of the supporters might even have opted for the Wembley win over promotion that season. Possibly they would have wanted their moment in the sun and would have been prepared to wait before their favourites took their place again in the top flight. Who knows?

I don't think Os and Mick could play in the same team. Genuinely, I never thought their styles were compatible. They clashed and did not complement each other. It was Lawrie who put them together, so he must have thought they could dovetail, but I rarely saw evidence of this. You might find it strange when I say one of their biggest assets was their football intelligence, they knew their way about a football field and were good team men. But, to my mind, their styles just didn't seem to gel. It was the same with myself and Alan Ball. We only played in the same team a few times, but I think if we had both been honest we would have held up our hands up and admitted we were too similar and, on the rare occasions we were playing beside each other, it looked like two men doing the work of one. That was never going to work.

I've lost count of the amount of times Chelsea and Southampton fans have asked me to choose between Mick and Os. Who would have been my preference to play alongside? Well, I am in the privileged position of having played with and against two very talented players, a couple of lavishly-gifted professionals. Mick was always on the go as he looked to utilise his pace at every opportunity. His record tells you he could score goals, 157 strikes in 391 league games is good going. And, of course, the fans loved him. He made his first-team debut at the age of sixteen, gave the club thirteen years service before his move to Manchester City and then he returned two years later. Is it any wonder he is still such a revered name around the club?

While Mick liked to hare around, Os was a bit, shall we say, more relaxed? He let the ball do the work most of the time, but he was a wondrous sight when he got into his stride. He was well-built and powerful with fabulous poise and balance. His timing in the air was just about impeccable. Okay, he was tall, but that doesn't necessarily mean you will be good in the air. It's all about knowing when to make that run and when to take off. Look at Denis Law, for instance. The Lawman was no skyscraper, but he was one of the best headers of a ball I have ever seen. He could spring with incredible agility and seemed to be able to hover in the air above defenders while the ball was in motion. He could snap his neck muscles at the precise moment of impact and on these occasions goalkeepers had that sinking feeling that their next move would be to fish the ball out of the back of their net.

Both Mick and Os knew how to look after themselves, too. That was important. I was acquainted with a lot of footballers who possessed an abundance of skill who just did not want to know when the boots started flying around. If a defender got the opportunity to smell fear, his opponent might as well have packed up and gone home. People talk about the attributes of Mick and Os and often overlook the basic one of bravery. They were never intimidated. So, two good professionals anyone would be delighted to have in their team. That's why I am still puzzled to this day that they did not spark together as I would have expected.

Basically, to answer the question, I cannot separate two players with God-given skills. I would rather discuss their special qualities and the ability they possessed to share joyous moments to fans wherever football is played. Southampton and Chelsea followers were fortunate to see these guys at the peak of their considerable powers. They brought a lot of happiness to so many supporters. And a few of their team-mates, as well.

For my part, I will never forget the presence of Mick and Os in the Wembley dressing room as we prepared to go out and face the favourites of Manchester United. 'We're here to win the FA Cup,' said Mick Channon. 'We'll prove we're good enough to lift this trophy, mark my words,' added Peter Osgood. And both played massive roles on a historic day for Southampton.

I would like to think I made a small contribution, too. It was superb to be afforded the occasion to say thank you to Southampton followers for making my stay at the club so pleasurable. But, as the great man said, all good things must come to an end.

Chapter Forty-Three

WINNERS ARE REVERED – HISTORY MAKERS

I ADMIT to feeling aggrieved and insulted when I read Lawrie McMenemy's words in a recent book, 'A Lifetime's Obsession', when he stated 'coming second was the biggest moment in my football career' when he reflected on Southampton's runners-up place to Liverpool in the First Division in 1984.

I could hardly believe my eyes when I looked at that quote. I checked it out a couple of times to make sure I had not misread it. Nope, there it was in black and white and it was my old manager's take on the completion of season 1983/84. Biggest moment? What about the little matter of actually winning the FA Cup eight years earlier? That set of players had silverware to show for their efforts throughout an arduous campaign. It gave the Southampton public something to cheer for the first time in decades, a Wembley triumph that will live forever in their memory banks, something to pass onto their grandchildren.

Those words from McMenemy hurt. I am not being overly sensitive, I simply believed winning the FA Cup in 1976, beating a much-fancied Manchester United from a league above us, was extra special. So, for the manager to dismiss that feat in such a manner certainly riled me. Okay, I understand where my former gaffer was coming from. It is most certainly a highly laudable achievement for a club such as Southampton to come close to being hailed as the best in the country.

So, for a team that had returned to the top flight in 1978, there was a lot to applaud. But I make no apologies for insisting nobody remembers who came second. The league programme is a marathon and the best team should win the championship. Liverpool, rightly, were acclaimed for their endeavours, especially when they went all the way in Europe, too. That's what the rest of the world will remember, not the fact Southampton were second. But if you want to talk about the FA Cup in 1976, there's only one name that matters and that is Southampton.

Back then, the FA Cup was the most glamorous and prestigious knock-out competition in the world. It had a global audience of goodness only knows how many millions. English football was the envy of so many other countries with the pomp and ceremony of the big day at Wembley. It has been devalued today, unfortunately. Businessmen look at the financial aspects and there is more to be earned in the league. Foreign managers will often rest some of their key players when the Cup games come around. That's a shame.

I am still so proud to be one of twelve Southampton players, the starting eleven plus substitute Hugh Fisher, to possess an FA Cup winner's medal. I am also so honoured to have played in all eight games in the historic success, scoring three goals and setting up the famous winner for Bobby Stokes. I have nothing but happy recollections of that run all the way to Wembley and sharing such joyous moments with the people of the city in the glorious aftermath where we were all involved in one wonderful massive celebration.

I have never mentioned Lawrie McMenemy's declaration to any of my team-mates who played that afternoon. They may see it differently from me. However, I don't think there were any street parties in Hampshire in the summer of 1984 as an accolade to a team that came second.

Chapter Forty-Four

PELE AND THE CHICAGO CONFRONTATION

A BRIGHT and warm Wednesday afternoon in New York on May 22 1977 will live with me forever. It's not easy to forget being chased around the pitch by the world's greatest footballer.

I was playing in opposition to Pele as my club took on the superstar-laden New York Cosmos in a North American Soccer League fixture at The Giants' Stadium. It was the perfect setting for a football match and a fair-sized crowd turned out to see the team that could boast the Brazilian genius, his fellow World Cup-winning compatriot Carlos Alberto and much-vaunted Italian striker Giorgio Chinaglia and, if that was not enough, West Germany legend Franz Beckenbauer was due to arrive in a couple of months' time. They were probably backed to become football's answer to the famed basketball team, the Harlem Globetrotters. If I hadn't been playing that afternoon, I would have paid the admission to see that lot.

Growing up in the Gorbals in Glasgow, I was first made aware of the name Pele when he played for the South Americans in the 1958 World Cup Finals in Sweden and actually scored two goals as a seventeen-year-old unknown - in Europe, at least - in the 5-2 triumph over the hosts to lift the glittering prize in Stockholm. Everyone knew the name Pele and kids in the playground all wanted to be called after the great Brazilian. And, yes, that included yours truly.

They say you should never meet your heroes for fear of being disappointed. You could say I had the fear of being booted over the stand when I met one of mine! Okay, it wasn't quite as extreme as that, but, clearly, Pele and I would never be Christmas card buddies after our altercation when he was thirty-six years old and earning a King's Ransom with the Big Apple outfit as part of the vanguard of big-name players to get football - or 'soccer', as it was known to our American cousins - off the ground and into the awareness of sports fans in the country.

George Best, I believe, had been the number one target for the Cosmos. Let's face it, Bestie was a football promoter's dream. He had the good looks, the Irish charm, the girls loved him and they would have added considerably to attendances up and down the country just to get a glimpse of the Manchester United idol. He had been dubbed the Fifth Beatle as he swapped back pages for front pages and his magnetism was obvious. Bestie was only thirty when he signed for Los Angeles Aztecs in 1976 and was a massive draw at the gate. He had a season in California before joining Fulham in 1977 and then returning to LA later that year. There is no doubt he had everything the Cosmos franchise cried out for, but he opted for the Aztecs and, later on, had spells at Fort Lauderdale Strikers and San Jose Earthquakes. I suppose, though, Pele wasn't a bad second choice!

Okay, what had I done to annoy the Great Man? Let me rephrase that - what had the Great Man done to annoy me? The game was moving along at a brisk pace and the supporters seemed to be enjoying what was on show. It was obvious Pele had shed none of his God-given talents. He skimmed across the Astroturf playing surface, controlling and passing the ball with ease as he gracefully twisted and turned this way and that to drive opponents to distraction. An imaginative writer with a penchant for a flowery phrase called it 'poetry in football boots'.

It was clear he took his role seriously as an ambassador for 'the beautiful game'. He wasn't there to top up his pension. Admittedly, a lot of players from Europe were brought to The States to participate in 'The Great American Dream' who were past their sell-by date - hopefully, not myself - and were there for a fast buck. Pele saw it as his duty to make the spectacle as entertaining as possible against us as he elegantly swept his way across the pitch in the iconic Cosmos strip.

But, it was equally evident, Pele had not lost the desire to be a winner. He and his team-mates had arrived at our place looking for a victory. He was streetwise, that's for sure. He had acquired talents for survival following a couple of decades of playing at the top for Brazil and Santos. He knew when to lean in to players and knock them off balance, he could utilise his excellent upperbody strength as well as anyone I have ever seen. And if you won the ball off him, you had to earn that right. Pele surrendered possession lightly to no-one.

We had been getting up close and personal on a few occasions as he worked his way through his repertoire. I thought of stopping and applauding every now and again, but I didn't think that would go down too well with boss Bill Foulkes or my team-mates. As much as I admired my adversary, I didn't appreciate a bit of sneaky gamesmanship when he tried to nick a goal. As I recall, it was goalless at the time and our keeper Mervyn Cawston, all the way from Norwich, came off his line to gather the ball in his penalty area. With everyone retreating back upfield to get into position before his anticipated clearance, I noted Pele had hung around. I didn't think he was waiting for Mervyn's autograph,

As the netminder explored his options before firing the ball down the field, Pele, with incredible speed and uncanny reflexes, flicked out his boot and knocked the ball up and out of Mervyn's hands. Our bewildered shotsopper stood there open-mouthed as Pele completed the cheeky manoeuvre by heading the ball into the empty net. He threw his hands in the air and shouted: 'Goal!'. I wasn't having any of that. I thought he had put in a high boot with his studs showing and it was clearly a foul. I attracted the referee to the flashpoint incident and, thankfully, he agreed with me and immediately chalked off the goal.

Pele was not happy. This was a guy who had scored over 1,000 goals for his club side and had claimed crucial efforts in two World Cup Finals, but he was fuming that he had been denied on this occasion. He glowered at me. I don't suppose I helped my case by telling the match official he should book the offender for dangerous play or, at least, ungentlemanly conduct. Listen, the amount of dollars in the franchise sponsoring the Cosmos, Pele could have gone on the field with an Uzi machine gun and he wouldn't have been sent off. The fans paid big bucks to watch the Brazilian and there would have been a riot if they didn't get their money's worth. We won the game 2-1. It had been an interesting ninety minutes.

Funnily enough, I had first witnessed Pele in the flesh back on a cold Monday evening in October 1962 when I was just sixteen. It was during my spell at Leeds United and innovative manager Don Revie took a squad of young boys, Billy Bremner and Peter Lorimer were among the lucky travelling party, to Hillsborough to watch Santos in a glamour friendly against Sheffield Wednesday. Pele's side were the South American club champions at the time and I recall a crowd of some 50,000 cramming into the ground to get a glimpse of the extraordinary footballer who had captured the world's imagination four years earlier in Sweden.

The visitors won 4-2 and Pele thumped in a penalty-kick. Amazingly, thousands of the home fans cheered his goal. Playing for Wednesday on that occasion were goalkeeper Ron Springett, skipper and defender Don Megson and midfielder Peter Eustace who all became team-mates and great personal friends when I joined the Yorkshire club three years later. I thoroughly enjoyed the education of studying Pele, but I could never have realised he would be paying close attention to me one day!

I had another meeting with Pele and the New York Cosmos at Soldier Field in Chicago. I was eager to get out there and square up to my hero. Before the game, the players of both teams were introduced individually and that meant you would go out, take a bow and then join your colleagues. Well, that's what we all did with the exception of just one man. Yes, you've guessed, The Great Man himself, Pele.

His name was blasted over the stadium tannoys, samba music blared out and the Brazilian took off on a lap of honour round the trackside, smiling and waving at the cheering supporters. Meanwhile, all the other players were standing around with their arms folded wondering when we might be given the okay to get on with the actual game. As I recall, it was unseasonably cold that day, but it didn't prevent Pele from savouring the moment. It was clear he was the A-lister and we were the supporting cast. A small price to pay, I suppose, for sharing a pitch with one of my boyhood idols. Even when I was twelve years old and marvelling at his unbelievable skills as a teenager leading Brazil to their first-ever World Cup triumph - at the time of writing, they have now lifted the trophy a record five times - and I will always remember discovering his real name, Edson Arantes do Nascimento. Thank goodness he shortened it to Pele.

Looking back, I realise I was on the same football pitch as genuine football royalty. I had a couple of moments with Pele, but the game at our place was played entirely in the right spirit. Pele was well aware he was the main attraction, but he was not a selfish showman. Pele possessed that uncanny ability to hit the ball instantly to a team-mate who couldn't possibly have been in his vision, but he would be aware of their movement and exact location. Before a pass arrived at his feet, he was ready to launch it elsewhere. It was an impossibility to anticipate his next move.

And, yet, at the end of that particular Sunday afternoon, I found myself shaking hands with Pele after an exciting encounter and, to make it even more special, I had been on the winning team. He spoke very little English, despite his previous two or three years in America. He smiled and said: 'Good play'. I reckon he had forgotten the May evening chasing me around Chicago in our previous incarnation. I replied: 'Thank you, Pele'. It was most certainly an experience sharing a moment with one of the greatest footballers who will ever grace the game.

My American odyssey didn't last too long, nineteen games and nine months in total, but it had been extremely interesting participating in an entirely new environment with so many different cultures. Bill Foulkes, the head coach who took me to The States, also brought in my good friend Willie Morgan and West Ham's Bill Jennings as he scrambled to put a squad together for a new season. The owner was a very approachable chap by the name of Lee Stern who also had the franchise for the Chicago Football (American-style) team and the local baseball outfit. You could say he was a big-hitter (no pun intended).

Bill, as I have said, worked at Manchester United while I was there and I knew he was a hard-working professional who would do his utmost to give the people of Chicago a team of which they could be proud. However, the game was very much in its infancy since Clive Toye, a one-time Fleet Street newspaperman, and Phil Woosnam, a former Welsh international who had played for West Ham, Aston Villa and Atlanta Chiefs, got together to hatch the ambitious plan to bring the game to the country. As well as Chicago Sting and the New York Cosmos, there were teams with such wonderful names as Washington Diplomats, Connecticut Bicentennials, Rochester Lancers, Dallas Tornado, Las Vegas Quicksilvers, Minnesota Kicks and Vancouver Whitecaps.

There were slogans plastered all over billboards and advertising on TV and newspapers informing us that 'Soccer Is A Kick In The Grass' and that 'Soccer Players Do It For 90 Minutes'. One piece of information which may be relevant if it is the all-important question in 'Who Wants To Be A Millionaire?' is the origin of the Chicago Sting name. 'The Sting' monicker came from the 1973 movie of the same name which was set in the city and starred Paul Newman and Robert Redford as a follow-up to their first film together, 'Butch Cassidy and the Sundance Kid', which, of course, was a massive box-office hit. Just remember where you read this snippet of info when you are rich and famous.

My introduction to my new team-mates was in Florida on April 16 when we were due to play Tampa Bay Rowdies, whose big star was Rodney Marsh. This was the sort of stage the flamboyant Englishman would have loved with all the razzmatazz and suchlike. John Boyle, my old Scottish team-mate at Chelsea, had played for them and, in fact, took over as head coach in June when Eddie Firmani quit. There were a few recognisable names from English football such as Len Glover, ex-Charlton and Leicester City left-winger, former Crystal Palace keeper Paul Hammond and Derek Smethurst, another one-time Stamford Bridge performer. Davie Robb, the former Aberdeen and Scotland striker, was also in their squad - or roster, as they preferred to call it in America.

It was quite a baptism. There were around 33,500 spectators in the arena at the kick-off and they were there to be entertained. I actually quite enjoyed it apart from one small fly in the ointment - we were turned over 4-0 with Smethurst, in particular, putting our defence to the sword with a double. Lesson learned. We played them again the following month at our place and beat them 4-3. I have to say it did take a little getting used to and it did feel like a bit of a holiday training in the sun, but I was there to play football and do my best for my new team. Bill Foulkes, who had been at the club since its formation two years earlier, had created a good team spirit and they were a great bunch of guys.

The downside was that every team in the league had to have five America-born players in the roster. Nothing against these guys on a personal level, my team-mates were super blokes who wanted to learn, but it was fairly evident they couldn't play. Football was new to them and it showed. They would have been brought up playing American Football which is an entirely different sport, of course. There's not a lot of footwork with a ball, for a start.

But, my goodness, they gave the game their best shot and I was always impressed by their endeavours. Simply put, it's not possible to learn practically overnight how to run full-tilt with a ball at your feet. These guys were athletes and their fitness levels were quite astounding, but that meant little when an awkward little sphere refused to be brought under control. American keepers had good hands, but they thought they were playing basketball at times and that does nothing for attempting to keep the ball out of the net behind them. Some were fairly agile, but their work on angles and anticipation left some coaches pulling out what was left of their hair.

I lived about forty minutes by car from where we actually played our games, but the training ground was a little closer. Part of my deal was free accommodation and a car. I drove an American model, a Chevrolet Camaro which was something you would expect Telly Savalas to zip around Manhattan during an episode of Kojak. The apartment was first class and it was obvious the club had spared no expense in helping me settle into my surroundings and making me comfortable. I took to the city very quickly. I thought it was beautiful and there were so many leisure parks dotted all over the place where you could relax.

The beach was in the middle of the city. Believe it or not, there were bus tours to the former homes of Chicago-based Mafia gang leaders. I really had no hankering to meet a relative of Al Capone, old Scarface himself, so I avoided that 'attraction'. I had no intention of 'sleeping with the fishes'. I had seen 'The

Godfather', the first of the blockbuster trilogy, starring Marlon Brando, and that was as close as I wanted to wake up in bed with a horse's head for company.

While I was in Chicago, I took in some American football and baseball games. I am afraid they didn't quite get me on the edge of my seat. In plain language, I thought they were fairly dull and boring. However, the fans knew how to make the most of a sporting occasion. Entire families would turn up at our stadium's huge car park at nine or ten in the morning, deposit their vehicles, many of them enormous campervans, and begin to unload all the barbeque equipment. A band would be playing from about midday and the well-nourished supporters, after devouring a landslide of hot dogs and suchlike, would go to the stadium where the volume would be cranked up a notch. Then they would take their place, shout and wave at all the wrong things before returning to the car park to continue their festivities. It started to empty around ten o'clock in the evening.

That was one of the happy memories of my experience in The States, but, of course, there is always the flip side. Later in the season, we lost a few matches in succession and Bill Foulkes was removed from the head coach's position. Bill had been in at the start back in April 1975, but at the end of August 1977, he was out of a job. You can't keep a good man down, though, and a year later he returned to take charge of Tulsa Roughnecks and also had a spell at San Jose Earthquakes before calling time on his personal American experience. I can't thank Bill enough for allowing me the opportunity to experience the NASL and, of course, meet the one and only Pele.

Willy Roy, a German who had moved to Chicago with his family at the age of six, took over as head coach. He had been a record goalscorer with the club in indoor football and was knowledgeable and enthusiastic and, thankfully, we began to put some better results together. At one stage, it looked as though we would get to the league play-offs, but we lost narrowly and, basically, my stay in The States was about to come to a halt.

After a pitstop in Oslo in January 1978, I returned home and wondered what surprises lay in store. I can reliably inform you Sincil Bank in Lincoln will never be mistaken for The Giants Stadium in New York.

Chapter Forty-Five

SEVENTEEN YEARS AS A PRO COME TO AN END

IN the back of my head I can hear the words of my headmaster from Holyrood Senior Secondary, Mr McKie, as I set out on my football career: 'What if you break your leg?' He also informed me the life span of a footballer was four and a half years. My answer to the headmaster was: 'If I get injured, I can always pick up on college or university later on. But to be a top player, I have to start as early as possible.'

Tommy Docherty must have been suffering from Jim McCalliog withdrawal symptoms. After signing me for Chelsea and Manchester United, my old gaffer was going for the hat-trick at Derby County. I must admit I was flattered.

I had returned to my home in England after a two-game stop in Oslo at FK Lyn following a season with Chicago Sting in the North American Soccer League. I was coming up for my thirty-second birthday, but I didn't reckon I was quite ready to retire.

The boss had taken over at the Baseball Ground in September the previous year when he was asked to rescue a Derby team in all sorts of trouble after Dave Mackay's successor, a bloke called Colin Murphy, had been sacked following only five wins in thirty-five games. In a results-driven business, a sequence like that will undoubtedly invite a P45. My old manager had been slowly and surely getting his ideas in place and I was surprised to discover I was part of them as he prepared for season 1978/79.

He got in touch to ask me if I wanted a role as an assistant coach with the youths. I would also be registered as a player and it gave me something to ponder. I would be sharing youth team duties and I would be squad member. Derby were in the First Division and, naturally, it was tempting to link up again with one of the game's most compelling and charismatic characters. I had asked for time to think it over and The Doc agreed. At the time, I did not know if I wanted to stay in the game, I wasn't 100 per cent sure about the management side of it, either.

It was then I learned my ex-Leeds United team-mate Willie Bell, who had won a couple of Scotland international caps at left-back in 1966, wanted me to get in touch with him. He had taken over as manager of Lincoln City in the Third Division a couple of days after Christmas in 1977. He replaced another Scot, a chap by the name of George Kerr, who had lasted a mere six months in the post. He had taken over from Graham Taylor who had gone to Watford and had a ten-year career at Vicarage Road. That led to three years at Aston Villa before he got the call to become England manager in 1990 where he spent three years as the country's international supremo. Naturally, he had been a tough act to follow.

I had got on very well with Willie and his wife May who had been neighbours during my short time at Elland Road. Naturally, I got in touch with Willie and he didn't waste too much time in telling me he wanted me to join him at the club. To be honest, I didn't even know where Lincoln was! We met up for a chat to see what might transpire and Willie outlined his plans for the team which involved myself in a player/coaching role. He offered me a two-year contract and, of course, I told him of the interest from Tommy Doc who had also put together a twenty-four month deal. It's always nice to feel wanted.

I don't like to keep people dangling, so I realised I had to make up my mind quickly. I phoned The Doc to tell him about Willie's offer and that I had decided to accept it. I thanked my old boss for remembering me and I apologised if I had let him down. It was never easy to say no to Tommy Docherty. I've always been my own man and I didn't want to share responsibilities with another coach. The Doc understood and wished me all the best.

I wanted to find out about management first hand and I reckoned I would get a better opportunity of that with Willie Bell at Lincoln City. I was delighted to accept the deal and on September 21 1978 I went into the coach's dressing room for the first time. I have to admit it was a little odd. I had spent my entire career mixing with the players and getting involved in the banter and discussing all sorts of things with team-mates. This was different.

Willie was a very enthusiastic coach, had great ideas for the club and was willing to go that extra yard to bring success. I found him a refreshing chap altogether and I admired his attitude and outlook in life. He always saw the good in players and people. That was a praiseworthy trait in anyone's personality as football got more and more cut-throat. I went into my new role with my eyes wide open. I was aware there was a dividing line between being a coach and a player and the trick was to pull off a reasonable balancing act. It was essential to differentiate my playing side of things with coaching.

Sounds easy enough, doesn't it? Actually, it can be a delicate manoeuvre and you have to get it absolutely spot on or you face the threat of falling between the cracks. Look at Bobby Charlton, for instance. He had all the experience in the world after a successful seventeen-year career at Manchester United while making 106 appearances for England. He left Old Trafford for Preston North End to become manager in 1973. The following year, at the age of thirty-seven, he decided to get the boots on again to combine the roles. He lasted a year and, remember, we are talking about an individual who must have picked up a hint ot two playing under Matt Busby and Alf Ramsey, two knights of the realm recognised for services to football, but he still decided to chuck it after one season.

As a player, it is mostly about yourself as an individual whereas as a coach it is a collective and how to help other players and the team. So, obviously, there is a lot of responsibility in combining the roles and you have to get everything spot on. I looked forward to it. I could still get the kit on, get out there, get stuck in and attempt to put things right on the pitch if required instead of standing helplessly on the touchline. It was a fresh challenge and I was up for it while I wanted to see where it would take me on my football journey.

Willie Bell's idea was to get the players to actually play football, get the ball down, knock it around, keep possession and probe for openings. Sadly, the players had been schooled in an entirely different way by Graham Taylor. They were used to the long ball that could often bypass the middle of the park, lumping it from one end of the pitch to another. The ball would spend so much time in the air that it would come back to earth with snow on it. You could always spot a midfield player in this division because he was the guy with a crick in his neck watching the ball fly over his head for ninety minutes. Okay, a slight exaggeration, but you get the idea. It certainly wasn't football for the purist.

My team-mates struggled to adjust to Willie's philosophy. To be fair, the boss did not want to compromise his idea of how the game should be played. Standing around a tactics board with a piece of chalk is one thing, putting those thoughts into action is another. The players would nod and agree with the manager when he spoke to them and then cross that white line and do something else altogether. Some players can take things in and attempt to implement them during the game, but others, alas, choose to ignore or forget the instructions and information and continue to do their own thing. Old habits die hard, unfortunately. Football is an emotional game and the best plans can often go wrong. Players are human beings and not robots and just cannot be programmed.

Willie persevered, but it was obvious he was growing frustrated and, to be honest, I couldn't blame him. The manager always tried to be upbeat, but, in the confines of the coach's room, he would confide to me his frustrations in some of the players who just could not change or adapt to the system he believed would take Lincoln to a superior level and, hopefully, promotion. In these moments, it's easy to become exasperated.

However, there were some moments of laughter along the way. I recall an evening when we were playing at Brentford and we were not performing too well. We were in our away strip which was green and white stripes against the home side who were, of course, playing in their traditional red and white stripes. We had not played too well and we trooped in at half-time. The boss was waiting for us. 'What's happening out there?' he queried. 'You keep giving the ball away.' Willie looked at a young player, Glenn Cockerill, and asked: 'Are you colour blind?' There was a brief silence before Glenn answered: 'Yes, boss'. We all fell about laughing at the response and, to be fair, Willie apologised to the player. It lightened the mood for a moment, but, unfortunately, although we did play better after the turnaround, we still lost 2-1.

On the coach home, Willie fretted about the team's first-half performance. Clearly, it wasn't what he was looking for from his players. I suggested he give the squad the following day off and let them contemplate their individual contributions. It might get them dreading Friday and provoke a reaction for the game twenty-four hours later. We desperately needed points as we dropped like a stone down Division Three and you reach the stage where you will attempt anything to arrest the slide. All of this, of course, was a learning curve for me.

The following Saturday, we managed a 1-1 draw at home to Walsall. At that stage, we had won only one league game, a 2-1 home victory over Tranmere Rovers on the opening day of the campaign on August 19. Then came the depressing run of seven losses - five in succession - and one draw before we picked up that point against Walsall. On top of that, Lincoln had gone out of the League Cup at the first hurdle, 3-1 on aggregate to Bradford City. These were grim times for the club. I could see the pressure mounting on my friend and it was obvious the shadow of Graham Taylor loomed large. His mind-numbing so-called tactics of hammering the ball from one end to another had brought some sort of success - maybe that's what it took at this level where actual football would be frowned upon - and some of the players were more comfortable involved in that environment while the fans bought into it. I was in the middle, between the rock and a hard place.

A week after the draw with Walsall, we went down 2-0 at Blackpool and that was followed by a goalless clash at home to Colchester. At least there were six goals in the next game, but, alas, four were put into our net by Gillingham. On October 21, we were thumped 3-0 at our place by Swindon Town and two days later Willie was sacked. I felt so sorry for my mate, but it just wasn't working. I didn't like to see a long-time friend suffering. I gave him ten out of ten for effort and endeavour, but no matter what he attempted, the horrible sequence of results just kept stacking up. Ten losses in fourteen games with only one win brought the inevitable conclusion.

Willie didn't leave the post before wishing me well and he took the time to advise about what may happen regarding my position. Typical of my friend, he probably believed he had to take some sort of responsibility for bringing me to the club in the first place, but I reassured him I would be contacting the Professional Footballers' Association to be given guidelines. I took training that day and kept it simple. Before we went through the usual routines, I asked the secretary to book the local golf club for the following day where we could have a spot of lunch. I thought it would give me the opportunity to have an informal chat with the players to clear the air. If anyone had anything to say or get off their chest, that would be their chance. We could start with a clean slate with a game due at Southend at the weekend.

The chairman requested to see me in the boardroom. I was eager to discover where I stood in the midst of changes at the club. As anticipated, he told me it had been an extremely difficult decision to sack Willie as he was a gentleman and so well respected within the club and the community. He insisted he had no option in an effort to stave off relegation. However, the decision had been made and it was now time to look to the immediate future. The chairman asked me to take over as manager in an interim basis and also requested I apply for the postion in a full-time capacity.

I told him I would accept the responsibility as caretaker manager only if there was no outside interference and I was completely in charge. However, I also informed him I would not be applying for the job as I had never done so at any other stage in my career. He agreed with both my points and wished me well. The following day, the players came in for training and I had asked one of the backroom staff to instruct them not to bother changing into their kit. I told him I wanted a word. Deliberately, I kept them waiting until the last minute. When the bus arrived, I went into the dressing room and told them we were heading for the golf club and a spot of lunch. Their faces lit up, probably in a fair bit of relief.

My idea was to lessen the pressure on the players and take the opportunity to have a bit of team bonding at the same time. There was a little bit of psychology involved, of course, and I thought a change of scenery might put them at ease while I got my points across in a bid to save the club from the drop. It was clear time was an enemy. I had to hit the ground running and the players had to be in complete tandem. We were all in it together and I had to get that message across to them. Pronto.

On a personal level, I had to believe in myself and draw on the experience I had gathered from my games at club and country level from the many managers who had played a role, large or small, from Don Revie, as a teenage amateur, to Willie Bell, as a veteran campaigner, and everyone in between. I realised I could pick up the phone and call my many contacts for advice, but I decided against it. I determined I would sink or swim by my own decisions, I was going to do it my way. I had to change a playing system that hadn't worked and had cost a good friend his job. I had no intention of suffering the same fate.

I decided we would have to defend from the front and our strikers would have to adapt very quickly to putting in an extra shift. We did not have the luxury of players standing on the halfway line waiting for the ball to be fed forward. They had to put pressure on the opposing defenders and I didn't want to see a rival centre-half nonchalantly strolling out of defence without a care in the world. I wanted my guys down on top of him to disrupt the rhythm of the team who were doing their best to hammer another nail into our Division Three coffin. We had to be tighter in midfield, supporting the attack and the defence, and, basically, the defenders had to do their job. They had to make sure every 50/50 ball became 60/40 in our favour.

I was excited about the challenge and had individual meetings with senior players. I wanted to hear their thoughts and I was determined they knew exactly what I was demanding of them and their team-mates. I wasn't interested in dealing in grey areas, everything had to be in black and white. They had to know what they needed to provide in the crucial forthcoming weeks and months. We were coming into November and we all knew there was a fair chance the team that occupied that rock-bottom position by the turn of the year normally remained there until the end of the campaign and relegation was officially confirmed. The time to address the problem was right now.

The team was as well primed as I could possibly make them by the time we travelled to Southend on October 27. We lost 2-0 and the journey back to Lincoln was far from pleasurable, I can assure you. Losing is a bad habit to adopt in a business such as football. Mistakes are cruelly punished. A week later, we lost 1-0 at home to Mansfield Town. The players had tried hard and worked well in both games and had nothing to show for their efforts. I wondered what was around the corner. I would soon find out when I received a call from the secretary to be at the ground at 8.30am on Monday, November 6.

I duly turned up at the appointed hour to be told we had a new full-time manager. I was informed Colin Murphy would be taking over and the club would make the announcement to the media at midday. Colin Murphy? Yes, the same Colin Murphy who had been sacked by Derby County after five wins in thirty-five games to make way for Tommy Docherty. I was surprised and disappointed, but I did my best to keep an open mind. Later in the morning, I met Murphy and he told me he was looking forward to working with me. I was far from happy. Look at the situation from my point of view. I had played for some top clubs, won an FA Cup medal, scored the winning goal for my country against the world champions at Wembley and I was being asked to take orders from a bloke who had never kicked a ball in league football and had failed at management with another club.

I explained my situation and Murphy asked me to stay on as his assistant. I had to be blunt. I told him: 'I don't think it will work between us. We come from different football backgrounds. I think it's best that you bring in your own coach and I'll stay on as a player.' I saw little point in us sharing a dug-out when there would be too much friction. I thought honesty was the best policy and I believed I was doing him a favour. I was a player again and I was back in among the guys I had bossed only a couple of days earlier.

In the first training session under Murphy, I sensed disaster around the corner. He claimed one of the main problems with the players was the lack of fitness. I have no idea who in their right mind devised a training exercise where players had to run down a hill. If you have ever had to race down a slope, you will know how difficult it is. It certainly won't do anything for your fitness, but it will give you every opportunity to twist a knee, buckle an ankle or break a toe. I was beginning to feel like Jack Nicholson's character Randle McMurphy in the movie, 'One Flew Over The Cuckoo's Nest'. I reckoned it was time to go.

I asked the club to pay up my contract until the end of the season, about six months' wages, and Lincoln and I could part company on fairly amicable terms. I was told by the chairman the club could not afford it. I was there for seven or eight awkward weeks and Gordon Taylor, the PFA boss, stepped in to mediate between myself and the club. I got my financial dues and was set free. Under Murphy, Lincoln lost sixteen league games - six in a row - from thirty games. They drew eight, won six and were relegated. They were also knocked out of the FA Cup in the opening round by Blackpool.

Did I have any regrets about going to Lincoln and not joining Tommy Docherty at Derby County? This may surprise you, but the answer is no. Tommy Docherty would probably have mollycoddled me at the start of a coaching career and, as you may have detected by now, that is not my style. I am my own man and I'll stand or fall by my own decisions.

After a spell away from the game, Gordon Taylor, the chairman of the PFA, got in touch to sound me out about a position that had become vacant at Runcorn, a Northern Premier League club. I am not one to dismiss something out of hand and I thought I would have a look at what was on offer. Obviously, they could not afford huge wages, but I could supplement my income with some commercial work during the week. The players trained on a Tuesday and Thursday and played on a Saturday. I found the standard wasn't too bad, but it was obvious I needed someone in beside me who knew the league.

Altrincham were the team in the league with the money, I believe Manchester City chairman Peter Swales was involved, and they could afford the best players. It was hardly a level playing field. However, there was an honesty about the place which I found refreshing. I found I was constantly swimming against the tide and it does get tiring, especially when you feel someone has just placed a piano on your back. I was aware I had to make a monumental decision.

It was time to say farewell to an old friend. I was thirty-three years old. It had been one helluva ride.

TESTIMONIALS

"I always enjoyed playing with Jim over a few years at Chelsea, was great to see how his career blossomed even more after he left."

Ron Harris, Chelsea FC

"Jim was quite rightly always confident amongst some of the best players, he really did come in and put his stamp on the Club. We especially needed midfield players and he was just what we hoped for, he came to Chelsea and quickly became one of the boys."

John Hollins, Chelsea FC

"The first time I actually met Jim we were only schoolboys. He was at Holyrood High School and I was at Our Lady's High School in Motherwell, and I remember hearing about him before we met at 15 just before he went to play for Scotland Schoolboys. When Jim came to the youth team at Chelsea, he was quickly signed professionally and the next thing we knew we were on tour in Australia. Jim was always a skilled and confident player, when we were 18 we played against the West German National team and I remember the Doc was telling Helmut Schön about these two 18 year olds from Scotland and we very nearly got the opportunity to train with them! Jim and I were always the youngsters, I remember us going down for breakfast after that famous night in Blackpool, asking coach Harry Medhurst where the rest of the boys were, and he quickly replied they've been sent home!"

John Boyle, Chelsea FC

"Jim was a really nice lad and an exceptional player, much more advanced than his years. When he came to us he was only 19 but you'd never have known it and he made a big and fast impression on all of the team. A couple of things I remember about him more than anything, he was such a family man he brought his parents and all his siblings down to Sheffield Wednesday to meet everyone. And of course, the other thing I'll never forget was when he scored the two exceptional goals that helped us get to Wembley, and he celebrated with a hop and a forward roll! For me, he was one of the best."

Don Megson, Sheffield Wednesday FC

"Jim was a very likeable young man, I'm 76 now and still remember his company and how impressive he was to watch on the pitch. I can remember we travelled to Hong Kong and Singapore together and had some great laughs. Then when I went to Newcastle he went to Wolves and we played against each other but Jim still invited us all to his house after the match! He could see a pass a mile off, and score the goals, and most importantly to me he was a great team player – an all rounder which was rare."

David Ford, Sheffield Wednesday FC

"First impression was what a good footballer he was at 19 years old! He could not only play the game, but he knew how to look after himself on the field. Jim was a serious footballer, I never once saw him go into a game or training without giving it 100% and his full attention. We'd have fisticuffs if I didn't take it seriously! But we'd always leave training arms around each other ready for the next match. Our team were renowned for winding each other up, we knew our dressing room as "The Dragon Court" where we'd catch one of the players out, provide the evidence, call the witnesses and give the verdict! We only managed to get Jim on trial once, and when the day finally came Eric Taylor had been begging us to sit in on a hearing – so we let him chair!"

Peter Eustace, Sheffield Wednesday FC

"Jim had already got a reputation when he arrived to Wolves, because obviously he had been one of the youngest players in the FA cup final – everyone knew about him. We were sure he'd be so big-headed, but he was the total opposite, a great lad with a natural talent. That was a mark of a good man and a top class footballer. I still laugh when I remember Jimmy's first car, his beloved Alfa Romeo, everyone had to be careful around the Alfa, his car was probably more respected than Jimmy! He really was a credit to the club, and we were all sad when he left even if we understood it."

John Richards, Wolverhampton Wanderers FC

"He was always a great player and a good lad, he was highly regarded in football before he even got to us and we met him. I was impressed with him from the first time we played together, I genuinely enjoyed playing alongside him. He was a runner! He could run forever and get to the other side of the defense to score before anyone was even close."

Derek Parkin, Wolverhampton Wanderers FC

"One of the best left-halves (midfielders) I've ever seen! Jim was faster than most, but he could also create opportunities, he could pass, he could dribble and the only person that came close in my mind was Jim Baxter. I was delighted when Doc signed him, and I was absolutely gutted when he left Man U, I didn't know I was going to be next, mind! I really got to know Jim more it was when we were playing in America, we were together all the time, we loved playing the game there, what memories."

Willie Morgan, Manchester United FC

"Jim was obviously a very talented player, cool as you like on the ball – which is not an easy thing to do in football especially playing at the highest level. At the time, like all clubs we had great camaraderie in the dressing room, you had to be a part of the set up and be one of us. Jim quickly became one of the lads as if he'd played for years, but he had great partnerships on the pitch and friendships off the pitch. It really was a different generation, we all did everything together and Jim was happy to be the life and soul of the dressing room."

Lou Macari, Manchester United FC

"Everyone loved Jimmy to bits, I remember when I first joined the club I went straight to Spain with the lads and we got on the drinks, I'll blame Jimmy for that one! All the lads were down to earth, even though you expect the odd bighead when you get to Man United! Jim was a midfielder, he knew what he was doing and wasn't scared to try things on the pitch. He nearly got me banned from playing before I'd even played a game! Jimmy and I shared digs together, and thought it was a good plan to go for drinks before my first match, and then first thing the next morning The Doc had me in the office telling me not to let Jimmy Mac lead me astray, but obviously I didn't listen. I must admit I was disappointed when he left, but now I see it led him to the FA Cup final even though our club missed him. That move and the FA cup was a great achievement for him and his new club and we were so proud."

Stuart Pearson, Manchester United FC

"He was pretty good when he turned up! Jim came into our midfield with a bunch of records and as a Scottish international. Laurie McMenemy had a knack of signing really good players, and he proved his point when he signed Jim and we got to the cup final for him to lay on the ball to Bobby Stokes for that winning goal. Jim had great vision, a good touch, but I used to do all his running for him mind! He saw things before the ball got to him, and he'd already planned what he was going to do and how to open up the defense. We had good fun, good times and a good bunch of lads and laughs."

David Peach, Southampton FC

"Jim in one word? Magic! He was a different class when he joined us, a fabulous player, he could see things before anyone else knew what was going on. Just even thinking about the goal from Bobby Stokes in the Cup Final – he saw Bobby before Bobby even knew it and Jimmy put the ball forward and it really was a fantastic ball. We became really good friends and had many a drink and celebration together, he was one of my best mates at that club. The night before the Cup Final he told me to go see Laurie McMenemy and tell him we couldn't sit in the hotel all day we were bored! The boss said we could have a couple of pints each, thank god we still won or we'd have all been fired! They really were the good old days."

Jim Steele, Southampton Football Club

"We took the piss out of him at first. Especially me and Ossie who remember him for becoming the 'World Cup Winner" for the Jocks at Wembley in 1967.

That Dell dressing room was a right laugh and we used to goad Jim when he first arrived – making him out to be one of those vagrants with his belongings hanging from a stick over his shoulder in a red and white spotted handkerchief because he'd travelled the land and been to that many clubs before pitching up in the car park on Milton Road.

How many was it?

I remember him at Chelsea when I was still a kid, then Wednesday, then Wolves and he came to us from United if I remember rightly.....

He seemed to have been a prominent figure wherever he went when few of us changed clubs as often as he did, but he was always dangerous.

Not quick (never quick to my mind) but always cute and technically brilliant.

Most importantly, he was (and still is) a fucking Jock.

Me, Bally and Ossie hated the Jocks. Strange that so many of them became my best mates really! The Dell's dressing room always had plenty of them throughout my career, lads like Eric Martin, Hughie Fisher and the ultimate lunatic in Jim Steele. We'd goad, banter and bully each other all the time. Not daily, but hourly!

It was great fun and we'd have a few battles in the old concrete gym that was Southampton's state of the art facility back in the day behind the West Stand. The 'North v South' matches were never friendly and blood could be shed in those sessions but as silky as Jim was, he could also look after himself.

I can still see the passes he'd pick out for Ossie, Stokesy and me. He only needed half a look and because he had such ability, he'd deliver the ball to suit our own individual strengths.

Jim was like Bally in that sense – he could see things quickly, slow time down and damage teams from deep positions.

When he was a youngster he'd hurt teams by getting forward into the box, like he did at Wembley in '67, but by the time he arrived at The Dell in '75 he was more of a playmaker, a quarterback almost.

He'd penetrate defences with the ball as long as those of us up front did our job by capitalising on his supply.

I'm chuffed Bobby did that in the Cup Final. That pass was typical of Jimmy Mac and he was a big part of our Cup win.

We were a bunch of rascals as I'm sure Jim will describe us as in this book.

All I know is that he played a major part in helping the team I supported as a kid to win the one trophy I dreamed of growing up.

That has bonded us together forever.

I've not mentioned the volley against Bradford because I'm sure Jim has spent a chapter on it already!

A top lad and a great player.

He's still a Fucking Jock though!"

Mick Channon, Southampton Football Club

"I didn't really know Jim that well until we went to Wembley, but as soon as we got to that game on the pitch I knew how good he was. He really was a smashing player, and good fun to play alongside which is always a bonus."

Bobby Lennox, Scotland National Team

"Jim was always professional, he was very much a team player, trying to always make passes and include everyone in the beautiful game. He was well-known as a player in England by the time I met him, but he made a fantastic addition to the Scottish team."

John Greig, Scotland National Team

PHOTOGRAPH INDEX

1. 1st photo at St. Francis Boys Guild.
2. St. Luke's Boys Club - Pat Crerand (Celtic and Scotland).
3. Signing for Leeds Utd with Don Revie and my brothers.
4. Cup winners at St. Luke's Boys Club.
5. 1st Gorbals & Holyrood schoolboy to be picked for Scotland Schoolboys.
6. Holyrood Senior Secondary team with Mr D Cuddihy.
7. Glasgow Schoolboys.
8. Scotland Schoolboy.
9. 1st photo in Leeds Utd strip.
10. Scotland Schoolboys team to play England at Ibrox.
11. Warming up at Stamford Bridge.
12. Chelsea tour - Australia.
13. Chelsea tour - Australia.
14. Waving to the Chelsea supporters at the Bridge.
15. Chelsea team photo with Harry Medhurst (Physio).
16. Chelsea v Glasgow select (3-0 to Chelsea).
17. Lost in thoughts. Moving to Sheffield Wednesday.
18. Signing for Sheffield Wednesday. Tommy Docherty and Alan Brown.
19. Football Weekly - Sheffield Wednesday.
20. Having a cup of tea with Mum and Dad.
21. Peter Bonetti saving my goal-bound shot at Villa Park in the semi-final of the F.A. Cup.
22. Scoring against my ex club, Chelsea, in the semi-final of the F.A. Cup.
23. Meeting Denis Law - my football hero.
24. Sheffield Wednesday team photo at Hillsborough.
25. Scotland training before England game (1967). Myself, Denis Law, Billy Bremner and Bobby Lennox.
26. Scotland team line-up at Wembley (1967).
27. Debutants 1967. Ronnie Simpson, Bobby Brown and myself.
28. Tussling in mid-field with Bobby Charlton.
29. Baxter on the ball, Bremner and McCalliog in support.
30. Walking towards Baxter and my team mates.
31. Celebrating with my team-mates.
32. How the goals were scored.
33. Ronnis Simpson (36) McCalliog (20) celebrating together after beating England (1967).

34. Signing for Wolves with Bill McGarry.
35. Travelling to Scotland for my 2nd cap v Russia at Hampden.
36. At the Savoy Hotel, London with the England team after the game at Wembley. Myself, Bobby Lennox and Denis Law.
37. Wolves Football Weekly.
38. Scoring for Wolves v Saints at The Dell.
39. Opening my garage in Penn Road, Wolverhampton with the Chairman, Mr Ireland, and Derek Dougan.
40. Wolves team photo.
41. Scoring for Wolves v West Ham.
42. Exchanging penants before the 1972 UEFA Cup final v Spurs.
43. Playing against Juventus at Molineux.
44. Scotland squad in Glasgow.
45. Manchester United team photo (1974).
46. Scoring my 1st goal for Man Utd against Newcastle at Old Trafford.
47. My best football pal, Willie Morgan, watching my 1st goal from another angle.
48. Myself and The Doog celebrating (Wolves).
49. Celebrating with Sammy McIlroy after my goal against Everton at the Theatre of Dreams.
50. Bending a free-kick around the wall v Everton at the Stretford End.
51. Change of strip at Man Utd.
52. Posing with Mick Channon, Peter Osgood and Peter Rodrigues.
53. Southampton team photo.
54. Scoring with a volley at Valley Parade. A new free-kick routine with Oss.
55. Relaxing with my team mates at Southampton.
56. Saints after winning the F.A. Cup at Wembley 1976.
57. Celebrating with the F.A. Cup at Wembley 1976.
58. At Southampton Town Hall with Bobby Stokes, our goal scorer.
59. Saints team showing off the F.A. Cup to Mike Reid at the TV studios.
60. Pele (Mr Angry) chasing me after he had a goal disallowed. New York Cosmos v Chicago Sting (1977).